SECRETS REVEALED

The Kremlin

"The Kremlin is a center of political intrigue, undermining tactics, temporary alliances, betrayals, sudden falls and equally sudden rises, mysterious disappearances and deaths, suicides that look like murders, and murders camouflaged as suicides . . . "

Mikhail Gorbachev

"One of his classmates recalls, 'We all got drunk as lords and didn't remember a single thing the next day. [Gorbachev] alone remained sober as a judge throughout the whole evening, and remembered everything. Our suspicions grew stronger when we were sent out to serve internships. Some went here, some went there: to courtrooms, to the prosecutor's office, to prisons for regular criminals . . . [Gorbachev] began to avoid us and stopped studying: he was beginning another career . . ."

The KGB

"The KGB has replaced the government, the Party, and the ministry of foreign affairs, while of course continuing to control the armed forces. Behind the scenes, it is functioning with far greater effect than is apparent to outside observers of the Kremlin stage . . . "

D0034264

BEHIND THE HIGH KREMLIN WALLS

Vladimir Solovyov &
Elena Klepikova

Translated by Guy Daniels
in Collaboration with the Authors

BERKLEY BOOKS, NEW YORK

To our correspondents in the USSR,
whom for the sake of their security we cannot name here,
but without whose help we could have written
neither this book nor our earlier one about the Kremlin.

This Berkley book contains the complete
text of the original hardcover edition.
It has been completely reset in a typeface
designed for easy reading and was printed
from new film.

BEHIND THE HIGH KREMLIN WALLS

A Berkley Book / published by arrangement with
Dodd, Mead & Company

PRINTING HISTORY
Dodd, Mead & Company edition published 1986
Berkley edition / March 1987

ISBN: 0-425-09716-1

A BERKLEY BOOK ® TM 757,375
Berkley Books are published by The Berkley Publishing Group,
200 Madison Avenue, New York, New York 10016.
The name "BERKLEY" and the "B" logo
are trademarks belonging to Berkley Publishing Corporation.

PRINTED IN THE UNITED STATES OF AMERICA

10   9   8   7   6   5   4   3   2

Contents

Introduction:
The Limits of Understanding

What the World Knows About the Kremlin, and What the Kremlin Knows About the World

Where are the control consoles of the chief world powers?

The president of the United States governs that country from an elegant private dwelling on Pennsylvania Avenue. The British prime minister works in a rather small brick residence on narrow Downing Street. The French president lives in the splendid Élysée Palace.

The Soviet empire is governed from an impregnable medieval fortress on Red Square. The fate of all mankind hinges more upon what happens behind its high, thick, crenelated walls than it does upon what takes place on the other side of the planet in the White House. Another kind of wall—an invisible one of mystery, secrecy, spontaneous rumors, and deliberate disinformation about the Kremlin—stirs the imagination of people in the free world, who have a large appetite for information and are used to having it satisfied. It's no wonder that the Kremlin, the most secretive place on earth, is also the most intriguing.

What goes on in that epicenter of the Soviet world? How does power change hands there? Who makes those decisions so crucial for humankind? In particular, who makes them when there is seemingly no one in control of the government because the Soviet leader is terminally ill, like Brezhnev from the late seventies on, or Andropov and Chernenko during almost the entirety of their brief reigns? Is it not strange that it was during such a period that Afghanistan was annexed? That a Korean airliner was shot down? That worldwide terrorism, at least partially instigated by the Kremlin, flourished and took on such scope that it is now threatening the very existence of Western civilization?

Which is more important for understanding the Kremlin: the fact that Mikhail Gorbachev has a sense of humor and a wife who is modern, chic, and ambitious, or the fact that, among the baker's dozen (in Russian, "devil's dozen") making up the ruling Politburo he heads, there is not a single military man? On the other hand, there *are* three police generals: KGB Chairman Victor Chebrikov, Vice-Premier Geidar Aliyev, and Foreign Minister Eduard Shevardnadze. All three of them are experienced intriguers and plotters. It is hardly likely that this record-breaking number of officers from the punitive agencies got into the Politburo because Gorbachev wanted it that way; after all, only a few years before, the presence of only one such officer, Andropov, in the Kremlin was sufficient cause for carrying out a coup d'état and removing Brezhnev's bureaucratic mafia from power.

How are Gorbachev's character and views affected by the fact that he was born during the years of collectivization? That as a teenager he spent more than a year in German-occupied territory? And, finally, that he made his political debut in the years when the Stalin era was in its death throes?

How are the Kremlin mafias put together? What is

the Kremlin Olympians' attitude toward their own people, and what is the people's attitude toward them? What is the people's role in Kremlin politics?

It is not the Russian soul that is mysterious, as the world was taught by the great Russian writers of the nineteenth century, but rather the incentives and actions of the dozen men entrenched in that impregnable fortress in the very center of the Russian capital who are obsessed to the point of paranoia with the secretiveness, as with something indispensable to their continued existence. Life in the Kremlin goes on in an atmosphere of even greater secrecy than the military maneuvers of the Warsaw Pact countries or the testing of new Soviet missiles.

That is why the Kremlin persecutes so harshly those of its subjects who decide to declassify certain secret aspects of its monastic rules and medieval customs. An "oath of silence," rather like the Mafia's vow of *omertà*, is extracted even from members of Kremlin families. When one of them violates it, the Kremlin goes into a state of shock, from which it does not recover for a long time. We recall the panic caused in the Kremlin by the defection of Stalin's daughter, Svetlana Alliluyeva, and the publication of her memoirs about life behind the Kremlin walls. The Kremlin's shock was so great that KGB Chairman Vladimir Semichastny was dismissed because his organization had not prevented that perfidious act of defection and, along with it, the leaks of Kremlin information. By its own standards, betrayal of the Kremlin is an even greater crime than high treason. And it did not rest easy until seventeen years later—a period during which both the KGB and the Kremlin itself underwent several changes of top leadership—the "prodigal" daughter returned to the land of her father, who had been politically resurrected just at that time. (Her return was the result of a complex operation carried out by Soviet secret agents over a period of many years.)

It has been jokingly said that the chief Kremlin secret is that it does not in fact have any secrets—a state secret that the Kremlin carefully guards against outsiders and enemies. If this is true, the Kremlin has succeeded brilliantly in disinforming the West: witness the acute interest taken by the rest of the world in everything that happens in the Kremlin.

At this point, the reader may legitimately ask: How with all these safeguards is it possible to penetrate Kremlin secrecy? We shall go into the matter of our sources at the end of this book. Here we shall say just this: It is not a question of the possibilities but of the *necessity* for the West to attempt such penetration—and by no means merely out of idle curiosity. That very necessity, once recognized as vital, itself broadens the possibilities although we do not and cannot have any hope of obtaining, at any time in the near future, tape recordings of Politburo sessions or of private conversations among its members. This does not mean, however, that we are totally helpless before that wall of secrecy that the Kremlin has tried to put up all along the perimeter, stretching for thousands of miles, of the empire it governs—the last one on earth.

That wall plays a double role: It keeps the outside world from gaining reliable knowledge about the Soviet Union, and at the same time it keeps the Kremlin leaders from learning what is really going on outside its borders. Their self-imposed isolation doesn't only give the West a distorted picture of how they live and what they are up to; it distorts the Kremlin's own notions about life in the West, especially in the United States. It is a wall of mutual ignorance, although the Kremlin, as its inventor, has an unchallenged copyright on it. The ignorance of each party is comparable to that of the other. Readers of this book will have to decide for themselves which is greater: the West's ignorance of the Kremlin, or the Kremlin's ignorance of the West. About one thing, however, there can be no doubt: Mutual ignorance is dangerous, because it leads to tactical mistakes, paranoia, and military panic.

There are many examples of both kinds of ignorance. For one, is it not astounding that the invasion of Af-

ghanistan by Soviet forces just before Christmas 1979—
an invasion that had been carefully planned by the
Kremlin over a long period of time—came as a complete
surprise to both Western journalists and Western intelligence services? When it finally happened, it was precisely those who, by virtue of their official duties or the
kind of profession they practiced, should have surmised
that it was impending who began *post scriptum* to
dream up explanations for it, each one more fantastic
than the one before it: the USSR's eagerness to gain access to the Indian Ocean and the warm-water ports of
the southern seas, or to move toward the oil fields of the
Arabian Peninsula, which are so vitally important to
the West, and so on. Even more absurd, however, were
the well-nigh unanimous predictions in the American
press that Afghanistan would become a Russian Vietnam. (The reasons why that did not happen, and could
not happen, are given in the appropriate section of this
book.)

Or another example. By the spring of 1982, Andropov had carried out his secret-police coup and taken
power away from the ailing Brezhnev. Yet even at that
time, almost none of the American Kremlinologists
were able to predict that the all-powerful regent would,
after Brezhnev's death, become the official Soviet
leader. Most of them reasoned that he would not, solely
on the basis of the fact that not once in Soviet history
had a chief of the secret police become chief of state, as
if what had not happened in the past could not happen
in the future! Why, in a full-fledged police state, should
fifteen years of service in the secret police be an obstacle
to becoming the top leader? That Western miscalcula-
tion was due to ignorance not only of Russian history
and Soviet realities but of the elementary laws of logic.

At the time, we were among the few—if not the only
ones—to predict Andropov's accession to power, in articles published in *The Los Angeles Times* and *The An-
tioch Review*. We mention this not in order to brag
(there's nothing to brag about: Andropov was already
the de facto Kremlin leader) but only to give another ex-

ample of wrongheaded American notions about what
goes on in the Kremlin. (A curious note: although or-
dinarily our articles appear in several dozen periodicals,
that one was accepted only by the two mentioned
above.)

The most remarkable Western delusion took place
after Andropov was officially proclaimed the fifth
Soviet leader. The empire's former top cop was declared
by leading American newspapers to be a liberal, a
"Westernizer," a polyglot, an aesthete, and an intellectual. Mikhail Gorbachev, too, underwent a metamorphosis of this sort in the world press, although he had
received his share of praise and compliments even
before he became the top Kremlin leader. It happened
on the occasion of his visit to Great Britain in late 1984;
the British press, naturally, headed up that preinaugural
campaign.

In this connection, it's not a bad idea to compare
the tone taken by Western journalists in writing about
their own leaders with the one they take toward the
Soviet leaders. The contrast is striking. If British and
American voters had to choose, say, between Margaret
Thatcher and Yuri Andropov—or between Ronald
Reagan and Mikhail Gorbachev—and if they heeded the
opinions of many British and American papers in cast-
ing their ballots, the two graduates of the Kremlin
school of politics would make it into the White House
or No. 10 Downing Street by a landslide.

One more example: the notion, widespread in the
West, that the Soviet Union is a country with a Communist ideology. What is the notion worth if, as happens to be the case, true believers in Communism can
more readily be found in any Western country (including the United States) than in Russia, where in order
to ferret one out you have to send Diogenes on a search
with his lantern on a bright sunny day? The country is
governed by a ramified police bureaucracy, solidly
based on centuries-old traditions of Russian imperial
rule, that makes hypocritical use of Communist slogans.

More than a half-century ago, Spanish philosopher Ortega y Gasset wrote, apropos of Russia's postrevolutionary ideological camouflage, "I'm waiting for the publication of a book that will translate Stalinist Marxism into the language of Russian history." Unfortunately, such a book has for some reason not yet appeared; and what philosophers say is beyond the grasp of practical politicians. The struggle against leftist ideology, of which the USSR is still thought to be the locus, is thus becoming more and more reminiscent of Don Quixote's famous joust with the windmills. On the other hand, that mistake in identity makes things much easier for the Soviet Union in its own struggle against Western civilization, since some of the blows aimed at the former fall on an ideology that has no direct, practical relation to it.

When we were living in Russia, we were truly amazed by Western misconceptions about our country. Here in America, we have changed our angle of vision. Our Soviet experience has remained with us, but we are now gauging the country we left behind us from a safe (or relatively safe) distance. The shift in our perception can be compared to the difference in impressions that a zoo makes on its permanent residents, locked up in cages, and those it makes on visitors—free people who just happen to drop in. The two of us, having given up citizenship in one superpower to become citizens of another, are now no less amazed at how ignorant the inhabitants of the Soviet zoo are about life outside it, and especially the ignorance of its privileged inhabitants, the people in the Kremlin. Is it not incredible that one Soviet leader should have asked a Canadian professor recruited by the KGB about the massive persecution of Jews in the United States? Or that another, after the mid-term congressional elections of 1982, congratulated an American diplomat on Reagan's election to a second term, getting a whole two years ahead of the story?

It may come as a surprise to our readers that the Kremlin demigods, from Stalin to Gorbachev, have used as their most reliable source of information on just about everything the Russian-language broadcasts of the BBC and the Voice of America—broadcasts that they themselves jam and forbid their subjects to listen to.

The information the Kremlin leaders get from their staffers passes through a great many filters. It is shaped to meet their expectations and fashioned to fit their prior conceptions, however out of date they may be. Usually this is "favorable" information, as smooth as toothpaste coming out of a tube. The Kremlin leaders themselves encourage biased and highly selective processing of the news, both domestic and especially foreign. The result of that complex, multistage processing of information is a finished product that differs as much from the real facts as do canned fish from live ones darting about in the sea. There is only one way out from that hermetic circle for a member of the Kremlin elite to get real facts in a real context: listen to foreign radio stations.

It is reliably known that in Stalin's dining room there was a big, polished wooden cabinet with a winking green eye: a Telefunken radio set that his wife's brother had brought back from abroad. Even the author of a highly laudatory biography of Stalin, who had access to classified Kremlin materials, acknowledges that fact, although he writes that Stalin

> always intended to have the Telefunken removed from the dining room, . . . but kept putting it off until tomorrow, and even joked about his own procrastination and the fact that he himself, Stalin, in his position and with his high categories of Marxist thought, was not invulnerable to little foibles and predilections in everyday living.

During the war, when the Soviet news agencies were issuing communiques from the front that had been doctored (by Stalin himself), the suspicious tyrant did not put much faith in the reports from his own commanders—he would push the button on his foreign-made radio set and, holding his ear close to it, get the war news from the Russian-language broadcasts of foreign radio stations. That was how he first learned that his son Yakov had been taken prisoner. (Yakov was later executed by the Germans.)

Unfortunately, we do not know whether Khrushchev listened to the Voice of America and the BBC when he was in power. But after he was removed from office and became a pensioner, he definitely became a regular, avid listener to those broadcasts. According to his closest relatives, what interested him more than international news or fascinating gossip was political information about his own country—information from which he had been forcibly isolated.

The Russian writer Felix Kamov, who now lives in Israel, told us (when all three of us were still living in Moscow) about a meeting in 1977 between a group of Jewish *refuseniks* and Brezhnev's minister of internal affairs, General of the Army Nikolai Shchelokov. Shchelokov frankly told them that he had learned from a Voice of America broadcast made the evening before about a Jewish demonstration in Moscow that had been broken up by policemen—who were of course under his own authority. Even when it came to something that happened in his own ministry, the minister learned about it from a foreign radio broadcast!

Brezhnev himself, no less than his ministers and very likely more than his predecessors, was extremely fond of listening to short-wave radio. He especially liked to do it when he was in Zavidovo, that "bit of paradise," as the inhabitants of nearby villages called it, the woodland area not far from Moscow with Kremlinites' hunting lodges, where members of the Politburo spend time hunting, relaxing, holding sessions, and even entertaining foreign guests. In order to assure undisturbed and "clean" reception of foreign radio broadcasts for the Kremlin Olympians, this area is left free of jammers—of which we ourselves found confirmation more than once when we were in that vicinity. (We could hear the faint sounds of jammers only in adjacent areas.) One of the superintendents of the Politburo's hunting lodges in Zavidovo told us that Brezhnev preferred Japanese-made short-wave receivers; that he tried not to miss a single evening broadcast by the Voice of America; and that he took a special interest in its analysis of the alignment of political forces in the Kremlin and in the odds put on each of his potential heirs, no doubt so that he could render the most likely one harmless in good time.

As for Andropov, when he was KGB chairman he listened to foreign radio broadcasts as part of his job. At KGB headquarters, located on Dzerzhinsky Square, a big short-wave receiver with a whole forest of antennas that pick up virtually all the radio stations in the world is an indispensable working tool not only for the chief of the KGB but also for all his deputies, department heads, and on down. Since few of them know foreign languages, they listen only to Russian-language broadcasts. According to a credible story, Andropov preferred the BBC to the Voice of America because the former's reportage was "clean"—unburdened by ideology. As a matter of working routine, KGB personnel listen to all the morning broadcasts not only to get fresh news about their own country and the world but also to check it against information from foreign agents. All this is in addition to its routine round-the-clock recording of any and all transmissions—in Russian and in the languages of the other peoples making up the USSR—from Western stations, ranging from the Voice of America to the Voice of Israel. These are then taken down by stenographers, typed up by typists, and, finally, filed in huge ledgers that are kept, in chronological order, on iron bookshelves in special archives for the internal use of KGB staffers. They are, however, available to some Soviet journalists and propagandists, who use them as a basis for writing anti-American and anti-Zionist articles—and sometimes even entire books, such as the recently published *The Poisoned Voice of the Airwaves*, *Beware: the Deutsche Welle!*, *The Anatomy of Lies*, *The Real Face of Zionism*, *A Whole Army of Scribblers*, *Anti-Communism on the Airwaves*, *The Undeclared War Against Poland*, and many others. It is because of the access to those archives given to Soviet journalists (a profession we practiced when living in the USSR) that we know of their existence.

Along with eyewitness accounts of the Kremlin elite's predilection for foreign broadcasts, we offer herewith one of its own members' *viva voce* admission of that vice. The man in question is Grigori Vasilyevich Romanov, Mikhail Gorbachev's chief rival, who lost out in the power struggle with the latter. Romanov is the only Politburo member we have met, and we have each met him more than once, on "business" occasions. Perhaps we should refer to him as a "future and once" Politburo member, because at the times we encountered him he was not yet a member, and he has since been expelled.

At the time, we were living in Leningrad, where he was Party boss. One day the magazine *Aurora*, where one of us (Elena Klepikova) was working as an editor, made an "ideological blunder." It printed an article about the "moral feats" of scientists, in which the author mentioned academician Andrei Sakharov, the father of the Soviet hydrogen bomb, as a model of morality, along with Einstein, Fermi, and Oppenheimer. This was after Sakharov had published his book *Progress, Coexistence, and Intellectual Freedom* in the West, but before the Soviet press had launched its vitriolic campaign against him. At that moment, the ostracism of Sakharov had the form of a ban on mentioning his name in print.

That ideological lapse was regarded as scandalous. Romanov himself summoned the editors of *Aurora* to the Smolny, the Leningrad Communist Party headquarters since the Revolution, and chewed them out for their lack of vigilance. Most likely the magazine's editor-in-chief, Nina Kosareva, really didn't know anything about Sakharov's "delinquencies." At any rate, what she said in her own defense at the Smolny sounded completely sincere; it was convincing from the viewpoint of the *Aurora* staffers attending the meeting (where they had no right to speak up), including Elena

Klepikova, who reports the following dialogue:

"How was I supposed to know who Sakharov was and what crime he had committed?"

"What do you mean, 'how?'," Romanov shouted. "Why, the Voice of America talks about him on broadcasts from morning till late at night!"

Kosareva was a naïve "Party lady" who had grown up as a Komsomol (Young Communist League) member during the harsh years of the Stalin era, when listening to the "voices of the enemies" was considered a very serious crime. There was a tone of dignity and inner righteousness in her response to Romanov: "None of us ever listens to the Voice of America—neither I nor the members of my staff."

Plainly, it seemed to her that she had found a way out of the situation and had proven her Party loyalty. But what she said made Romanov even more furious. "Well, you're wrong. You *must* listen! To the Voice of America and the BBC and the *Deutsche Welle*!"

It was such an amazing pronouncement that Romanov, noticing that the editors' faces were gaping in astonishment, fell silent for a moment. Then he added a caveat: "Not, of course, so as to take hostile propaganda on faith, but so as to become familiar with the enemy's poisoned weapon. You must do that not as ordinary citizens but as workers on the ideological front. And most important: Don't believe a word of it, no matter what they say!"

The most recent example of the Kremlin's radio addiction was furnished to us in a conversation with a traveling Soviet official who in 1985 had occasion to be in the Kremlin at a formal reception in honor of International Women's Day, March 8, only a few days before Chernenko's death and Gorbachev's inauguration. When the Kremlin "aristocracy" (along with Valentina Tereshkova, the first woman cosmonaut), wearied by the ceremonies, had left the rostrum and were moving toward the hall where a sit-down dinner for special guests was to be held, Gorbachev began to hum a tune familiar to most of those present. He hummed, that is, until Gromyko—who after Andropov's death had taken over the role of mentor to the "crown prince"—came over to him and whispered an admonishment into his ear. We can confirm indirectly the eyewitness's report of that tableau; the BBC's signature theme is in fact a very catchy tune. The intriguing thing here, however, is that even in his choice of foreign radio stations, as in so many other things, Mikhail Gorbachev was following in the footsteps of his chief sponsor, Andropov. Of course, it is also possible that at this critical time the very-soon-to-be Kremlin ruler was busy picking up from the airwaves the Britishers' impressions of his visit to their islands two and a half months earlier.

The question is: How much is the Kremlin leaders' political outlook influenced by their regular listening to the "enemies' voices"? Or to put it another way: Would things in the world be different if Reagan read *Pravda* every morning and watched Moscow TV's news program *Novosti* in the evening? It might be objected that this is not an apt comparison: Not only *The New York Times* and Dan Rather but also the more biased Voice of America differ sharply from all the Soviet propaganda media: radio, TV, and newspapers. Yet if, as is reliably known, Brezhnev, of the wide range of subjects covered by the Voice of America, was mainly interested in international gossip about himself and his confederates and rivals, one may reasonably assume that the other members of the Kremlin mafia listen to foreign broadcasts to the Soviet Union out of strictly "mercenary" motives.

As a matter of fact, every Politburo member must be very curious to learn just what his political position in the Kremlin is in the judgment of Western commentators and whether or not he has any envious enemies and rivals whom he himself may have failed to sniff out, what with the outward unanimity in the Politburo's close-knit clan, the members' pledges of loyalty to one another, and their common oath of fealty to the general secretary. Or whether (God forbid!) he has been declared in the Western mass media to be next in line for the Kremlin throne—which would put him in a very ticklish and precarious position, because all members of that powerful lodge keep constant watch to see whether one of their number has moved up politically. There have been many cases when someone prematurely declared crown prince by Western commentators has not only failed to come into his inheritance but has been utterly cast down from the Kremlin Olympus by his vigilant comrades, owing to that untimely disclosure of his political ambitions. That was what happened to Alexander Shelepin, Fyodor Kulakov, Kirill Mazurov, Petr Masherov, and Andrei Kirilenko—all unsuccessful crown princes, or even tragic ones. The most recent of the Kremlin's miscarried off-spring was Grigori Romanov, who suffered a crushing defeat in his long-drawn-out struggle with Mikhail Gorbachev.

Some correspondents once asked Gromyko about what had happened to certain former Politburo members; he replied with a smile, "You know, our Politburo is like the mysterious Bermuda Triangle: whoever is thrown out of it vanishes without a trace."

So it is hardly any wonder that Mikhail Gorbachev, four days before he mounted the Kremlin throne, should in a moment of distraction have nervously hummed the signature theme of the BBC; for him the BBC was a vitally important source of information about his chances in the final phase of the power struggle, when his predecesor was at death's door.

The lives of those in the Kremlin are mainly given over not to seeking solutions for domestic and foreign affairs but rather to jousting for power. That struggle goes on continuously; it does not end with the election of a general secretary of the Party (the top political post in the empire). Sometimes, indeed, the struggle is renewed with greater force *after* such an election; the most vivid example of that was Stalin, who after coming to power gradually destroyed all his rivals—many more imaginary rivals than real ones. But all the other Kremlin rulers too, beginning with Lenin, have got into power by means of a coup and have hung on to it by means of repeated countercoups. Is it not significant that of the "magnificent seven" Soviet top leaders, five have seized power while their predecessors were still alive?

For that matter, those predecessors sensed—and sometimes knew for sure—that their comrades in arms were undermining them. Former President Richard Nixon recalls that one evening when he was sitting next to Brezhnev at a state dinner in the Faceted Palace of the Kremlin, he "looked directly across the room at a several-times-life-size mural of Christ and the Apostles at the Last Supper. Brezhnev said, 'That was the Politburo of those days.' " To which Nixon replied, not very wittily and certainly not very fittingly, "That must mean that the general secretary and the Pope have much in common."

The conversation fell flat because the leader of the militantly atheistic state turned out to know more about biblical mythology than the president of a country that on every possible occasion emphasizes the Judeo-Christian roots of its culture. "The Last Supper" is a symbol of perfidy and betrayal, for it was at the love feast that Christ foretold that one of his disciples would betray Him and another would deny Him. That is the classic formula for life in the Kremlin: Stalin betrayed Lenin, Khrushchev betrayed Stalin, Brezhnev did the same to Khrushchev, and Andropov did likewise to Brezhnev. And each master was denied by all those who wanted to survive under the new one—by so many, there is no counting them.

To this, one might add that the number of members of Brezhnev's Politburo at the time of Nixon's visit to Moscow was exactly the same as the number of those present at the gathering of Christ and his apostles in Jerusalem, so that Brezhnev's hint to Nixon could be taken in only one sense. But judging from Nixon's memoirs, he completely failed to grasp that.

With neither an electoral system nor a hereditary principle of succession, the Kremlin is a center of political intrigue, undermining tactics, temporary alliances, betrayals, sudden falls and equally sudden rises, mysterious disappearances and deaths, suicides that look like murders, and murders camouflaged as suicides. Some of the aforementioned traditions survived Stalin's death; others were restored by Andropov and his cronies, who are now the rulers of Russia's destiny and that of the people under Russia's sway.

The new era in Kremlin life began not with the inauguration of Gorbachev in March 1985 but three years earlier with the palace coup carried out in the Kremlin shortly before Brezhnev's death by Yuri Andropov, the chief of the secret police. Despite his brief tenure and the fact that during more than half of it Andropov conducted business from the Kuntsevo Hospital by "remote control," he radically changed the character of life in the Kremlin and hence the life of the entire Soviet empire.

Our primary concern is with the recent years in the Kremlin: from Andropov's coup in 1982, through the interregnum of the figurehead Konstantin Chernenko, to the accession of the new generation of Kremlin leaders headed by Mikhail Gorbachev. We shall of course discuss Gorbachev in greater detail than any of his predecessors—which does not mean, however, that we rule out a few amusing and edifying accounts of recent doings in the Kremlin that will help us to understand that power center as it is today.

Drawing on materials we have gathered and adhering to the documentary genre, we try to portray the Kremlin from within, as it really is and not as it appears to be to beholders on the outside, however curious their stares. And we warn the reader that in many respects the Kremlin reality is very different from the image of it that is common currency in the West.

1. A Throne on a Deathbed

> To think is easy, and to act is hard.
> But the hardest thing in the world
> is to act in accordance with your thinking.
>
> —GOETHE

CERTAIN NUMBERS RECUR in the career of Yuri Andropov in a strange, almost cabalistic way. For example, the number of years during which he was KGB chief was exactly the same as the number of months during which he was head of the state: fifteen. The similarity is striking, if not tragic, for if Andropov had not had those fifteen years of experience in the KGB, he would never have made it to the top of the Kremlin hill. The very thing that Western augurs took to be an insurmountable obstacle on his road to supreme power was in fact the surest means of achieving it. During his long service in the KGB, Andropov was able to get that secret punitive-espionage organization out from under the Kremlin's control, and he took so much power into his own

1

hands that, toward the end of the Brezhnev era, it exceeded that of the official chief of state. True, by the outset of the eighties, Brezhnev was very different from what he had been when he began to rule in the midsixties, after the overthrow of Khrushchev. As a feeble old man who had had several strokes and heart attacks and who had become rather slow-witted, he was no longer in any condition to offer strong opposition to the intrigues of his chief of secret police. Yet he could not have failed to realize that Andropov's campaign against corruption in the top Party echelons was actually an operation to undermine his own power and that of his sprawling bureaucratic mafia, which in Moscow was named "the Dnepropetrovsk mafia" after the Ukrainian city of Dnepropetrovsk. Brezhnev was born not far from there and had graduated from the metallurgical institute in that city. It was there that he married, that his children were born, and that he began his career, at first as an engineer, then as deputy mayor, and finally as a Party functionary. But most important of all, it was there that he struck up friendships with the people he later brought to Moscow and installed in some of the empire's highest positions: as secretaries and department heads of the CC (Central Committee), premier, deputy premier, and ministers, not to mention numerous posts below that level. In the capital, Muscovites openly talked about an invasion by the people from Dnepropetrovsk who were "occupying" Moscow by the late seventies.

When Brezhnev was largely incapacitated by illness the governing of the country was taken over increasingly by the Dnepropetrovsk mafia, whose members found more gratification in their own prosperity than in the well-being of the empire. Andropov attacked that mafia ruthlessly; as chief of the KGB, he had its mighty apparatus at his disposal. It was a battle against corruption, and at the same time it was a struggle for power. It reached its decisive stage in 1982—the most eventful, stormy, and tragic year in Kremlin life since the death of Stalin.

In accordance with the traditions of the organization

he headed, and with his own personal principles, Andropov was not exactly squeamish about the means he used to reach his goal. For him, the end justified any means. His immediate goal was to dispose of Brezhnev's protégés, and his ultimate goal was to do the same with Brezhnev himself. As early as the first months of 1982, several of the last men who had served as props for Brezhnev's weakened regime suddenly vanished from the Kremlin stage.

One of them was Andrei Kirilenko, Brezhnev's Party deputy and trusted comrade in arms, who was the number-two man in the Kremlin. After a rather simple frame-up of Kirilenko's son-in-law (he had allegedly sought political asylum in England but his attempt had been nipped in the bud by vigilant KGB agents), Andropov smeared Kirilenko to the point that he was forbidden to attend sessions of the Politburo, of which he was still a member.

A few weeks later, Andropov dealt Brezhnev another blow. This time he physically eliminated a Brezhnevite who held a high post in Andropov's own organization, the KGB. The man in question was General Semyon Tsvigun, who was married to the sister of Brezhnev's wife. Brezhnev had appointed Tsvigun as Andropov's first deputy. His real assignment (as opposed to his ostensible duties) was to spy on Andropov. Tsvigun justified the trust placed in him by Brezhnev; he had remained loyal to his exalted relative by marriage rather than to his immediate superior. But that loyalty was to cost him his life. Until the very last day of it, he tried in every way to obstruct Andropov's investigation of a case involving some diamonds that had been stolen, allegedly with the complicity of Brezhnev's daughter Galina. Galina Brezhneva was in fact very fond of fine jewelry. But she had plenty of money and connections to get them legally, so that there were no grounds for Andropov's charge. That fact served as the basis on which Tsvigun built his niece's defense.

Tsvigun's office was of course in the KGB building on Dzerzhinsky Square. It was there that, on January 19,

1982, he was found dead, with a bullet in his head. Since his office was close to Andropov's own, the latter must have heard the shot that killed the man who had been spying on him.

The last man who tried to intervene in the Kremlin power struggle at this stage of it was Mikhail Suslov, the Party's chief ideologue. Suslov was apparently convinced that there was enough clout in his prestige alone to restore, after so many inroads had been made in Brezhnev's power, the status quo ante. But after a violent quarrel with Andropov, the seventy-nine-year-old Suslov had a heart attack, and he died the next day. Three days later, on January 29, 1982, taking advantage of the fact that Brezhnev and his depleted retinue were attending Suslov's funeral in Red Square, Andropov ordered the arrest of Galina Brezhneva's closest friends. She herself was summoned to KGB headquarters for interrogation. By this time, neither her father, the official leader of the USSR, nor her husband, General Yuri Churbanov, the first deputy minister of internal affairs, could do anything to defend her.

In May 1982, after sweeping the Kremlin clean of many Brezhnevites—having had some of them killed, others arrested, still others fired, and having frightened all the rest—Andropov named himself a secretary of the CC. He assumed the functions previously performed by Kirilenko and Suslov, although at the same time he kept for himself the general command of the KGB. This was in fact a palace coup, notwithstanding the camouflaging of it by Party ritual (calling a special session of the CC plenum, "discussion," "voting," and the like). Thus, on the last lap of the Kremlin derby, Andropov, who only a few years before had been an outsider and a dark horse, suddenly emerged as the favorite and finished first.

The only difference between the Kremlin power struggle and a race in sports is that in the former the finish line was a relative concept: one could not tell in advance just where it would be. But it could be brought closer by hastening the event that marked it: Brezhnev's death.

Since he was an old man, seriously ill, whose death had often been predicted and had even been falsely announced several times, one did not have to look far to find a basis for presuming the innocence of the person in whose way that old man stood. In our biography of Andropov, we wrote that, however fierce the power struggle had become by 1982, we would like to think that Brezhnev died a natural death. But we now have to acknowledge that new facts have dissipated that wishful thinking like so much smoke.

Although by the spring of 1982 Andropov was actually in power, its trappings were still being worn by Brezhnev; it was urgent for Andropov to find a way out of that constitutional dead-end. He stepped up the campaign to smear Brezhnev. For the first time, TV cameras showed him as he actually was—old and feeble, incapable of governing the country. Rumors that his closest friends, his relatives, and even he himself were implicated in graft were widely circulated. But Brezhnev still clung to his high offices, no doubt less of his own will than at the urging of top aides, who realized that his departure would mean the end for them, too. Then Andropov prepared an exhausting work schedule for Brezhnev, one that would have been hard for even a healthy man to cope with; it required that he attend and makes speeches at meetings and conferences, traveling in Russia and abroad. If Brezhnev had died a natural death, it would have been the best way out of that continuing crisis for Andropov. But the old man heroically bore up under the demanding ceremonial duties imposed on him.

In the spring of 1982, while Brezhnev was visiting a tractor plant in Tashkcnt, in Central Asia, a catwalk crashed down on him. But his luck held even in that case: by a miracle, he was not killed. Injured, he was flown in a special plane to Moscow. The plane was met by an ambulance that took him to Kuntsevo Hospital. A grand welcome at the airport had been scheduled—including Politburo members, reporters, and TV cameramen—but it was canceled under the pretext that he had had a stroke on the plane. However, word of the attempt on his life was leaked by nurses and nurse's attendants at the hospital, where he was being treated for minor injuries, scratches, and bruises. No sooner had he recovered than he again began appearing at public ceremonies and making speeches.

In late September 1982, Brezhnev traveled to Baku, the capital of Azerbaijan, where Andropov's protégé Geidar Aliyev was all-powerful boss. Aliyev arranged a lavish reception for the aged ruler, and along with it, a malicious practical joke that was witnessed by the whole nation—there was detailed TV coverage of everything that happened to Brezhnev on that ill-fated trip. He was to give the welcoming speech at a great rally of Azerbaijan's Party members. When he mounted the rostrum, he began to read a text that had been palmed off on him. At first he did not notice that it wasn't his speech at all and had nothing to do with that rally. The TV cameras caught not only that gaffe but also the commotion in the hall, the hurried consultations among Brezhnev's aides, and one of them half-running up to him to give him the right text.

Brezhnev evidently surmised that this was yet another of Andropov's tricks. Putting aside the phony text, he smiled and said, "What just happened is not my fault, comrades. I'll have to start over again." Then, unshaken, and even with dignity, he read the forty-minute speech of welcome to the Communists of Azerbaijan.

Right after that incident, two jokes that made a mockery of Brezhnev popped up in Moscow. In one of them, it seems that, after giving a speech, he reprimands his speechwriter for having handed him a text that took a half-hour to read, instead of the fifteen-minute one he should have gotten. "But Leonid Ilich!" the speechwriter replies. "There were two copies, and you read through both of them."

The other was a bit of black humor. Brezhnev mounts the rostrum, takes the text of a speech out of his pocket, and begins to read . . . his own obituary! When he notices the confusion in the audience, he stops and takes a closer look at the text. "Damn it all, I've done it again! I put on Andropov's jacket instead of my own."

November 7 was drawing near. Andropov had special hope for that day, when the sixty-fifth anniversary of the Bolshevik Revolution was to be celebrated. The forecast was for very cold weather, and Brezhnev's doctors had firmly insisted that he must not review the military parade from atop Lenin's Mausoleum because there was a risk of hypothermia, which is especially dangerous to old people. But Andropov had demanded that he make an appearance, maintaining that his absence on such a day would be wrongly interpreted by the Soviet public and foreign observers. The rules of protocol for Soviet holidays were binding on all and were strictly observed. Andropov took advantage of that fact.

In making his decision to go, Brezhnev was probably heeding the call of duty more than the advice of his impatient heir. In any case, three days before his death, the aged ruler, supported on both sides by aides and pausing at every step to get his breath, made his painful way to the rostrum atop Lenin's Mausoleum, where he stood for several hours, his benumbed hand raised in welcome. It was ten degrees above zero. His old blood gave him no warmth, and the muscles of his swollen face were stiff. That was his farewell to all he had once held sway over: Red Square, Moscow, Russia. Within a week his comrades would mount that same mausoleum, and his successor, Yuri Vladimirovich Andropov, would open the ceremonies at his funeral.

That would be the first in a series of funerals in Red Square that continued for a whole twenty-eight months, until the relatively young Mikhail Gorbachev became Russia's leader. With all those funerals, as much alike as peas in a pod, held in the very center of the empire's capital, people forgot that, despite his old age and illnesses, Brezhnev bore up under the grueling test of November 7 that Andropov had insisted on; also that in the evening, as if nothing had happened, he attended a formal reception.

Foreign guests who were present that evening noted that he looked no worse than usual. And during the next two days, his health showed no signs of having worsened; he didn't even seem to have caught a cold. Yet less than three days after that, he died.

On the morning of November 10, after having breakfasted and read *Pravda,* he went into his bedroom, followed by bodyguards assigned to him by Andropov. A few minutes later, they returned to the living room and told Victoria Petrovna Brezhneva that her husband had suddenly died. She leaped up from her chair and rushed toward the bedroom, but the bodyguards barred her way. One of them tried to calm her and made her sit down on a sofa, but no one hastened to call a doctor. Then Victoria Brezhneva was led away; she didn't see her husband's body until two days later—in the Hall of Columns of the House of Unions—embalmed, in an open coffin bestrewn with flowers.

Unfortunately, our information does not take us beyond that point. However, many of our Moscow acquaintances have no doubt that Brezhnev met a violent death. Jokes like the following, of which there were many, became commonplace in the new Andropov era:

"What do you think, Yuri Vladimirovich: Will the Soviet people follow you?"

"Oh, yes. Because if they don't, they follow Brezhnev."

And, in fact, the people did follow their new leader of their own free will. This was because the people's political ideals and those of their leader (the fifth since the Revolution) converged to a rare degree, even though the policeman's club wielded by Andropov struck the backs of the common people.

"Come to rule and reign over us. Our land is great and rich, but there is no order in it." Judging from the old chronicles, the Russian people, in the early Middle Ages, issued that invitation to occupy the princely throne. The people's age-old dream of order was embodied in the political ideal of a strong and ruthless ruler. There is good reason why they have fond memories of those high chiefs, even though the rulers did not pamper the people and were hardly distinguished for their gentle ways: Ivan the Terrible, Peter the Great, Joseph Stalin. Andropov's appearance on the Soviet political horizon was a response to the people's yearning for a strong and imposing personality at the helm of power; it was not only due to his skills at intrigue and plotting, which he had displayed to excess during his struggle to wrest power from Brezhnev's bureaucratic junta. By themselves, they would not have sufficed.

The main argument that Andropov used against Brezhnev was incontrovertible: During his eighteen-year rule, he had been concerned only with amassing titles, orders, prizes, gifts, honors, and other outward signs of power. Brezhnev and his clique had exhausted the country, perhaps irreversibly. They had brought Soviet agriculture, already unprofitable, to the brink of collapse. They had made the national economy dependent on foreign capital investments. They had weakened the reins of government within the country and in Eastern Europe. They had retreated before America in the Middle East, a key region of the world. In the matter of military technology, they had brought the Soviet Union down to the level of a second-rate power.

The whole question is: What did Andropov set up in opposition to his predecessor's regime? From the outset of his rule, Andropov adopted a stern domestic policy. He had to fight on two fronts at the same time: against the Party VIPs, who were negligent of their duties and corrupted by power, and against the common people, who were no less corrupted by sloth, indifference, and drunkenness. In his heart of hearts, Andropov was a naïve idealist. He wanted to restore order in the Soviet empire by means of harsh and highly publicized police campaigns. His goal can be given different labels: the ideal of a police state, the idyll of a police state, the illusion of a police state, a utopian police state. But the name doesn't change anything. Andropov himself, unlike Brezhnev, was a man of puritanical bent; he was opposed on principle to any luxuries, and tried to establish a standard of austerity and discipline throughout the USSR. He used police methods not only because other methods were unknown to him but primarily because he regarded others as ineffective in combating the nation's customs. Being a policeman both by virtue of his working habits and by deliberate choice, he acted in accordance with his thinking, which, as Goethe put it, is "the hardest thing in the world." He surely knew what another German, Karl Marx, had said of Peter the Great: "He rooted out barbarism by barbarous methods."

On January 31, 1983, no more than two and a half months after Brezhnev's death, Andropov showed up without warning at the Sergo Ordzhonikidze Machine-Building Plant in Moscow. He made a tour of the plant's shops, much as a sharp-eyed owner would; he stopped at machine tools and chatted with workers. On the subject of the country's critical economic condition, he spoke frankly, straight out, and exactingly, which hadn't been done in the Soviet Union for a long time:

"What, then, is the way out of such a situation? . . .

"And where, to use Lenin's words, is that link that must be seized in order to stretch out the whole chain? That chain is big and heavy. And although we can't boil everything down to discipline, it is with discipline, comrades, that we must begin. . . .

"I would like the comrades to understand correctly that the problem of strengthening discipline does not apply only to blue-collar workers and engineering-technical workers. It applies to everyone, beginning with the ministers."

From the very beginning, Andropov found the right tone in talking to the common people, who were of course flattered that the demands placed on them were also binding on their masters. The method was well known and unerring. A classic description of it was given by Wilkie Collins in *The Moonstone,* when the detective, Kaff, wins over the servants in Lady Julie's household by beginning his search in the wardrobe of the mistress of the house herself.

Andropov kept the promise he had made to the workers at the Moscow machine-tool plant. When it came to cleaning the house he had inherited by bypassing the legitimate Party heirs, he did all the floors, including the top one, simultaneously. It looked as if it was even more interesting for him to clean the upper floors than the lower ones. In the fifteen months allotted to him by fate, he managed to do quite a lot.

Andropov carried out a large-scale purge of the Soviet Olympus: the apparatus of the CC, and the Council of Ministers. During the long years while Brezhnev was slowly dying, those who dwelt on that Olympus had got used to thinking of themselves as immortal, and they had actually come to seem immortal, like Greek gods or the members of the French Academy. But Andropov's seizure of power showed them to be the most ordinary of mortals, tainted by the peccadilloes that mortal flesh is heir to. Taking advantage of this, Andropov escorted the would-be Olympians down the mountain and into retirement.

He drove more than a third of the high officials out of the places that they had made cozy and warm by sitting in them for so long and replaced them with reliable KGB cadres. At the same time, he shook up the provincial foundations of the Soviet power structure: out of 150 provincial Party bosses (actually, local satraps), forty-seven—again, almost a third—were dismissed. In the small Urals republic of Bashkiria alone, 160 high-ranking officials were victims of an exemplary purge. In the Ukraine, where Brezhnev was born, out of twenty-five first Party secretaries, nine were removed; and in Kazakhstan, once Brezhnev's fief, seven out of twenty. In Moscow itself, there were rumors about a secret Andropov circular letter ordering a substantial reduction in the bureaucratic staff in general. The Lubyanka, the Moscow political prison through which Stalin had sent hundreds of thousands of "enemies of the people" to the other world, was now crowded with Brezhnev's minions, accused of bribe-taking and other kinds of corruption. To the obvious satisfaction of a public longing for spectacle, Andropov had several of them shot. The victims included Brezhnev's bosom buddy Yuri Smelyakov, chairman of the Technology and Industrial Export Agency, and Yuri Sokolov, manager of the Eliseyev Delicatessen Emporium and supplier of scarce victuals to the Brezhnev household and to the elite of the Moscow cosmonauts.

In Moscow, people were waiting (some with fear, others with impatience) for the next act of the show being put on by Andropov: the trial of his personal enemy, Nikolai Shchelokov. Shchelokov had been successively removed from the post of minister of internal affairs only a few days after Brezhnev's death, expelled from the CC and then from the Party, stripped of his general's rank and reduced to enlisted status, and ultimately arrested. At the same time, his son was sent to a labor camp in Siberia as a parasite. In Moscow, it was said that ex-General Shchelokov would be sentenced to death for corruption as an example.

But that trial, like many other moves planned by Andropov, was destined not to take place; the show was interrupted by some extraordinary events not foreseen by the director. Those events occurred in Moscow in March 1983, only a few months after Andropov's accession to power.

After the arrest of her husband and son, Madame Shchelokova was left alone in the huge apartment on Kutuzov Prospekt, abandoned by her friends. She was in despair; but what she did can hardly be explained as simply an act of vengeance. More likely, she had decided that the only way to save her husband and her son was to destroy their personal enemy physically. She had never liked him and had once told Brezhnev's wife, a good acquaintance of hers, that he had paranoid delusions. Andropov lived in the same building, so she took her husband's pistol and ambushed her neighbor on the stairway when he arrived home late one evening from the Kremlin. She managed to fire at him several times before she was cut down by his bodyguards. But since it was the first time she had ever used a firearm, all she succeeded in doing was to wound Andropov in the side. This wound was enough, however, to put the energetic ruler on the sidelines for a time.

Indeed, precisely at this time, the second half of March 1983, some extraordinary events took place in the Kremlin. Item: A solemn ceremony marking the one hundredth anniversary of Karl Marx's death was unexpectedly canceled. Item: For the first time, TASS failed to publish a routine report on the weekly Thursday session of the Politburo, which meant that there had been no session. Item: Marshal Ustinov, the minister of defense, left in his plane for an official visit to Hungary early on the morning of March 23, but no sooner did he arrive at the airfield in Budapest than he changed planes and unexpectedly returned to Moscow.

Andropov disappeared from public for the first time since he had come to power. Although he again appeared in public less than two weeks later, he was a different man: he walked unsteadily, his hands trembled, and he could not manage without assistance. Many people in Moscow are inclined to believe that the wound given him by Madame Shchelokova played a fateful role in his life.

In the summer of 1983, we received an account of her attempt on Andropov's life from Moscow. Our source was quite reliable but was not in possession of all the facts; his information could only have been third-hand, or at best second-hand. Our source reported to us that, during this same period, an editor from the Political Literature Publishing House had been summoned by the new KGB chairman, Victor Chebrikov, and ordered to make urgent preparations for the publication of a book about the attempt made on Lenin's life by Fanya Kaplan, a Social Revolutionary, on August 30, 1918. The time allotted him was very brief by Soviet standards: three months. When the editor asked who the author was, Chebrikov told him that the book would consist only of documents that had been kept in KGB files and that had never been published; they would be put together by a KGB consultant, Associate Professor N. D. Kostin. He added that the manuscript would be delivered to the publishing house within the next few days.

The publication of several other books was immediately postponed in order to give the green light to the KGB. Three editors were assigned to work on the book (instead of one, the usual practice); and at the Red Proletariat Press, where it was to be printed, all workers' vacations were canceled. In short, extraordinary measures were taken.

The whole thing was all the more strange in that the attempt on Lenin's life was very rarely written about in the Soviet Union. Since 1925, not so much as one monograph on it had appeared; the idea was to avoid mentioning that precedent. Our source saw a direct connection between the attempt on Andropov's life and the KGB's commissioning of a book about the attempted assassination of Lenin.

The publication of the book in the autumn of 1983 under the title *A Shot at the Heart of the Revolution,* and the printing of two hundred thousand copies, which were immediately bought up, indirectly confirmed the reliability of our correspondent's report about the attempt on Andropov's life. It was confirmed in another way, too: On the anniversary of Andropov's inauguration, *Izvestia* ran an article about Fanya Kaplan's attempt to assassinate Lenin; it noted significantly that the event was "of topical interest even now." That remark would have been meaningless if the attempt on Andropov's life had not actually been made.

As a replacement for Shchelokov (who had avoided standing trial only because he beat his persecutors to the punch by committing suicide), Andropov appointed General Vitaly Fedorchuk, the brutal former KGB chief in the Ukraine, as minister of the interior, and assigned two other KGB generals as his deputies. Acting as a team, the three of them carried out a colossal purge of the regular police. In Moscow alone, more than two hundred high-ranking police officers were arrested, not to mention ordinary policemen, for whom the common people felt less pity than they did for the partocrats. (It is the regular police who deal with most of the common people; the KGB gives its attention to the intellectuals.)

Once again, Andropov had found a way into the hearts of the populace, which for centuries had usually blamed the courtiers for everything and had excused the tsar. And if the "tsar" proclaims a crusade against the director oppressors of the populace, the regular police and the officials—even if it is done only with a view toward seizing power or strengthening it—he is assured of popular support.

But Andropov himself was not long able to make use of that support. His visit to the workers at the Moscow machine-tool plant was his first and, alas, his last act of "going to the people." Four months after his accession to power, he was physically just as feeble as the Brezhnev whom he had ridiculed as a doddering old man. Unlike him, however, Andropov stayed on the job until his last hour, and he died at his workplace, a ward converted into an office in a suburban hospital. The hospital is located in Kuntsevo, a residential community near Moscow, in the middle of an old park, around which runs an insurmountable stone wall with barbed wire on top of it. The central control panel for governing the country was temporarily installed in that hospital in the fall of 1983, so that for a good six months, Kuntsevo replaced the Kremlin.

This added a bit more radiance to Andropov's heroic halo, which had been partly created by himself—something of which even his severest critics were not entirely insensible. Historically, Andropov undoubtedly belongs on the long list of the world's evil men, although because of the brief span allotted to him he was not able to fully realize his potential for criminal acts. And yet by virtue of his paradoxical fate, his dramatic struggle against death, and his unflagging labor up to the last hours of his life, Andropov also belongs among the tragic figures of history; he is a match for some of the characters in Shakespeare's chronicle plays or in the *Annals* of Tacitus. This certainly cannot be said of

Brezhnev, Chernenko, or, for the time being, at any rate, Gorbachev.

In the fall of 1983, Andropov again disappeared from view—not for ten days, as in March, but for twenty, thirty, forty days. As the days, weeks, and months passed without his reappearance, many people began to suspect that he was not on the job at all, as had been the case with his predecessor during the last years of his life and as would be the case with his successor throughout his thirteen months as general secretary. But exactly the contrary was true. Andropov's political strength was in inverse ratio to his physical state: as his health worsened, his power grew stronger and stronger. He continued his purge of the Party and government apparatuses; more and more of his people were made members of the Secretariat and the Politburo itself; and his police revolution in the bureaucratic state was expanded, reaching into the most remote corners of the empire. Ultimately, this led to a paradox very rare in world history and unique in the history of Russia; Andropov was never so all-powerful as just before his death.

The most striking proof of his political omnipotence —and also, perhaps, of the insanity that Shchelokov's wife had told Brezhnev's wife about—was his ordering the shooting down of a Korean airliner with 269 people aboard on the night of September 1, 1983.

Former Soviet pilot Victor Belenko, before defecting in his MIG-25 to Japan, had flown an SU-15 fighter plane like the one that destroyed the Korean airliner, and he had done a tour of duty at the Kamchatka base whose radar first picked up the KAL. Belenko pointed out the first stage in the immediate communication from the local Air Defense control tower to the central command. The moment a radar picks up an unidentified plane flying within one hundred kilometers of the Soviet border, its position is reported to the Soviet command center in the city of Kalinin, not far from Moscow. This is standard operating procedure.

The next link in this centralized system of command was pointed out by the chief of the general staff, Marshal Nikolai Ogarkov, at his press conference: "Soviet Air Defense Forces operated in full contact with the Government's authorities."

In his memoirs, Khrushchev offers irrefutable evidence of the governmental level at which this kind of military action is decided on. He tells how, on May 1, 1960, at 5:00 A.M., he was awakened by a telephone call from the minister of defense, Marshal Rodion Malinovsky, who reported to him that an American U-2 spy plane had crossed the border with Afghanistan and penetrated into Soviet airspace in the direction of Sverdlovsk. Khrushchev ordered Marshal Malinovsky "to shoot down the plane by whatever means he could." A few hours later, when Khrushchev was standing on Lenin's Mausoleum reviewing the May Day military parade in Red Square, Marshal Sergei Biryuzov, commander in chief of the Air Defense Forces, violated protocol and came up to him and whispered into his ear that the U-2 had been shot down and that the American pilot, Francis Gary Powers, had been taken prisoner.

This same centralized military-bureaucratic communications system also functioned smoothly during Andropov's rule, although the occasion in question involved not a military plane with only one person, its pilot, but a passenger plane.

When the Korean plane, after crossing the Bering Sea, was over Kamchatka and first showed up on the Soviet radar screens, Soviet fighters scrambled from various air bases. One after another, they followed the wayward jumbo jet as it strayed in and out of Soviet airspace. For two and a half hours, in the predawn mist over the Sea of Okhotsk, at least eight Soviet fighter planes followed the off-course airliner, passing it on like a football from one zone to the next. In accordance with orders, they did this surreptitiously, in no way revealing their presence, so as not to put the crew of the KAL on guard—so it wouldn't realize its fatal error and promptly get into radio contact with Japanese ground control.

During those two and a half hours, word about the "intruder" was passed through sclerotic bureaucratic channels and the tangled system of intermediate links up to the central control panel in the Kuntsevo Hospital, and direct instructions were issued from there.

As the Korean airliner, still with its menacing (although stealthy) escort, was approaching the wooded hills of Sakhalin, the order to destroy it had already been received by the local base of the Air Defense Forces. One pilot, Vasily Kazmin, had only one order as he took off in his jet fighter to intercept the Boeing 747: attack the KAL plane (which from the very beginning he called "the target"), and do so by surprise, unawares, so it could not report the presence of its pursuers to anyone. Military secrecy was strictly observed throughout this long operation, whose aim was to "terminate the flight" of the airliner.

At the request of the U.S. government, Victor Belenko analyzed the tapes of the conversation between the Soviet pilot and ground control. Six minutes before the destruction of the KAL plane, Kazmin, in accordance with previously received orders, deployed his SU-15 behind and below his moving "target" into an attack position and reported that his missiles were "locked on the airliner and ready to strike." Unexpectedly, however, he received an order to break the missile lock-on and move closer to the KAL plane. Belenko commented that the pilot's voice "reflects disgust at the order." Those two minutes of "indecision on the ground" were in fact minutes of cold-blooded resoluteness and precise calculation. Before the target moving across their radar screen was destroyed, the ground dispatchers had to see that it was brought exactly to the dividing line between Soviet and international airspace. They did this so the wreckage of the plane, shot down in Soviet airspace, would fall into international waters, to eliminate any responsibility on their part for its fate. "Over the island of Sakhalin, warning tracer bursts were fired along the course of the intruder aircraft. . . . Shortly afterward it left Soviet airspace and flew on toward the Sea of Japan.'' This was the version the Soviet government insisted on during the first forty-eight hours after the Boeing jumbo jet was blasted out of the skies—before the tapes of the conversations between the Soviet pilots were made public at the UN.

When Andropov authorized the order to destroy the airliner, he must have been thinking least of all of a confrontation between the superpowers. But he wanted to wreak vengeance for the humiliating failure of Soviet military technology above the Bekaa Valley during the war in Lebanon, when the Israelis, without losing a single aircraft, had destroyed 104 Syrian MIGs; for his powerlessness to do anything about the American RC-135 spy plane that was regularly patrolling the Kamchatka region and that was ''constantly playing on our nerves,'' as the commander of the Far Eastern Air Defense Forces put it; and finally, for the imposed role of peace-lover that Andropov had to play with a view to preventing the deployment of American missiles in Europe—which later proved impossible. The only way the former KGB chief knew to demonstrate to the rest of the world its vulnerability in the face of Soviet might was the terrorist way. Because of that way—political self-assertion through a terrorist act—under Andropov's dictatorial regime any foreign aircraft straying into Soviet airspace would be welcome.

But his scheme was foiled when the details became known. After that, denials were futile. So the Soviet Union then declared unequivocally, through many mouthpieces, that in similar circumstances it would again destroy a civilian aircraft. Andropov went for broke and, figuring that the best defense was a strong offense, shifted all the blame for what had happened onto President Reagan, claiming that he had sent a spy plane into Soviet airspace under the guise of a passenger plane. That theme was eagerly seized upon by Western journalists, and they have so thoroughly masticated it that we need not deal with it here at all. Andropov's accusation—absurd and harsh to the point of heedlessness

—burned all bridges to the normalization of relations with the West, and it destroyed the image of peace-maker, defuser of world conflicts, and advocate of disarmament that he, for tactical purposes, had so stubbornly foisted upon mankind. Thus, Dr. Jekyll was once and for all transformed into Mr. Hyde.

But far from weakening Andropov's prestige within the country, his performance only strengthened it, not only among his military-and-police bullyboys but among the common people of the empire. During the many centuries of their servile existence, the common people of Russia have become used to interpreting mercy as weakness, sadism and barbarous treatment as strength, and fear as respect. The suffering that has been the lot of those people has embittered and hardened them and has made them ruthless toward other nations. The moral values that inspire Western civilization are unknown to them, or if known, they are incomprehensible. Why then should one be amazed—as Western correspondents in Moscow were—at the common people's unanimous support of the Soviet military action against the civilian aircraft?

The Marquis de Custine, a well-known author-traveler of the nineteenth Century, compared the Russia of Nicholas I to a garrison. In order to function successfully as an empire today, however, Russia must also be a police torture chamber. In a paradoxical way, the enemies of the empire, both the real enemies and the imaginary ones, are the source of its negative inspiration, the grounds for its political, police, and military consolidation. Thus, the empire's fear of collapsing brought Andropov to power, with his ramified apparatus of coercion and his well-worked-out methods of violence. The common people of the empire, haunted by that fear, welcomed the drop in its level, which was brought about by increasing the functions of the state at the expense of curtailing the already-skimpy civil liberties of the individual.

So if Andropov was looking for popularity among the Russian masses, he found it. And thanks to the fact that his rule came to an unexpected end only fifteen months after its beginning, like President Kennedy in the United States, he was transformed from a reality into a myth (with due allowance, of course, for the different political tastes of the American people and the Russians).

When Andropov was on his deathbed, he issued an ultimatum to the United States and kept his word. After NATO had begun to deploy Pershing-2s in Europe, he broke off the Geneva talks about intermediate-range missiles. In the Soviet Union itself he launched a campaign of unprecedented scale against America and the U.S. president personally, with huge street demonstrations, meetings at industrial plants, and TV shows. Near the very end of Andropov's life, the anti-American rhetoric reached an hysterical pitch as the Soviet newspapers began to compare Reagan to none other than Hitler. In part, this campaign stemmed from an inferiority complex, a sense of impotence. Andropov surely felt humiliated: on the part of his country, because it was lagging so hopelessly behind America, and on his own part, because he was so feeble physically in comparison with Reagan, a man older than he. By now, anti-American rhetoric was all he had left.

Every morning a government motorcade would leave Kuntsevo, where the top Kremlin leaders have had their residence since Stalin's day, and speed along the cleared center lane (the so-called green lane) of the Kalinin Prospekt with headlights on and extra bodyguards ahead, behind, and on both sides, and disappear into the gates of the Kremlin. Exactly at 5:30 P.M. it would reappear from there and, signaling with varicolored lights rotating on the domes of the cars, speed out of town and back to Kuntsevo. The police would stop all traffic, and the passersby would try to guess which car Andropov was in. "Most likely he's in that black limousine in the middle of the motorcade, the one with the window-curtains drawn"—such was the guess of the Western correspondents, and for the moment it satisfied the world's curiosity. But only for a moment, because everyone soon figured out that this was a fraud, and there was no question that it had been devised by Andropov himself.

Again, in November 1983, just before the solemn evening ceremonies in the Kremlin's Palace of Congresses celebrating the anniversary of the Revolution, one of the masters of ceremonies, wearing a red armband and a beaming smile, assured the foreign guests with complete sincerity that Andropov would certainly appear this time. But then the Politburo members, in a close-knit bunch, made their appearance, and once again Andropov was not among them. At this point something happened that was unprecedented in Kremlin history: the members of the Politburo took their place in the presidium, and in the very center they left an empty armchair, a symbol of the invisible but dread presence of Andropov among them. That armchair created an ominous atmosphere for the ceremonies, which were more like a funeral. The most nervous of all were the Politburo members seated on both sides of that empty armchair, "waiting for Godot." It was plain that until the very end of the evening, most of them didn't know whether Andropov would show up.

Andropov had time to repeat once more this trick of leaving an empty armchair: on December 28 at a session of the Soviet parliament. The oldest member of the Politburo was the seventy-eight-year-old cadaverous-looking premier, Nikolai Tikhonov; because of his venerable age, he had difficulty understanding what was going on around him, not to mention in adapting to the new Kremlin rules. By mistake, he almost sat down in Andropov's armchair. Stopped in time by his Politburo colleagues, he took the next seat, from which during all the rest of the session he kept glancing with undisguised terror at the chair in which the invisible ruler was sitting.

Finally, if the ghost of Hamlet's father was free to stroll about Elsinore, why wasn't the spectre of the Kremlin's mysterious master free to stroll about it, since he himself was incapable of such movement?

The way the Politburo members scheduled their activities during the last days of Andropov's life testifies to how poorly informed they were about the state of affairs at Kuntsevo Hospital. The day before his death, *Pravda* reported that his protégé Geidar Aliyev was preparing to leave within the next few days for a brief working visit to Syria. And on the next day, *Pravda* informed its readers that the Politburo's commission on educational reform was holding a session. That session was attended by four Politburo members, two of whom became, each in turn, the top Soviet leader (the sixth and seventh): Konstantin Chernenko and Mikhail Gorbachev. If even one of them had known that Andropov was dying, the session would certainly have been canceled or attended by replacements from among the lower-ranking partocrats.

Even Igor Andropov, the day before his father's death, was in Stockholm, speaking at the European Security Conference, declaring that the Western countries were "deliberately planning a nuclear war." He didn't leave Stockholm until February 9; when his plane landed at Sheremetyevo Airport in Moscow, his father was already dead.

To sum up: The state of Andropov's health was unknown both to his son and to such loyal followers as Geidar Aliyev and Mikhail Gorbachev. Even Minister of Foreign Affairs Andrei Gromyko was denied access to Andropov's hospital ward and merely talked to him on the telephone, according to a Gromyko aide. Yet all of these men belonged to his "kitchen cabinet," or more accurately, his "hospital cabinet." This means that not a single member of the Politburo knew exactly what was going on behind the high walls, festooned with barbed wire, of the Kuntsevo compound, where Stalin had died and where Andropov was now dying. The only link between Andropov and the Kremlin elite was KGB Chairman Chebrikov, who, although he was a general, served as a messenger for the sick man, keeping the state of his health totally secret.

It remains an open question whether the Politburo members were ignorant of what was happening with their chief in Kuntsevo Hospital because he concealed his condition from them or because he himself did not realize the seriousness of his own condition and hoped to recover. We have no sure answer to that question, although we are inclined to accept the latter explanation and suppose that the sharp and irreversible downturn in Andropov's health came unexpectedly, both for him and for his doctors. That conclusion is also supported by the medical bulletin on his death. Needless to say, there was not a single word in that bulletin about the wound from one of the bullets fired by Madame Shchelokova, which some reports have as a major factor in Andropov's death.

One can only guess how things would have gone for Russia and the rest of the world if Andropov had been granted not fifteen months but two or three times more, at least several years, in his post as official leader of the empire. Certainly, however, those would have been years of more confrontations between the superpowers and a greater number of risky "adventures" and anonymous acts of terrorism, both in Russia and abroad, more eventful and sensational years than those that did follow Andropov's death. However loyal to him his epigones may be, they are a far cry from him; a copy cannot compare with the original.

We say this with no regrets whatsoever.

2. The Duel at the Tyrant's Coffin

IN EARLY FEBRUARY 1984, the body of Yuri Andropov was lying in an open coffin profusely adorned with flowers and wreaths in the Hall of Columns of the House of Unions, on the same dais where, fifteen months before, the body of his predecessor, Brezhnev, had lain in state, and where, thirteen months later, the body of his successor, Chernenko, would do the same. Tens of thousands of Muscovites were filing by to pay their last respects to him, and many were weeping out of sincere grief. (At the coffins of Brezhnev and Chernenko, no one wept except for immediate relatives.) At the same time, a half-mile away in the Kremlin, a struggle was going on for the post that he had left vacant: that of Party chief, the highest in the empire.

Every day, in accordance with protocol, the members of the Politburo would visit the coffin. They would stand there for a few minutes as part of the guard of honor, then go back to their complex cloakroom ma-

neuvers. On one occasion, Andropov's landsman, Mikhail Gorbachev, stopped by in a private capacity and, in
a special gesture, as though he were a member of the
family, sat near the coffin for a while with the deceased's widow, Tatyana Filippovna, and children, Igor
and Irina. With that gesture he emphasized, for millions
of Soviet and foreign TV watchers, his personal devotion to his patron, without whom he probably would
still have been vegetating in the provinces as Party boss
of the Stavropol Territory in the Northern Caucasus.

But Gorbachev had had good luck with the fief he
held from the Party. Although all administrative units
of the USSR are theoretically equal, some, as Orwell
said, are "more equal." In particular, by no means all
of them have sanitariums for the higher Party elite. But
the Stavropol Territory has several of them, including
Krasnye Kamni (Red Stones) in Kislovodsk (*kislaya
voda* means "acidic water"), which was visited from
time to time by Kremlin dwellers. From these famous
mineral springs, rich in carbonic acid, hydrocarbonates,
calcium, magnesium, dolomite, and sulfates, the political careers of two other Party bosses of the Stavropol
Territory, Mikhail Suslov and Fyodor Kulakov, had
taken their rapid rise. Both of them, once in the Kremlin, had sponsored the young Mikhail Gorbachev. Yet
for his transfer to Moscow in the winter of 1978, Gorbachev was indebted only to Andropov, who was at that
time KGB chairman; Andropov regularly traveled to
Krasnye Kamni beginning in the late sixties. He did this
chiefly in order to "take the cure" but also partly out of
nostalgia: the sanitarium was located only a few miles
from Nagutskaya Junction, where he had been born on
June 15, 1914. (The Cossack village of Privolnoye,
where Gorbachev was born seventeen years later, and
where his mother, Maria, still lives, is northwest of
Kislovodsk.)

Each time Andropov made this trip, in accordance
with protocol he would be met by Gorbachev in his capacity as Party boss of the territory. Gorbachev would
accompany him to Krasnye Kamni; he also visited him

there on several occasions. Gorbachev's visits were made unobtrusively and without excessive pomp—which he knew Andropov disdained, unlike the other Politburo members, most of whom preferred more luxurious government dachas elsewhere in the Caucasus, in the Crimea, on the Baltic, or in the Ukraine.

According to the recollections of former patients at that elite sanitarium (for example, two high-ranking defectors, Arkady Shevchenko and Mikhail Voslensky), Andropov stayed in an isolated cottage that was in fact his government dacha. And he socialized with no one except KGB officials who regularly came from Moscow to see him. (Even while on vacation, the chief of the secret police did not forget his official duties.) His stays at Krasnye Kamni were shrouded in secrecy, and aroused acute curiosity in the other vacationers—curiosity that could not be satisfied, however, because day and night Andropov's dacha was ringed by KGB agents in civilian clothes. The only person for whom Andropov made an exception was Gorbachev: the guards allowed his limousine, with its Stavropol license plates, immediate access to the secluded dacha. On one occasion, people even saw a small motorcade, including one limousine from Stavropol, set out in the direction of Nagutskaya Station. It seems that the hospitable local boss, Gorbachev, had arranged for his high-ranking landsman a sentimental journey to his old stamping grounds. But the journey was made incognito, at Andropov's insistence, since he disliked publicity, not only for professional reasons but also for personal ones. We do not know whether, on that occasion, the top cop managed to recover *le temps perdu* or only experienced a few pleasant moments associated with his memories of childhood.

Soon, however, the modest cottage in Krasnye Kamni was transformed from an idyllic vacation spot into the bridgehead from which Andropov launched his crusade against corruption. This was done at the prompting of his young friend and landsman, Mikhail Gorbachev.

At this point we must explain to Western readers what

every Soviet schoolchild knows. Neighboring provinces enter into competition with one another over all kinds of economic, cultural, and other indices; those competitions are called "socialist" so as to exclude any "bourgeois" taint of money-grabbing, deceit, or envy. Actually, though, precisely these traits determine the nature of the "socialist competitions"; and the one between Mikhail Gorbachev's Stavropol Territory and Sergei Medunov's Krasnodar Territory was no exception. But in that competition, the role of the vanquished was predictable for Gorbachev, not only because the land in the Krasnodar Territory was more fertile than his own land but primarily because Medunov, a protégé of Brezhnev, was accountable to no one but himself and could falsify his indices just as he pleased with no fear of an audit. Brezhnev himself generally tried to avoid offending his friends, regarding that as a breach of the code of friendship, and he in turn gave no credence to the complaints of others about them, figuring that they were smears by either their enemies or his own. This system of patronage, rake-offs, protectionism, and the promotion of his friends was the basic mechanism of his regime, and Andropov, in his post as KGB chairman, studied it in every detail before setting out to undermine Brezhnev. But he did it by proxy, acting through Gorbachev against Medunov, Brezhnev's protégé. Andropov had a compromising dossier on Medunov; it had been prepared by Gorbachev, who was not only earning brownie points with the powerful KGB chief but was settling old accounts with his neighbor to the west.

At the very end of 1978, even before Andropov had "fixed Medunov's wagon," he had managed, with the support of Mikhail Suslov, the cloakroom kingmaker, to get their mutual protégé Gorbachev transferred to Moscow as CC secretary for agriculture. It was important to Andropov to have readily available his chief, if secret, witness against Medunov. As for agriculture, the following year witnessed the beginning of those catastrophic crop failures in Russia that are still ongoing and that can be compared only with the "seven lean years" in the land of the Pharaohs predicted by Joseph. The agricultural collapse would have ruined the career of any other overseer of the empire's agriculture (as had repeatedly happened in the past with Gorbachev's predecessors), but it didn't leave a scratch on Gorbachev's political reputation and in no way interfered with his very rapid rise up the Kremlin ladder. This shows once more how much more important secret Kremlin intrigues are than overt failure or success in management or economic matters in general.

So it was that Andropov moved one of his most reliable people into the Kremlin to replace another he had close at hand, Vitaly Vorotnikov. Vorotnikov had helped Andropov—as vigorously as Gorbachev, but more overtly—in his struggle against Medunov. The Brezhnev mafia dismissed Vorotnikov from his post as deputy premier of the Russian Republic and sent him in honorary exile to Cuba as the Soviet ambassador.

Before Vorotnikov's return to the capital; before another Andropov protégé, Geidar Aliyev, was brought there from Azerbaijan; and before Victor Chebrikov was named KGB chairman, Gorbachev was Andropov's only reliable supporter in the Kremlin. (This is not counting Minister of Foreign Affairs Andrei Gromyko, who during the struggle took a wait-and-see position and did not side with the victor until it was obvious who it would be.) Gorbachev was the only person in the Kremlin close to Andropov, a man incapable of human closeness, tight-lipped and a loner. But it was not merely their joint campaign against Medunov, or the patron-protégé relationship between the older man and the younger one, that had brought them close together. When he went to Krasnye Kamni, Andropov usually brought his wife with him and they and Gorbachev's family got to know each other well. The initiative in this was taken by the hospitable and enterprising Raisa Gorbacheva, which is one of the reasons why Moscow rumors gave her credit for her husband's rapid rise in politics. In any case, Gorbachev had good reason to sit for a few minutes with Andropov's family near the coffin of his late sponsor. It would have been strange if he hadn't.

Once shown on television, however, that gesture took on symbolic coloration, especially since Andropov's lying in state and the "election" of his successor were prolonged even by Kremlin standards. Between Andropov's death and the proclamation of the new Soviet leader, four whole days passed in tense waiting and all kinds of guessing. Who would take his place? A private visit by a Politburo member to the coffin of the ruler was unheard of in the entire history of Kremlin funerals. In that charged atmosphere, the visit became evidence, presented *urbi et orbi*, of the special ties between the deceased patron and the living protégé. But the decision as to who would fill the vacancy left in the Kremlin did not, alas, depend on the television audience. And those on whom it did depend did not need evidence from television, since they were well informed as to the close relations between Andropov and Gorbachev. Indeed, the capital's upper Party circles were the source of a rumor (which we have not been able to verify) that Andropov and Gorbachev were not only landsmen but relatives, although distant ones.

But ties between friends, persons born in the same part of the country, or even kinfolk do not constitute a political testament. And even if such a testament had existed, in written or oral form, it would by no means have been binding. Thus, all during Soviet history up to that time, not a single number-two man in the Kremlin had become the number-one man.

This time, however, it seemed that Andropov—unlike Lenin, Stalin, Khrushchev, or Brezhnev—had finally managed to regulate the process of succession in the Kremlin; also that his henchmen from the punitive organs (the armed forces, the regular police, and the KGB) would see to it that the will of their patron was carried out and that the transfer of power to his successor went off smoothly. That probably would have happened if only one of Andropov's protégés in the Politburo had been a Party secretary. (That, along with being an ethnic Russian, is an absolute prerequisite to becoming general secretary.) But there were two of them: besides Gorbachev, there was also Grigori Romanov. A third Politburo member who was also a secretary was Konstantin Chernenko, but he was out of the running in view of his advanced age, the diseases that afflicted him, his lack of ambition, and the fact that he was not on the Andropov team, being a member of the Brezhnev clan.

The first two were formally the only pretenders to the post of Party leader. Both were CC secretaries, Politburo members, relatively young (although with a difference of eight years between them), ethnic Russians, and born in the countryside. (But of course, countrysides vary: Gorbachev was from the fertile South, with its "black earth," while Romanov was from the North, with its very poor, ashy, and swampy soils.) Fate had paired them in an artificial and false way, based on the kind of criteria used in questionnaires: age, position, social and ethnic background. Actually, they vied with each other like Gladstone and Disraeli (or, to use a Soviet analogy, like Stalin and Trotsky). Political life in the Kremlin gradually took on the character of a desperate struggle between them, at first covertly, when Andropov was close to death, and then more and more overtly, while Chernenko was in that same state. At various stages in that struggle, other members of the Kremlin elite became involved in it, some on Romanov's side, others on Gorbachev's.

Sometimes the struggle surfaced publicly, and the world officially learned of its latest victims. The first time this political duel was brought out into the open was at Andropov's coffin, a situation that was almost romantic, like Don Juan's duels in graveyards.

What was Andropov thinking of when he gave Gorbachev and Romanov parallel, equal positions, thereby involuntarily setting them at each other's throats? He had such a limited number of his own people in the Kremlin when he seized power there, and he had such an acute need for proponents of his police-state policy, that he quickly summoned to Moscow those men who had proven their efficiency by ruling harshly and sternly in their own domains. Thus, Vorotnikov was brought to Moscow after he had cleaned out, as if with an iron broom, what was left of Medunov's team in the Krasnodar Territory. Vitaly Fedorchuk, who had gained notoriety in the Ukraine for his very fierce reprisals against dissidents, up to and including murder, was named minister of internal affairs, replacing Andropov's old enemy, General Shchelokov. And Geidar Aliyev, a professional KGB man since his youth, who in the Republic of Azerbaijan in the Caucasus had waged such a harsh campaign against corruption that the death sentence for economic crimes became a fixture of everyday life, was brought into the Politburo a few days after Brezhnev's death; he was named first deputy premier under the nominal premiership of the seventy-eight-year-old Tikhonov.

As for Romanov, during his thirteen years as Party boss in Leningrad, he had contrived to turn that city—architecturally the most European of Russian cities—into a bastion of dark reaction, a stronghold of Russian ethnic chauvinists and neo-Stalinists, plunging its inhabitants into an atmosphere of fear that had disappeared in Moscow after Stalin's death and was partially restored only under Andropov. Fear, whose level in Moscow depended on the political weather, became in Leningrad a stable sign of the political climate. If Dickens had been in Russia at the time, he could have written yet another *Tale of Two Cities*. For Moscow and Leningrad, although only 650 kilometers apart, became almost as politically different from each other in the post-Stalin era as Paris and London in the late eighteenth century. The paradox of Leningrad, which in the USSR is called "the cradle of the Revolution," is that, although it has preserved its revolutionary spirit, it has turned that spirit around. It is revolutionary in its reactionary practices; it is avant-gardist and pioneering, but in the opposite direction. That tendency, which at first glance is self-contradictory, is clearly characterized in a Soviet joke: "Forward to Stalin!"

Judging, however, from what happened after Andropov came to power, one may say that if Moscow is a kind of Potemkin facade turned toward the West and displaying to foreign visitors a greater degree of tolerance and civility than Russia actually has, Leningrad gives a view of the country that is not only more realistic and truthful but, more important, offers a better notion of the country's future. This is all the more reason why one should also notice the other side of the police regime in Leningrad under Romanov. It became a model city in terms of economic indicators, growth of labor productivity, discipline, order, and cleanliness. With the example of Leningrad, Romanov demonstrated to his Moscow supervisors and colleagues the effectiveness of, and the justification and necessity for, a return to Stalinist methods of leadership.

Ideologically, then, Romanov was closer than anyone else to Andropov when Andropov came to power. Since both his choices and his time were limited, the former chief of the secret police—who in general was not very sensitive to psychological nuances and was given, rather, to thinking up grandiose schemes—was compelled to blink at the individual differences and frictions between Gorbachev and Romanov, just as Lenin had to tolerate the rivalry between Stalin and Trotsky. Andropov himself had risen above his own personal biases and past conflicts with Romanov when he summoned the latter to Moscow from Leningrad in the summer of 1983.

While Andropov was covertly inventing and carrying out complex anti-Brezhnev schemes in his own interests at the end of the seventies, quite unexpectedly for him another anti-Brezhnev intrigue developed in the Politburo, one that Andropov came to strongly oppose rather than support. For him, the situation was like a chess game being played simultaneously on several boards; or, using a military analogy, Andropov had to fight on several fronts at once. In 1978, after winning the battle for Gorbachev and bringing him to Moscow, and while he was continuing the campaign against

Medunov, Andropov also had to accept a battle imposed on him from without. For a certain length of time, the "Leningrad Front"—where Romanov, although acting on behalf of others, was the central figure—was the cause for most concern to him.

Since Romanov's home base in Leningrad was far removed from the epicenter of the Kremlin struggle, his membership in the Politburo was no more than a formal honor, just as was the case with the Party bosses of the Ukraine and Kazakhstan. By himself, Romanov would of course never have undertaken any intrigues in that struggle; but he was the creature of his landsman, Premier Alexei Kosygin, and of the "gray eminence," Mikhail Suslov. They regarded Romanov, then the youngest member of the Politburo (in 1978 he was fifty-five, Gorbachev's age today) as a perfectly suitable candidate for the post of general secretary to replace the already-ill Brezhnev and to spite his Dnepropetrovsk mafia. Suslov and Kosygin had personal accounts to settle with this mafia that ranged from political ones to matters of life-style. Thus, both were opposed to détente, with its ideological concessions to the West, and both, being peevish ascetics, were irritated by the fondness of Brezhnev's entourage for sumptuous showiness, riding out to the hunt in the royal manner, and highly publicized gala receptions for foreigners.

At that time, in late 1978, stenciled political pamphlets about "the Zionist lobby in the Central Committee" and the "Zionist seizure of control over the Politburo" were widely circulating in Leningrad and Moscow. They declared that the number-one Zionist among them was none other than Brezhnev himself. This was apparently an allusion to his wife, who came from a well-to-do Jewish family. The pamphlets added that the last stronghold in the struggle against Jewish domination of the Kremlin was "the only three Great Russians in the Politburo: Mikhail Suslov, Alexei Kosygin, and Grigori Romanov."

By the end of 1978, the matter of Romanov's transfer to Moscow seemed so definitively settled that his Mos-

cow sponsors, Kosygin and Suslov, without waiting for
the decree of the Party plenum, made an overt move
against Brezhnev and began regularly to call their protégé to the capital to take part in conferences of special
importance or talks with foreign delegations. In effect,
they were bringing him into the government of the empire to replace Brezhnev, who by now was on the sidelines.

For example, in November 1978, a delegation of
American legislators headed by Senator Abraham
Ribicoff was received in the Kremlin by Kosygin and
Romanov—an extraordinary event, in complete violation of the Kremlin's strict, Byzantine protocol. The
"Connecticut Yankee" was taken aback by Romanov's
uncouthness, by his rude, abrupt interruptions of those
he was talking with and the interpreter, and by his
dismaying ignorance of foreign affairs. For his part,
Romanov was amazed by the lack of discipline in the
Democratic Party and by the fact that Carter could not
just order his fellow Democrats on Capitol Hill to be
more conciliatory toward the Soviet Union. During this
meeting, Romanov rudely reprimanded an interpreter
who he thought had given one of his titles incorrectly.
His behavior with foreigners in the presence of other
foreigners was the exact opposite of that with which his
future rival, Mikhail Gorbachev, charmed Western
dignitaries, thanks to which Gorbachev became "the
darling of the West" long before his inauguration in the
Kremlin. But during that meeting with the American
legislators, Romanov wasn't giving the slightest thought
to the impression he was making on them: he was striving—perhaps a bit too much—to please his mentor
Kosygin. And Kosygin by no means favored courteous
behavior toward representatives of a hostile nation.

So at that time in late 1978 and early 1979, when Gorbachev was just beginning to get used to the new situation in the capital, Romanov's chances of replacing
Brezhnev were very good. But then came an incident
that completely wrecked the plans of the "Russian
troika."

That incident took place at the wedding banquet of Romanov's daughter, which of course was organized not by Romanov himself but, as his rank demanded, by a whole staff of KGB men. When the merriment was at its height and the guests were properly under the influence, one of the ranking KGB men, disguised as a guest, unexpectedly rose from his chair and, imitating a long-outmoded Russian way of wishing the young couple happiness, dashed a cup onto the floor. The other guests followed his example, and soon the floor was covered with fragments of porcelain, to the evident displeasure of Romanov, who was instinctively apprehensive of riotous carryings-on. Besides, he didn't like to see property wasted.

And he was least of all capable of linking the joke about him as a direct descendant of the House of Romanov with the porcelain dinnerware, which, as was ascertained the morning after the banquet, had belonged to one of the most illustrious members of that imperial house, Catherine the Great. On the occasion of the family festivities being held by the "house of Grigori Romanov," the porcelain had been issued directly from the Hermitage by its curator, academician Boris Piotrovsky, whose colleagues at that world-famous repository of art treasures had nicknamed him "How Can I Serve You?" because of his excessive fawning upon superiors. (The services rendered to the KGB by academician Piotrovsky did not go unrewarded. On his seventy-fifth birthday in 1983, when all the power in the country was in the hands of the former KGB chief, Piotrovsky was given the title Hero of Socialist Labor and was awarded the Order of Lenin. No museum curator before him had ever been given that supreme government award, and none has been since.)

Amazingly, information about that ill-starred wedding banquet and the aristocratic affectations of the "heir" of the Romanov dynasty (Grigori Romanov was actually from a poor peasant family in the village of Zikhnovo in Novgorod Province) was promptly leaked abroad by the usually very-secretive milieu of the top

Soviet elite. The mass media of the free world, taking the story on trust, seized upon the myth proffered to them: that Romanov was a kind of *enfant terrible* in the Politburo. This caricature in no way corresponded to what he really was: a person undiscriminating and even primitive in his tastes, and extremely modest in his way of life. That contradiction, belatedly discovered by Romanov's Kremlin mentors only after the rumors about the scandal at the wedding banquet had reached them from abroad via a circular route, saved Romanov from stern punishment. He kept his Leningrad post and his nominal membership in the Politburo, although his transfer to Moscow was taken off the agenda.

"Operation Catherine the Great's Dinnerware" was one more sign that a new pretender, KGB Chairman Andropov, had entered the struggle for the Kremlin throne. Romanov got off rather lightly in the contest: the dinnerware used at his daughter's wedding banquet was wrecked, but not his limousine with him in it, as happened a year later to Petr Masherov, Party boss of Byelorussia and another potential Brezhnev heir. Actually, all the other Brezhnev heirs met fates much more unfortunate than Romanov's. Sometimes they were out-and-out tragic, as in the case of Masherov or that of Fyodor Kulakov, a full member of the Politburo and a national Party secretary, who in the summer of 1978 died suddenly under very suspicious circumstances.

But precisely the unfinished business with Romanov played a key role in the political destiny of Mikhail Gorbachev.

After all, Romanov was still in the Politburo, and he represented a threat to Andropov's covert encroachments on the supreme power in the Kremlin. That threat was at a considerable distance—650 kilometers—but it had not been completely eliminated. The "people from Dnepropetrovsk" understood and supported Andropov's attitude toward Romanov. They were alarmed by his political ambitions, which were still backed by Suslov and Kosygin, and they were unsettled by other things about him: by his stern temper and impolite manner, alien to the over-easy familiarity and buddy-buddy atmosphere that they instilled into Kremlin life; by the fact that he did not belong to their close-knit clan of kinsmen and landsmen; and by his being so unpardonably young in contrast to their average age of about seventy. For Andropov, whose date of birth was not much later than those of the Dnepropetrovians—although he was young in spirit, vigorous, and in two years would begin decisive reprisals against the Kremlin gerontocrats—Romanov's age was no less of a *bête noire* for him than it was for the people from Dnepropetrovsk. Since among the Party rules there was not one under which you could expel a person from the Politburo merely because he was fifty-six instead of seventy-six, the only way out was to find another "baby" for the Politburo—someone more obliging, less ambitious, and, most important, respectful of his elders. A good thing seldom lacks takers, and in this case it wasn't necessary to conduct a nationwide search or to publish a "boy wanted" ad, because the "boy" was ready at hand: Mikhail Gorbachev, the youngest of the ten CC secretaries, an inconspicuous, modest, and accommodating young man from the provinces. No doubt some of the Politburo members had surmised Gorbachev's role as an instigator in the Medunov affair, but in 1979 that story was still far from its finale, and Gorbachev was amiable and obliging with everyone in the Kremlin. There was no one else ready at hand who could serve as a counterpoise to Romanov in terms of age, since all the others on the second rung of the Kremlin ladder were considerably older. So on November 27, 1979, not long after the scandal in the "house of Romanov," exactly one year after his transfer to Moscow and just a month before the Soviet invasion of Afghanistan, the forty-eight-year-old Gorbachev was "elected" a candidate member of the Politburo. Eleven months later, on October 22, 1980, he became a full member.

So Andropov and Romanov, kindred ideological spirits and potential confederates, temporarily found themselves in opposing camps because of the Kremlin power struggle. A few years later, when they were no longer political rivals, Romanov finally got into the Kremlin on the team captained by Andropov, who thereby demonstrated, as it were, his objectivity and devotion to principle, putting them above personal feelings and memories of past unpleasantness. And Andropov set an example for his comrades: he gave his former enemy Romanov equal rank with his landsman, friend, and protégé Gorbachev, for whom he had a soft spot in his heart as a creator does for his creation. Moreover, it was Gorbachev who was sent to Leningrad to bring Romanov to the capital.

If Gorbachev was a general favorite in the Politburo, thanks to his obliging nature and artful adaptability, Romanov disturbed many members because of his abruptness and harshness. Yet everyone acknowledged his abilities on the job: his managerial skills, his capacity for work, the fact that he placed just as great demands on himself as on others, and his loyalty to Stalinist principles of governing the empire, which during the period of Andropov's police-state rule gained special popularity both in the Kremlin and outside the walls of the citadel. But Romanov himself, to whom everything had come thanks to his own sometimes strenuous efforts, with occasional vexing setbacks, could not but be irritated by a darling of fate such as Gorbachev. Besides, he knew that the latter had been taken into the Politburo as a counterweight to himself, a move that nullified his own age advantage over his Kremlin colleagues. Although Romanov had been in the Politburo for four years longer than Gorbachev, he had been five years behind him in making it to Moscow. Yet that didn't prevent him from taking a haughty attitude toward his rival. He himself was, after all, a Leningrader; and although Leningrad was in a province, it *was* its capital, unlike such a backwoods as Stavropol. Finally, Gorbachev's evasiveness and affability irritated the blunt, boorish Romanov.

Their rivalry was known to everyone in Moscow

because each made haste to strengthen his power base in
the capital and put together an apparatus of people
loyal to him. The struggle between them gradually
became a struggle between their political machines. In
this respect, Gorbachev had better luck than Romanov:
even while Brezhnev was still in power, he had managed
to get his second secretary for Stavropol, Nikolai
Kruchina, transferred to Moscow, first as deputy chief
of the CC's agriculture department, then as its chief.
And some time later he got him shifted to the post of
business manager of the CC, a very important one in the
power struggle. But Romanov, who had only been in
Moscow for six months by the time Andropov died,
when he managed to get his second secretary for Leningrad transferred to the capital, could get him no better
post than that of minister of industrial construction,
which could play no role in the power struggle. As a CC
secretary, Romanov was in charge of heavy industry
and the armed forces, something certainly more important than the failing agriculture over which Gorbachev
presided. But Andropov, not long before his death, had
given his landsman Gorbachev additional responsibilities: for Party cadres and ideology. His supporters included Minister of Foreign Affairs Andrei Gromyko,
while Romanov's included Marshal Nikolai Ogarkov,
chief of the general staff, with whom he saw eye to eye
in demanding greater economic bulwarks for the armed
forces. Romanov's speech in February 1984 to the
nominal electors of the nominal Soviet parliament contained the promise that the Party and the nation would
"equip the army and the navy with everything necessary." It was the strongest statement made by a civilian
leader during the election campaign on the need for a
strong defense.

Later, Marshal Ogarkov's temporary disgrace in the
autumn of 1984 and Gromyko's passionate speech
nominating Gorbachev in March 1985 confirmed the
positions the two had taken in the Kremlin power
struggle.

As long as Andropov was physically able to keep his

position at the helm of power, Gorbachev and Romanov supplemented each other; when he grew ill and took to his bed for the last time, they replaced him, despite their mutual hostility. But when he died, it was impossible to divide the post of general secretary between them. During the four days from his death to the "election" of his successor, they gave free vent to their political passions, and they did so in proportion to the time they had restrained them, had *had* to keep them in check, while Andropov was alive.

We do not know, and most probably never will know, all the details of the political duel between Romanov and Gorbachev at the coffin of their mutual patron. All that is known for sure is that the young turks who had no chance of winning the prize in that struggle—Geidar Aliyev, Vitaly Vorotnikov, and KGB Chairman Victor Chebrikov—tried to reason with the Kremlin duelists, calling upon them to be conciliatory, reasonable, and altruistic. But no way! Each claimed his intransigence was due to high ideals rather than personal ambition. Romanov fought under the populist banners of neo-Stalinism, national chauvinism, and imperial jingoism. Gorbachev, on the other hand, was ideologically neutral, almost indifferent. (His ideological passions had raged and then subsided long ago, late in the Stalin era, when he was a student.) He wanted to strengthen the empire by means of modest, palliative economic reforms; he remembered some of them from the days of Khrushchev's impetuosity and borrowed others from his mentor, Andropov. Each claimed to be saving the fatherland from the other, and neither intended to yield because each realized that if he yielded now it would be for good.

Neither was strong enough to overcome the other, so each preferred to "vote" for Chernenko, Brezhnev's "gopher," as a compromise; each hoped to regroup his own forces by the time Chernenko left the stage and then to seize power. That was the only reason for the unexpected outcome of that political duel, which left the empire without an official leader for four full days. If it had not been for Chernenko's venerable age, his numerous ailments, and the Kremlin duelists' conviction that his months (if not his days) were numbered, he would have had no more chance of getting the top spot in the Kremlin than of seeing his own ears.

If Andropov had lived for another year or two, or if he had taken a posthumous part in the selection of his successor, he would have chosen anyone but that seventy-two-year-old, colorless Party apparatchik, a prey to terminal illnesses who didn't have much understanding of anything. And to get *him* as leader after such a vigorous and bold adventurer as Andropov! During the fifteen months of his rule, the greater part of which he was ill, Andropov had managed to bring enough of his own trusted people into the Kremlin elite to assure himself an automatic majority in both the Politburo and the Secretariat, the two supreme organs of Party, and hence of government, power. Being an atheist, however, he was not in the habit of looking beyond the biological limits of his own life. He overlooked the fact that not only the majority in the Kremlin leadership but the unity of his group was assured only by him and no one else. He was the cornerstone of the structure that he had put together out of people loyal to him: without him, it must fall apart, and it did fall apart—immediately. Loyal to their master, his people were not bound to one another by any other obligations. And it was among them that the power struggle broke out, and not at all among the "young men" and the "oldsters," as most Western observers had figured it would.

Incidentally, the oldsters proved to be more ready to agree among themselves than did the young men. Andropov's death made them sigh with relief. The discord among Andropov's pupils instantly triggered the old men's instinct of self-preservation—one developed in them almost to a pathological degree back in the days of Stalin, when the struggle for political survival meant a struggle for life, as among primitive tribes. Most likely, none of them (least of all Chernenko) was dreaming of power or hoping for it: by their age, their ambitions had burned out. The power—or more accurately, its outer trappings—went to Chernenko, but it might just as easily have gone to Grishin, Ustinov, or Tikhonov. It didn't matter to which of those septuagenarians it went; for any of them it would have meant a secure old age, repose, stability, and honor, a solemn funeral in Red Square and a burial in the Kremlin wall (the ashes) or near it (the body). Power in the hands of any of them would have been impersonal power—a posthumous edition of Brezhnev, just as it became with Chernenko.

The old men carried a countercoup inspired by nostalgia—one rendered possible only by the antagonism between Gorbachev and Romanov, which was unrestrained by any Party rules of propriety.

That personal fight brought into play a paradoxical law that, for almost seventy years now, has invariably functioned when there was a changing of the Kremlin guard. The accession of each new Kremlin leader has meant not continuing the line of his predecessor but moving away from it, most often in the reverse direction, albeit within the parameters of the sluggish Soviet system. The Kremlin is characterized by interruption, not succession; by reaction, not continuity. It is a system of coups and countercoups, of political and ideological zigzags.

Recall the "big seven" Soviet leaders. From Lenin on, each acted in opposition to his predecessor's basic policies, and from Stalin on, almost each one followed in the footsteps of his predecessor's predecessor rather than of his own. In every respect, Stalin was more like a Russian tsar than a Russian revolutionary. Khrushchev adopted a policy of de-Stalinization and of restoring Leninist norms in the way the Party and government were run. Brezhnev started to restore the titles and names used under Stalin (general secretary instead of first secretary; Politburo instead of Presidium) and renounced Khrushchev's "thaw," but he didn't get far in the process of re-Stalinization, since he had succumbed to the temptation of détente with the West. Andropov resolutely returned to Stalin's tested police methods, but owing to the brevity of his rule, he did not reach a political orgasm like Stalin's Great Terror or his postwar "campaign against cosmopolitanism." Chernenko had less time than even Andropov, but he tried to turn the clock back and follow in the footsteps of his longtime mentor and boss, Brezhnev. As for Gorbachev, his model and example is undoubtedly his sponsor and teacher, Andropov.

Moreover, each new Soviet leader has been a usurper, because he took power contrary to his predecessor's will. Lenin came to power as a result of the Bolshevik Revolution of 1917. In his political "testament," after weighing all the pros and cons, he ultimately gave his preference to his longtime coworker, Trotsky, and very definitely insisted that Stalin be removed from the post of general secretary. Stalin, after he had seized power by means of force and perfidy, physically destroyed all of Lenin's old guard in a little more than a decade, and just before the curtain came down on this Party holocaust, he did away with his chief enemy, Trotsky, using a hired killer. Stalin's closest accomplice in his bloody rule, Lavrenty Beria—the man who committed and often instigated the era's most terrible and repulsive crimes (political in name but essentially just brutal murders)—was slated to succeed Stalin but instead was executed a few months after his master's death. And a few years later, Stalin's remaining aides—Molotov, Kaganovich, Malenkov, Voroshilov, and Bulganin—although they were allowed to live, were expelled from the Kremlin. Stalin himself was posthumously "exposed" by Khrushchev in his secret speech to the Twentieth Party Congress in 1956. Khrushchev's own turn came in 1964. In that year, a palace coup called the "Little October" (to distinguish it from the "Big October" of 1917) took the power away from Khrushchev. The new leadership headed by Brezhnev declared him a "voluntarist" because of his liberalizing and reformist policies. In 1982, Yuri Andropov, with leverage from an obedient KGB, carried out another coup, first appointing himself technical secretary of the Party and then, after Brezhnev's death, general secretary, bypassing the official heir, Konstantin Chernenko, Brezhnev's alter ego and personal choice. Under the guise of a campaign against corruption, Andropov removed many of Brezhnev's minions from power at all levels of the Soviet leadership. To replace them, he brought in "the iron young men"—as the Andropovcrats are called in Moscow—close to the throne. Although he could have quickly dismembered the Politburo that he had inherited from Brezhnev, he decided not to, since he wanted to confer an air of legitimacy on the power he had seized through intrigue, blackmail, and murder—confer it, at any rate, within the framework of the unwritten rules of the Party.

Although he took the long view of things and was crafty in his calculations, Andropov lost sight of the fact that the will of a dead man is not binding upon the living. His own death led to a new round in the Kremlin struggle, and the fighting in that round was so fierce that the few days between Andropov's death and his funeral did not suffice for it. Yet by Kremlin rules it was essential in that brief span of time to complete the job of electing a new general secretary. A way out from the dead end was found in the person of a compromise, interim, and ritualistic figure: the insignificant Chernenko. Yet by the law of contrasts that invariably comes into play when there is a changing of the Kremlin guard, it was to be expected that the Andropov team would regain the ground lost because of their own internal discord and the nostalgia of the Kremlin gerontocrats. After all, if even Brezhnev, overthrown by Andropov, was able to come back to power—however briefly and figuratively—with Chernenko's help, the dead Andropov had all the better chance of returning with the help of his loyal pupils in the Party and police apparatus.

Upon Chernenko's election, the fighting between Romanov and Gorbachev, far from coming to a halt, grew even fiercer. The whole question was: Did Gorbachev gain the upper hand in that struggle because (as two of our secret correspondents affirm) at the very last moment, he came up with the idea that saved the situation, the idea of temporarily transferring the power to a sick and none-too-bright old man, the person most unlikely to reach the apex of the Soviet hierarchy in all of Soviet history?

Gorbachev presided over the session of the CC at which Chernenko's candidacy for the post of general secretary was ratified. And two months later, he made the nominating speech at the session of the Soviet parliament that "elected" Chernenko "president" (officially, chairman of the USSR Supreme Soviet).

It was as if Gorbachev had renounced the political inheritance intended for him in favor of Chernenko, whom Andropov had bypassed fifteen months before, as if the injustice done by Gorbachev's mentor, Andropov, had been righted. This undoubtedly gained Gorbachev some points with the grateful gerontocrats.

3. An Intermezzo
With Konstantin Chernenko

> The old is dying, and the new cannot be born.
> In this interregnum, there arises
> a great diversity of morbid symptoms.
>
> —GRAMSCI

LET US NOW go back fifteen months to the death of another Kremlin leader, Brezhnev.

On the day of his burial with honors and pomp in Red Square, when his rival and successor delivered the funeral oration from the rostrum atop Lenin's Mausoleum, KGB agents were carrying out a search at the deceased's apartment on Kutuzov Prospekt. Even dead, Brezhnev gave Andropov no peace, although it is not known whether the search represented momentum from the power struggle or whether Andropov was covering his tracks and wanted to destroy evidence. It is hardly likely that we shall ever know exactly what his people were looking for in Brezhnev's apartment. But we do know one thing they found there: a solid gold samovar. And we know that because a living man fell afoul of the search made at the dead man's home. That person was Mohammed-Salam Ilyasovich Umakhanov, the Party boss of Dagestan and a CC member; he had given Brezhnev the gold samovar in the name of his little Caucasian republic on the shore of the Caspian Sea. Thus, Andropov found yet more evidence, by now superfluous, of Brezhnev's involvement in corruption, as if the dead man himself, from beyond the grave, had confirmed that his ruthless persecutor was right.

Before spreading this information among other Party officials for the purposes of their edification and of throwing a scare into them, Andropov sent some of his people to the Caucasus with orders to find out, at the home of Mohammed-Salam Ilyasovich Umakhanov himself, the details of this bearing of gifts in the oriental manner to the Moscow overlord. By way of justifying himself, the satrap of Dagestan could have cited Caucasian tradition and pointed to colleagues of his in neighboring republics and provinces who had also given gifts to Brezhnev, perhaps with less originality but just as lavishly, if not more so. His neighbor to the south, Geidar Ali Rza ogly Aliyev, then boss of the Moslem republic of Azerbaijan, had literally overloaded Brezhnev with gifts when the latter came to Baku six weeks before his death. Never in all the eighteen years of his rule had he received so many. But Aliyev was the kind of man who went all out no matter what he was doing, whether he was waging a life-and-death struggle against graft in his republic or playing up to the top men in the Kremlin. Indeed, he broke all records in that kind of flattery. For example, at the Twenty-sixth Party Congress in 1981 he contrived, in one fifteen-minute speech, to mention Brezhnev's name thirteen times, and none of the other thirty-nine speakers could compare to him when it came to the number, fulsomeness, and floridity of the praises he heaped on the aged leader. No doubt Andropov's people found gifts from Aliyev, too, in

Brezhnev's apartment, but right after Brezhnev's death, Aliyev was called to Moscow by Andropov; he Russianized his Moslem name (adding a patronymic) into Geidar Aliyevich Aliyev, and he assumed leadership of the nationwide campaign against corruption.

It may well be that among the items found at Brezhnev's apartment were gifts from still other neighbors of Umakhanov, including his neighbor to the north, Mikhail Gorbachev of the Stavropol Territory. But Gorbachev was already working in Moscow and was even rumored to be the Kremlin crown prince. So the kingpin of Dagestan could not cite the example of his former neighbors and did not try to explain to the KGB men who were interrogating him the difference between a gift and a bribe. All he did was offer to his uninvited guests a receipt for the purchase of forty kilograms of gold used in crafting the gift for Brezhnev, a document that was turned over to Andropov in the Kremlin. But Andropov had not spent fifteen years as chief of the secret police for nothing: he had the solid gold samovar weighed, and it proved to contain only twenty kilograms of gold. This time, in view of the seriousness of the case, which was coming to a head, he didn't send KGB agents to the Caucasus. Instead, the bountiful and enigmatic giver of gifts was brought from there to Moscow under guard.

But the investigation of Umakhanov yielded unexpected results, and Andropov was among those who had not been expecting them. The other twenty kilograms of gold had not been appropriated by the Dagestan Party princeling, as Andropov had no doubt supposed, but had gone into the making of another samovar also to be sent to Moscow. And Umakhanov admitted to whom it was to be sent: Konstantin Ustinovich Chernenko.

Umakhanov was removed from his post, not for corruption but for making a faulty forecast of the political weather, although the official explanation was different: "He interfered in a trial involving his relatives." But in the Soviet Union, who believes official explanations? Especially in that case, since Andropov took pains to see that the affair of the two solid gold samovars, which compromised two of his rivals—one living and the other dead—became widely known in Party circles.

Still, the affair was rather a contribution to the rumors about infighting between Andropov and Chernenko which actually had no basis in reality. Andropov never took Chernenko seriously. He was fighting Brezhnev's mafia as a whole, and not individual members of it. Of those members, Chernenko was the most harmless, as compared to the godfather, Brezhnev; his right-hand man, Andrei Kirilenko; or his minister of internal affairs, General Shchelokov.

Even while Brezhnev was still alive, Andropov's advisers, when foreigners started to talk with them about the rivalry between their chief and Chernenko, shrugged in contempt and called the latter a "country bumpkin." Not long before Brezhnev's death, Georgi Arbatov, a CC member and director of the Institute of America and Canada, declared outright that as a potential leader of the country, Chernenko was "unthinkable" and even indecent.

Chernenko was Brezhnev's man in the fullest sense of the word, in a way that no other associate of Brezhnev's was. By turns, he served his patron as flunky, orderly, valet, and secretary, sometimes doing all these things at once, and more besides. He saw to it that Brezhnev did not exceed the quota of cigarettes his doctors allowed him (no more than five a day), and he personally handed them to him from his cigarette case. When by reason of his deafness Brezhnev did not hear everything that someone was saying to him, or didn't grasp it because of his senility, Chernenko would shout it in his ear. He helped him to his feet when he had been sitting in a chair; he buttoned up his buttons; he led him away when he was drunk, supporting him on the stairs; he took him to the bathroom. On occasion, wearying of the long hours of conferring, Brezhnev would, without any warning, leave an enlarged session of the Politburo. (We have no information on the closed sessions.)

Chernenko would invariably tag along, and the two of them would organize a drinking bout at a dacha in the countryside. Of course, those drinking bouts were always Brezhnev's idea; but Chernenko would take part in them as willingly as in any other of his boss's activities, as when he handed him the text of a speech or a velvet cushion on which rested some decorations to be awarded. And he possessed one remarkable trait: Whereas Brezhnev would get tipsy after one drink, Chernenko never got drunk, no matter how much he consumed. He was very proud of his amazing capacity to consume alcohol, and ascribed it to his tempering in Siberia, a region so cold that the locals drink to keep warm, consuming even more than the inhabitants of Russia proper.

In the mid-seventies, Brezhnev started taking Chernenko along with him to meetings with foreigners. (Chernenko's baptism of fire came at the Helsinki conference among the heads of the European states, the USSR, the United States, and Canada.) Gray-haired, stoop-shouldered, with high Mongolian cheekbones and a typical peasant face, Chernenko filed protocols, opened bottles of mineral water, and laid napkins out on the table. No job was too lowly for him. At Vienna in 1979, he astounded the Americans: During the entire ten hours of meetings between Carter and Brezhnev, he said nothing at all except for a quickly mumbled remark on the weather in the Austrian capital. "The only impression I formed of him is that he was a 'dullard,' " recalls Malcolm Toon, the former United States ambassador to the Soviet Union. Even the Soviet delegates snubbed him, especially Minister of Foreign Affairs Andrei Gromyko and Marshal Ustinov, the minister of defense.

Far from feeling humiliated by the role assigned him under Brezhnev, Chernenko felt highly gratified by it, as a dog does when serving its master. A few days after Brezhnev's death, with Andropov in power, Chernenko was not playing the hypocrite when, in recalling the late leader, he said almost tearfully: "To be near Leonid

Ilich, to listen to him, to observe with your own eyes the acuteness of his mind, his inventiveness, his love of life: that was a school for all of us who had the good fortune to work side by side with him."

Flattery is wasted on a dead master, and it is especially not advisable when a new, living master is standing next to you. Chernenko was sincerely devoted to Brezhnev, although it is quite possible that an eagerness to be obliging was part of his nature: if not something he was born with, then a trait developed in childhood. At the age of twelve, he left home and hired out to work for a *kulak,* a well-to-do peasant. Subsequently, he worked for all manner of masters until he became the servant-friend of Brezhnev. It got so that Brezhnev simply could not do without him, either on the job or at home. They were neighbors in the same apartment building on Kutuzov Prospekt, and their wives were close friends. During the last years of Brezhnev's life, he even took Chernenko along with him when he went on vacation to Oreadna on the Black Sea. By this time, the master needed the servant more than the servant needed him. Their relationship was even the butt of a joke that went, "Brezhnev has been dead for quite some time, but Chernenko hasn't told him."

In the last volume of his memoirs, written not long before his death as a kind of political testament, Brezhnev gave a high rating to his bottle-buddy as a man "who would convince others, and could find the correct organizational forms," as a "steadfast fighter, receptive to the opinions of his comrades but unsparing of himself," and so on. Empty words, of course. Yet besides being a gesture of gratitude to Chernenko, they could be read as the dying leader's informal designation of his political heir. Although Andropov, a man of action, did not attribute any great importance to words —especially those of a man he had ceased to take into account long before the latter's death—he decided to insure himself, just in case. Using various pretexts, the censors, at his order, held up the publication of the last part of the memoirs in the magazine *Novy Mir.* The

November 1982 issue in which it appeared did not come out until January 1983, after Brezhnev's death, when his dying wishes were no longer of any importance.

After becoming general secretary, Andropov took as a model Lenin's democratic forbearance toward the weaknesses of his Party comrades and restrained himself and tried to ignore Chernenko's constant smoking throughout all Politburo sessions. Chernenko lit each new cigarette from the butt of the last, as peasants do to save matches. Andropov himself did not smoke, and tobacco smoke itself was distinctly irritating to him. He even complained to Rudolf Augstein, a correspondent for *Der Spiegel* (though without mentioning Chernenko by name) that smoking at the official Thursday sessions of the Politburo was a real problem.

One day his patience gave out. And when Chernenko had come to the end of one of his regular, long coughing spells, he asked him, "Konstantin Ustinovich, tell me confidentially, how long have you been smoking?"

With a touch of pride, Chernenko answered, "Since the age of nine, Yuri Vladimirovich."

"And do you really believe that will leave you unscathed? Just look at you, with your prolonged, racking cough! Comrade Chazov [a Kremlin physician and a CC member] told me you have emphysema due to smoking. I mention this so that, if you give no thought to others, you will at least think of yourself."

The person who told us about this incident added that the chat at the Politburo session had a most unusual result. Chernenko stopped smoking not only in Andropov's presence but altogether—and on that same day. He had been an inveterate smoker when serving inveterate smoker Brezhnev; but as soon as a man who was antismoking became his boss, he quit. Alas, that did not save him: it was too late. He died of pulmonary emphysema.

Both Chernenko's autobiography and his official biography recount in detail, with all the dates, what he did and what positions he held before 1933 and then from the early forties on. But they completely omit the mid and late thirties, the time of Stalin's Great Terror. The same odd gap is in the biographical note on Chernenko published on the front page of every Soviet newspaper after he became general secretary. Here are the dates given, first on one side and then on the other, of that chronology: 1929–30, 1930, 1931, 1933,——1943, 1945, 1948, and so on. Where are the missing ten years? What was Chernenko doing between 1933 and 1943? In biographical sketches, it is stated that before 1933 Chernenko served with the border troops and that upon completion of his military service he did Party work in the Krasnoyar Territory, where he was born. There is no mention of either the year when he completed military service or that in which he began his Party work. Left unanswered, therefore, is the question as to the specific duties Chernenko performed in the armed forces after his transfer out of the border guards.

Immediately after he was named to the supreme imperial post, the Soviet propaganda machine, its motor idling as it made use of old stereotypes, began to foster a half-hearted cult of Konstantin Chernenko. Speakers and journalists, using any pretext they could find—and sometimes none at all—began to mention his name and quote him. For example, Moscow Party boss Victor Grishin, in an electoral campaign speech made on February 21, 1984, only a week after Chernenko's inauguration, mentioned his name twenty-six times. *Pravda* printed a long article by his daughter, Elena Chernenko. And documentary filmmakers began shooting, in Kazakhstan, a film called *A Lad from the Border*. It tells the story of how, in the early thirties, young volunteer border guard Kostya Chernenko served on the boundary between Kazakhstan and China, and of the courage he displayed in combat against anti-Soviet bands. (The anti-Soviet bands in question were nationalist guerrillas who, like the Afghans today, were desperately fighting for independence—in their case, that of their small Central Asian countries—from Russia.) Since Chernenko did not serve in World War II, and since these episodes on the border provided the only dash of romantic color in his otherwise routine Party biography, Soviet newspapers and magazines laid heavy stress on them.

The day before the opening session of the nominal Soviet parliament that elected Chernenko the nominal president, the defense ministry's newspaper, *Krasnaya Zvezda (Red Star)* published an article by Lieutenant General Vasily Donskoi, commander of the Far Eastern Border District. Here is an excerpt:

> Those were hot times, with border guards in a constant struggle against the enemies of Soviet power. In clashes with bandits, Konstantin Chernenko demonstrated courage and manliness. He was a good shot with a rifle and machine pistol, and he threw hand grenades without a miss. He was a good horseman and always the leader of detachments sent to the border.

Alas, in the general's article, Chernenko's career breaks off at that point, and the reader is left in total ignorance as to what that good shot and skillful horseman did during the rest of the thirties, or whether he ever again had to make use of his skill with firearms. And yet such information is important in understanding not only Chernenko but the entire generation of the Kremlin elite to which he belonged.

We found an unexpected answer to that intriguing question in a Russian-language booklet published in West Germany in 1958 and called *Yezhovshchina (The Yezhov Reign of Terror)* after Nikolai Yezhov, the head of Stalin's secret police in the late thirties and chief architect of the Great Terror of 1937. The booklet deals with the bloody orgies of the secret police in the city of Dnepropetrovsk in the Ukraine. Its author used an appropriate pseudonym, A. Dneprovets, and made it clear that his brochure should be regarded as an eyewitness account. It looks as if this material on Dnepropetrovsk was smuggled out of Moscow to the West through secret channels. It is possible that this was done by Soviet officials favoring Khrushchev's policy of de-Stalinization who could not publish the material in the USSR, where even the world-famous anti-Stalinist speech Khrushchev delivered at the secret session of the Twentieth Party Congress, two years before the booklet about the Dnepropetrovsk terror appeared, was never published.

The details given by the author of the brochure (who wanted to remain anonymous for obvious reasons of personal security) testify to its documentary nature. Among other things, he tells about the executions carried out at night in the garage of the Dnepropetrovsk NKVD, the People's Commissariat of Internal Affairs, as the secret police was called in the thirties. Except for a few members of that punitive organization, two drivers, and the parking attendant, no one was allowed to enter the premises. One after another, the political prisoners were dragged out of the Black Maria and directly to the car wash, their hands tied and their mouths stopped with rubber gags. They were shot point-blank with small-bore rifles. Then the corpses were heaped into a truck, covered with a tarpaulin, and driven to the local Jewish cemetery. After each shooting, the attendant hosed away the blood so that in the morning no one could tell what had taken place in the garage during the night. The NKVD men called these shootings "weddings" because by morning they were either dead drunk or high on cocaine. Participation in these "weddings" was voluntary, and they were a kind of sadistic sport.

Among the dozen butchers named in this brochure is one Chernenko, who according to the anonymous author was deputy personnel chief of the Dnepropetrovsk NKVD in the late thirties. In 1958, when the booklet was published, Konstantin Chernenko was a little-known Party apparatchik in Moscow, so that any intention by the author of attacking the future Kremlin leader with the aim of discrediting him is completely ruled out. We have no direct evidence that the Chernenko named in the brochure and the sixth Soviet ruler were one and the same person, but several bits of circumstantial evidence, especially when lumped together, indicate that such is the case.

1. The very fact that in the official biographies, the autobiography, and the reminiscences of colleagues there is a cover up of what Chernenko was doing at the height of the Great Terror, when he was in military service. (Whereas in Stalin's time people were proud of such a past, after his exposure by Khrushchev they were afraid of it and took pains to conceal it.)

2. The border guard contingents in which Konstantin Chernenko served before 1933 were (and still are) directly subordinate to the secret police and are under its command. In the mid-thirties, when such real enemies of the Soviet regime as the Central Asian nationalist guerrillas had been put down and Stalin began to destroy his personal enemies, calling them "enemies of the people," many border guards were transferred to the "home front"; that is, they still came under the secret police but were now attached to its punitive organs.

3. On November 21, 1972, *Pravda* printed an obituary of Semyon Zadionchenko, who in the late thirties was first secretary of the Dnepropetrovsk Party Committee. It was signed by people who had worked with the deceased at various stages of his career, and one of the signers was Konstantin Chernenko. As has been shown by well-known English Sovietologist Leonard Shapiro, the only possible point of intersection between the careers of Chernenko and Zadionchenko was Dnepropetrovsk in the late thirties. (Shapiro did not know about the existence of the booklet by A. Dneprovets at the time he made his investigation.)

4. The first signature appended to Zadionchenko's obituary was that of Leonid Brezhnev, whose whole life was closely bound up with Dnepro-

petrovsk. It was under Zadionchenko that Brezhnev began his Party career, first as head of a
section (his biography does not tell us which
one), then as second secretary, and after the war
as first secretary. Once he replaced Khrushchev
as national leader of the Party, Dnepropetrovsk
became the main supplier of cadres for the
Kremlin. Many members of the sizable Dnepropetrovsk clan signed the obituary: CC Secretary
Andrei Kirilenko, General Nikolai Shchelokov,
General Konstantin Grushevoi, CC Business
Manager Georgi Pavlov, and Konstantin Chernenko, whose acquaintance Brezhnev is generally
supposed to have made in Moldavia. But Brezhnev served as Party leader in Moldavia for only
two years (as was later the case in Kazakhstan).
And although he did appoint a few of his friends
from Moldavia to posts in Moscow, he never
managed to put together either a Moldavian or a
Kazakh mafia. By contrast, the Dnepropetrovsk
one was for a long time a solid power base of his
administration, until Andropov began systematically to break it up. Furthermore, it is hard to
see how the complete trust Brezhnev placed in
Chernenko could have been due to a mere nod-
ding acquaintance in Moldavia after the war.
There is little doubt that their friendship,
strengthened in Moldavia, began before the war
in Dnepropetrovsk; both of them were then of an
age when it is easiest to form friendships. Chernenko was almost certainly serving there in "the
organs" (the secret police), which Brezhnev was
overseeing for the Party—something he acknowledges in his memoirs: "I had to deal with
matters which, although unrelated to the economy, . . . were likewise important"; and he
makes direct mention of "the security organs."
It was surely owing to a longtime friendship that
Brezhnev's bottle-buddy, hardly distinguished
for any special talents, ultimately reached very

high Party posts in Moscow, and that during his patron's last years he accompanied him on almost all his trips to this or that place in Russia, with one exception: Dnepropetrovsk.

That fact may be regarded as a fifth piece of circumstantial evidence—that in the late thirties Chernenko was with the secret police in Dnepropetrovsk. The reason for his not wanting to go there in later years may have been his fear of being recognized, because he was anxious to avoid compromising encounters and public scandals. Encounters of this kind sometimes happened when a victim who had somehow survived met by chance one of those who had persecuted him. This happened, for example, when Molotov, one of Stalin's henchmen now in retirement, while standing in line to buy milk, was recognized by a man whose sentence he had personally signed.

Brezhnev himself undoubtedly knew about his Dnepropetrovsk protégé's dark past, which the latter had had to conceal after Stalin's death. But at the same time, Chernenko must have known quite a bit more about Brezhnev than other Kremlin dwellers did. It is not known whose dirt on whom helped Chernenko to make a career that could be called unprecedented were it not for the famous story about the Roman Emperor Caligula and his horse, made a senator by his master. (But the horse was only a senator, not an heir!) Brezhnev and Chernenko were bound together by their respective pasts, but just what slush cemented their relationship is shrouded in secrecy. All the other members of the Dnepropetrovsk mafia, from former CC Secretary Andrei Kirilenko to the current chairman of the KGB, Victor Chebrikov, were in every respect more significant figures than Chernenko. Brezhnev himself has been called a mediocrity; but in comparison to his protégé, who was the quintessence of mediocrity, Brezhnev was another Abraham Lincoln. Chernenko's election as the sixth Soviet leader was the apotheosis of dullness, especially after the bright (perhaps even too bright) flareup of Andropov's political star. If Brezhnev's choice of Chernenko as heir was subjective, Chernenko's election by the Kremlin elite as its nominal leader had a more objective foundation and followed the principle of "negative selection."

When mediocrities are in power, the most mediocre among them is the ideal candidate for the position of top leader. In this case, he was also the sickest among the sick, since all of them were incurably afflicted with old age.

And he was not even a careerist. He was an industrious and willing bureaucrat wherever he was serving, in the Dnepropetrovsk secret police or in the Kremlin. Whereas Andropov put forth a tremendous effort to reach the top post in the Soviet empire, Chernenko came by it quite accidentally and no doubt to his own complete surprise. He received it gratis, as a spinoff from the power struggle between the Kremlin's young turks. As a matter of fact, he was neither power-loving nor ambitious nor an intriguer. He owed his career to a set of circumstances that proved to be happy for him, as well as to that perduring political crisis which began in the mid-seventies and which might better be called the degeneration of the aging Kremlin leadership. But the root cause of that decline is to be found in earlier Soviet history. For apart from two periods (which together represent ten years) of rule by exceptional men, Khrushchev and Andropov, political leadership in the Kremlin since the death of Lenin has been consistently mediocre. But mediocrity has never been an obstacle in the path to power. To the contrary, it has served as a kind of ticket for admission to the Kremlin Olympus.

It is hard to imagine anyone more mediocre than Stalin, especially when he is contrasted with such stars of the first magnitude as Lenin, Trotsky, and Bukharin. Trotsky called him just that, "The most outstanding mediocrity of our Party." Again, just compare Brezhnev with Khrushchev, or with any other member of

Khrushchev's Politburo. In his book *The Nomenklatura: The Soviet Ruling Class,* Mikhail Voslensky, a former member of that privileged class of high officials (although not a top-level one) who is now researching and writing about it, asks this question: "Whom does that elite endeavor to get elected as General Secretary? The strongest and most capable man? No, that member of the Politburo it regards as the least intelligent and most harmless."

In fact, fear of the brilliant, ambitious Trotsky on the part of Lenin's other heirs cleared the way for Stalin to seize power. And fear inspired in Stalin's other heirs by his bloodthirsty henchman Beria helped Khrushchev to take the reins of government into his own hands. (They had long regarded him as a knucklehead, and he himself enjoyed playing that inoffensive role in the eyes of his colleagues.) In that political context, the accession to power of the lackluster but devoted bureaucrat Chernenko should be viewed as a reaction to the strikingly energetic Andropov, who posed a deadly threat to the "Red bourgeoisie." In the same way, twenty years before, in reaction to Khrushchev, who had turned out to be anything but as innocuous as the Kremlin elite had at first figured, his tempestuous reign was brought to an end by putting Brezhnev's humdrum administration in place. Precisely then, after the palace coup carried out by the mediocrities in 1964 and called "the Little October," that the official Kremlin lexicon was enriched with the word *voluntarism,* meaning a political wilfulness, the rejection of collegiate leadership, and erecting one's own will into a principle of government. Using that word, the Party "aristocracy" distanced itself from Khrushchev and issued a warning to anyone who might want to follow his example in the future.

But however overdeveloped the instinct for self-preservation may have been among the ruling elite, it was by no means infallible, and it sometimes brought disaster upon those who had it, as happened in the case of Khrushchev. It had earlier happened in the case of Stalin, who proved to be a far greater evil for the elite (and not only for it) than Trotsky could ever have been. Trotsky would never have come anywhere close to what Stalin did with his mindless reign of terror on a cosmic scale, wiping out in only a few strokes a million and a half Bolsheviks, including most of those who had set him up against Trotsky.

As for Andropov, he was an exception. No one chose him, and no one was betting on him. He had worked his own way up to the supreme power by means of intrigues, plots, and terrorism against the Kremlin's "aristocracy," and above all against Brezhnev himself.

If there was anyone whom the Kremlin elite, frightened by Stalin and Khrushchev, chose unerringly, it was Brezhnev. It was not just that he was no dictator; he didn't once manage to be the sole, fully empowered ruler of the country. At first he shared the rule with two other men, Premier Kosygin and President Podgorny, under the constant ideological monitoring of Mikhail Suslov. And when that triumvirate fell apart in the second half of the seventies and Brezhnev supposedly remained the sole official ruler, his health failed him. One heart attack followed another; his powers of speech were impaired; his legs became wobbly. Just at that time, a deadly fight for power was developing behind his back, and he was in no state to intervene and defend his old friends, his landsmen, his protégés, his relatives, or even himself. Ultimately, as has so often happened in Asian and Levantine courts, the captain of the palace guard got the upper hand. (In his present-day status, he has many other duties besides heading up the guard.)

Brezhnev's secret was that he never ruled the country in his own person. But this didn't trouble him—at any rate, it didn't until he discovered Andropov's plot against him—because for him the trappings of power were more to be cherished than power itself.

Both Chernenko and Brezhnev were pretty much simple counters used by the Party-bureaucratic system that had put them in the top spot. They were both devoid of individuality, which in a totalitarian state is equated with "voluntarism" (to use Kremlin vocabulary). That trait had been displayed by Stalin and Khrushchev, who had betrayed the expectations of their Kremlin colleagues, and by Andropov, who covertly outplayed them. If we take a look at the first two, setting moral criteria aside, we find that like any two extremes, they resemble each other. Both were voluntarists, although in each case voluntarism took a different direction from the other: in Stalin's, toward mass political terror, and in Khrushchev's, toward liberal reforms. Under Stalin's command, the ship of state took a heavy list to one side, and he almost sank it in the bloody depths. Khrushchev, in saving it, caused it to roll to the other side—a phenomenon that was called, in a different figure of speech, "the thaw." Brezhnev's crew got the ship back on course and into the traditional Russian channel of bureaucratic rule without either liberal or tyrannical extremes. It was just what the partocrats expected of Brezhnev, and it was the reason for their support of him. After Stalin's bloody purges and Khrushchev's shakeup of the apparatus, the Brezhnev slogan "stability of the cadres" meant just what they wanted. It meant lifetime tenure for officials in high posts and the creation of Party peerage, a geriatric elite that ruled first in the name of Brezhnev and then in a slightly depleted state, after the minor massacre inflicted on it by Andropov, in the name of Chernenko. But Brezhnev, and not Chernenko, created the system, although at the same time he was its creature.

Outwardly, life in the Kremlin after the seriously ill Chernenko had been made its master seemed boring, sluggish, uneventful, and monotonous. It was amazingly remininscent of Brezhnev's prolonged death agony. The playgoer had to see all over again the play that had bored him in its first production—but with a new actor in the leading role: now the dying Chernenko was playing the part of the dying Brezhnev. It was an appearance of Brezhnev from beyond the grave, as if time had gone into reverse and was making footprints in its own tracks. And when on the international workers' holiday of May 1, 1984, the living corpses from the

Kremlin, headed by Chernenko, made their painful way to the top of Lenin's Mausoleum, it was almost a spectacle from *Inferno*. The Brezhnev era left the political stage unwillingly and sluggishly but took pleasure in the breather given it by the Chernenko intermezzo. Those dead men whom people had forgotten to bury pretended to be alive and now demanded political reanimation.

To borrow the language of Karl Marx, the audience was seeing performances by comedians in a period of history whose real heroes were already dead. "History does a thorough job and passes through many phases when it is bearing off to the grave one of life's outmoded formulas," he wrote. "The last phase of a world-historical form is *comedy*. . . . Why does history follow such a course? It is necessary so that mankind can *gaily* take leave of its past."

We don't know about that portion of mankind only indirectly affected by the Kremlin comedy; but the Soviet part of it followed the precepts of Marx, the founder of scientific socialism, and took leave of the Kremlin leaders (that is, Brezhnev and Chernenko; Andropov was another matter) without any signs of grief. On those occasions, black humor on the topical Kremlin themes of old age, disease, death, and funerals flourished with impunity.

"Why does Chernenko have three microphones in front of him when he makes a speech?"
"Two of them supply him with oxygen."

After Chernenko's first speech as the new Soviet leader, some worried doctors said to him, "Comrade General Secretary, you have advanced sclerosis, and it will be hard for you to govern the country."

"*I* have sclerosis?" Chernenko asked with real indignation. "It's Andropov who has sclerosis. He's already missed the second Politburo session."

A man who came to yet one more Kremlin funeral was asked by a policeman, "Do you have a ticket?"

"Yes, I have a subscription ticket."

Indeed, the reshuffling of the Kremlin oldsters was hard to take seriously. Chernenko did not invent that game of musical chairs; he was merely an ordinary player in it, despite the regalia of supreme power that he had come by accidentally. He was simply the most conspicuous product of political decay in the Kremlin, a process that had begun long before him.

Brezhnev's political longevity, in spite of his mental and physical feebleness, was an amazing phenomenon, both when viewed against the Russian historical background and when seen in the international context of his day. Although there had been Russian tsars and leaders who had governed longer than he, not a single one lived to such an advanced age while still in office.

During his term in office, the leadership of the majority of countries in the world, both democratic and totalitarian, changed hands, in some cases several times. This was true of France, the United States, Great Britain, both Germanies, Italy, Yugoslavia, Poland, Vatican City, Spain, China, India, Pakistan, Iran, Israel, Egypt, and even Uganda. After Brezhnev's death, however, the turnover in leadership picked up speed, because it was still old men who dominated the top Party echelon. During Brezhnev's eighteen-year sojourn in the Kremlin, the White House changed hands five times. By contrast, since Reagan has been in office, the Kremlin has had four successive leaders, three during Reagan's first term alone. And all three, including Andropov after the attempt on his life, were invalids, unable to walk, sit down, get up, or even button up their overcoats without assistance. They were always accompanied by a retinue of doctors and assistants, as the United States president is by bodyguards. They might have been shown off to the world as exemplars of Soviet medicine's undoubted success in gerontology but certainly not as viable leaders of a superpower.

The Kremlin itself has not been stingy in funding gerontological medicine, although access to its benefits has been strictly confined to Kremlin dwellers. To be convinced of the progress made in that most advanced and elite specialty in Soviet medicine, it suffices to compare the lifespan for males in the USSR, barely sixty-two, with the average age reached by Politburo members, seventy-seven (as of early 1985)—a whole fifteen years more! So much for social equality in the land of developed socialism. In the Kremlin, every man sets a record, and they certainly could qualify for *The Guinness Book of Records*.

During World War II, Stalin headed up one of the youngest government cabinets in the world, whereas in the first half of the eighties, the USSR had the oldest, in both the world's and in Russia's history. For example, Brezhnev was the oldest leader in that country's thousand-year history to die in office. Chernenko reached that office at a more advanced age, seventy-two, than any of his predecessors in that same thousand years. (By way of comparison, at age seventy Khrushchev was removed under the pretext of advanced age.) In 1985, the Kremlin had the oldest premier (Tikhonov, aged eighty) and the oldest minister of foreign affairs (Gromyko, aged seventy-five) in all of Soviet history. And Marshal Dmitri Ustinov, the oldest Russian minister of defense, who died ten weeks before Chernenko, was succeeded by a man of seventy-three, Marshal Sergei Sokolov—the first person of such advanced age to be appointed to that key post in the superpower structure. Out of 117 ministers and chairmen of top-level committees (the latter are also, in effect, ministries; for example, the KGB—Committee of State Security), more than one-quarter were older than seventy. The majority of them had got their ministerial sinecures under Khrushchev or early in the Brezhnev era. The oldest is Yefim Slavsky, born in 1898, who has been for almost three decades the minister of medium machine-building, a post to which he was named four years after Stalin's death; he is responsible for the production of nuclear weapons. Not surprisingly, this is the very industry in which the Soviet Union has begun to lag catastrophically behind the United States in the last decade, and its fright at the development of American technology is like the medieval fear of black magic.

In Moscow at the time, people were joking that in the Kremlin "middle-aged" meant seventy. But in comparison with the eighty-seven-year-old Slavsky or eighty-four-year-old Vice-President Vasily Kuznetsov (who had been a member of Stalin's Politburo), or for that matter the eighty-year-old Premier Tikhonov, the Kremlin's septuagenarians did not really look all that old.

This generation of men made their careers during the dreadful years of the Great Terror. Today they are rather amiable and, one would hope, harmless old men with gray or white hair—disease-ridden, feeble, and pitiable—who stir one's human sympathy more than they do associations with the era that engendered them, nurtured them, and advanced their careers. But that era left an indelible imprint on them and, through them, on all generations after Stalin's death, right up to the eighties.

They got their start in life early. After Lenin's old guard of Bolsheviks had been wiped out at all levels of the Soviet system, many yawning gaps had to be filled with new people right away. The screening was totally different from what it had been under Lenin before, during, and immediately after the Revolution. The brave were replaced by the cowardly, the principled by the unprincipled, the truthlovers by liars, the unselfish by careerists, and the able by the incompetent. Lenin sought out comrades in arms, even if they did not always agree with him, as was the case with Trotsky and Bukharin; but Stalin wanted obedient servants. The organism of the state was given a kind of blood transfusion, with the result that it was transformed into its own complete opposite. "Stalinism is above all the work of an impersonal apparatus on the downgrade from the Revolution," Trotsky wrote. It was indeed a counter-revolution of the faceless; this is no doubt more impor-

tant in understanding Stalin's litter of Kremlin leaders,
who cling to power as tenaciously as to life itself, than
are the individual traits of each one of them. Regardless
of whether they took a personal part in Stalin's crimes,
like Chernenko, or almost became victims of it, like
Tikhonov (Brezhnev saved him from nearly certain
death), or stood aside from the bloodbath of the struggle, like Gromyko—all of them walked over the corpses
of predecessors who had been tortured and killed, and
moved into positions that had been left vacant. Their
careerist instinct of self-preservation was an extension
of their physical instinct; under Stalin, to lose a position
meant to lose one's life. In order to survive that harsh
process of selection—in addition to Stalin's purges,
there was the war—one had to possess, or more accurately, to develop in oneself, a degree of tenacity,
adaptiveness, and cynicism not demanded in any other
period of Soviet history. The Kremlin became a school
of political—and under Stalin, physical—survival.
After his death, when the direct threat to their lives was
no longer there, those who had been through that school
kept the fierce grip that they had earlier got, as a result
of vicious fighting, on the top rung of the Kremlin ladder. Then, when the curtain was about to come down on
the Brezhnev era, they secured lifetime tenure of office,
like an aristocratic title or patrimony, but without the
right of succession for their heirs.

That victory, however, was in every respect a Pyrrhic
one. For they had merely won a single battle in a struggle being waged not only against the next Kremlin generation, or troublemakers in their own age bracket, but
against their own elderliness, against nature, against
God. It was a lost cause from the start, since death has
never been known to neglect a single soul under his
wardship on earth. Actually, they were "voluntarists"
to a greater degree than those to whom they applied that
Latin word, a word strange to hear even in standard
Russian, not to mention Kremlin jargon.

That accounts for the paradoxical outcome of the
duel between the rival "young men" in the Kremlin; the

revenge of the oldsters, a replay of the Brezhnev era and his posthumous One Hundred Days. It was as if the setting of the Kremlin drama had been shifted from our sinful earth to the nether world, where the dead Brezhnev overcame the dead Andropov with the help of the half-dead Chernenko and other "living corpses" in the Kremlin.

By that time, however, the viewer's attention span had been exhausted by Andropov, who had known how to intrigue spectators both in Russia and all over the world, but had not met their expectations because his reign had been so tragically brief. Disappointed by him and spoiled by the front-page news he had daily provided, they temporarily turned away from the Kremlin stage. And in truth, nothing happening there was interesting, certainly not the last, pathetic ceremonial appearances of just one more in a series of mortals, because the real action was once again, as in the days of Brezhnev's decline, going on in the wings. Not only was it much more interesting than the inaction onstage, but it was its total opposite. Behind the scenes, political passions were raging unslaked, a tumult interrupted only from time to time by the strains of Chopin's *Funeral March* coming from the stage on Red Square where yet one more funeral was being held.

4. The Empire's Secret Government: The KGB

> Every policeman knows
> that although governments change,
> the police remain.
>
> —LEON TROTSKY

THE RETURN OF the gerontocrats, headed by Chernenko, to power in the Kremlin in February 1984 gave rise to a situation that might be compared to prostration, a dead faint, lethargic sleep, or paralysis. Whatever the analogy, outwardly life in the Kremlin seemed to have come to an end. During all thirteen months of the nominal Chernenko era, there was not a single personnel shift in the top Party organs: not in the Secretariat, not in the Politburo, and not in the Politburo's "dressing room" for candidate members. An exception might be made for the case of Marshal Ustinov, the min-

ister of defense, whom death took from the ranks of the
Kremlin elite. But no one took his place in the Politburo. His position in the defense ministry was filled by
the seventy-three-year-old Marshal Sergei Sokolov, who
was not even a member of the Politburo; he was merely
a nominal defense minister under the nominal general
secretary, Chernenko, and under the nominal premier,
Tikhonov. The superpower itself was transformed into
a fiction, a phony empire of catalogues in which everything was listed but nothing was in place: not the general
secretary of the Party (who was also president and commander in chief), not the premier, and not the minister
of defense. God forbid we should look for what was behind those titles! It was just like the stage of the Globe
Theatre, where to indicate a forest, a river, or a tavern,
signs were held up that read "a forest," "a river," "a
tavern," and whether or not the playgoer could visual-
ize them depended upon his own imagination. "Think,
when we talk of horses, that you see them," Shakespeare told his audience. But there were no Shake-
speares at the Kremlin court, and no one needed any;
the deterioration in the leadership had gone so far that
no one cared any longer about providing a credible or
even a decent facade. It was enough that the Kremlin
games being played with imperial regalia and titles
pleasured those playing the games. All of them were so
old, so ill, and so indifferent that they simply did not
care about the onlookers—not those in other countries,
and especially not those in their own.

Yet amazingly, for all of the thirteen months that the
empire had no leadership and that the Kremlin ceased to
function as its control panel, the entity itself continued
to exist. The provinces did not revolt and secede; order
was not disturbed in the mother country; and the
peoples of the USSR remained loyal to their invisible
government, just as before they had been loyal to their
visible leaders. This was by no means due to momentum
from a previous regime continuing on through a brief
period of no government; momentum means the in-

evitable slowing down of movement, but in this case it was speeded up in several respects. Chauvinist propaganda was stepped up; censorship was tightened; dissidents were treated even more roughly, and political prisoners even more cruelly; and more pressure was put on Eastern Europe, whose leaders were prohibited from going to West Germany for meetings with its leaders that had been planned long before, and whose athletes were forbidden to go to Los Angeles to take part in the Olympic Games. Finally, the war in Afghanistan was expanded, and the Soviet troops there became even more brutal.

If the practice of medicine in the Kremlin had not been at such a high level and if Brezhnev had died a few years sooner than he did—say, before the invasion of Afghanistan—and if Chernenko had come to power right after him and not after Andropov, everything would of course have been different, and the Kremlin crisis would inevitably have provoked a crisis in the empire itself, although on just what scale it is hard to say. But during Andropov's several years as regent under the moribund Brezhnev, and in the fifteen months of his own rule, he had had time to reinforce the foundations of the police state, which had been shaken by the liberal, Khrushchev, and the bureaucrat, Brezhnev. He had enclosed the construction site with barbed wire, put up guard towers manned with guards loyal to him, and appointed contractors to continue work on the project. That is why, despite the brevity of Andropov's term as chief of the Party and the state, there is no good reason to doubt the existence of an Andropov era. That era began long before his inauguration and was continued without him. He was like the God of Descartes, who with a fillip set the world rotating and himself became superfluous, or in any case, not strictly necessary.

The Andropov era was an attempt to restore Stalinism in order to save the empire from a decline and fall. This lent strength and authority to Andropov's police measures and ensured their continued viability after his death. He put together a team of people loyal to him that, during the period when the gerontocrats there were trying to turn the clock back to Brezhnev, went on functioning as a kind of automatic pilot for the empire. Power was fragmented, redistributed, and shifted. The Kremlin ceased to be the real center of the Pax Sovietica and was temporarily transformed into a strictly ceremonial organ, a place whose tenants presented decorations to one another, received foreign guests, and performed other simple bodily movements that had no direct bearing on running the country. Whereas at the very inception of "the workers' and peasants' state" in 1917 the role of its president had been nominal, now for the first time in Soviet history the title of the leader of the Communist Party, the general secretary, had also become nominal. Chernenko held both of those posts, and for all practical purposes he had no power.

The Kremlin relinquished its suzerainty not only over the empire but over the central departments governed by it and formerly fully subordinated to it. Even the once-regular Thursday meetings of the Politburo's members were more and more frequently canceled owing to the illnesses of the Kremlin oldsters; when they did take place, rarely were all members in attendance. With the decentralization of power, each department, separated from the others by a distance of several kilometers and under no central control, was left to its own devices and was gradually transformed into a medieval stronghold in which the Party feudal lord had unlimited power.

For the first time in almost three decades on the job, Minister of Foreign Affairs Andrei Gromyko was free of interference by the Kremlin leader. It was no longer the general secretary of the Party—Khrushchev, Brezhnev, or Andropov—who determined the empire's foreign policy toward America and Western Europe, but Gromyko himself, who took no account of Chernenko's opinions, if indeed Chernenko had any. During meetings with foreign leaders in Moscow, Gromyko impatiently and rudely interrupted the general secretary, plainly dominating the talks.

Before then, Gromyko had always been somebody's mouthpiece and yes man: Stalin's, when he was with him at the Yalta Conference of the Big Three; Khrushchev's, when along with him, and even more forcefully, he pounded his fist on the desk at the UN during a speech by the delegate from Franco's Spain; Brezhnev's, when that general secretary was a "committed" proponent of détente; and Andropov's, when that ruler became just as "committed" an enemy of it and defended, crudely and with threats, his nation's piratical attack on the unarmed Korean airliner. Although Gromyko had always been a stodgy bureaucrat, Western print journalists, owing to their wishful thinking about the USSR, vied with one another in paying him compliments, calling him "the Russian Talleyrand," "the Soviet Metternich," and "the Kremlin Kissinger." (For that matter, there are other Kremlin leaders whom they have not exactly offended, as when they called Andropov a "liberal" and Gorbachev an "intellectual" and a "poet.") In a conversation with General de Gaulle, Khrushchev neatly characterized his minister of foreign affairs, saying that if Gromyko were ordered to take down his pants and sit on a block of ice, he would obey the order implicitly and sit there until he was ordered to stand up.

And now, when he was an old man of seventy-five, that faceless and voiceless bureaucrat finally found his own voice, not only in foreign affairs but in domestic matters as well. His voice, his vote, would be the deciding one when the time came, after Chernenko's death, to name the next Soviet leader—the seventh since the birth of the Soviet regime, and the sixth since Gromyko's career had been begun.

In another building, the Ministry of Defense on Frunze Quay, the man in charge was Marshal Nikolai Ogarkov, chief of the general staff, first deputy minister of defense, and de facto acting minister of defense under Dmitri Ustinov (a civilian even though he wore a uniform and had the title of marshal), who by that time was already old and sick. (He would die a few months later, in the winter of 1984.) Ogarkov was the most fervent advocate of the Korean airliner's destruction, a proponent of a nuclear first strike, and favored developing a Soviet "Star Wars" program. He aroused ever-greater suspicions among the Kremlin gerontocrats, including his immediate superior, Dmitri Ustinov, by his growing independence, so that they were already talking about his "Bonapartism," and even more by his alliance with Grigori Romanov, who directly supported his hawkish program and was demanding more and more funding for defense.

But the one who most feared that alliance was Mikhail Gorbachev. Although Romanov and Gorbachev held parallel and theoretically equal posts in the Party hierarchy, they preferred having some space between them and dug in, each with his own team, in separate buildings: Romanov remained in the Kremlin, while Gorbachev chose as his headquarters the CC building on Staraya Square.

Another building, housing the USSR Council of Ministers, was supposedly the domain of the nominal (and worthless) premier, Nikolai Tikhonov; he was so old that he dozed all the way through the long sessions of the Politburo, the parliament, and even those of the cabinet he headed up. His first deputy, Geidar Aliyev, the most colorful, able, and ruthless member of the Politburo since Andropov's death, took tremendous power into his own hands.

Aliyev stood out sharply against the solid gray background of his Politburo colleagues, and not only because of his distinct ethnic traits as an Azerbaijani. Tall, with the broad shoulders of an athlete; possessed of a splendid military carriage; clever and able to think for himself; and given to wearing English-tailored suits, silk ties, and Italian loafers, he called to mind a macho-style Hollywood actor. Set off by the sour, morose expressions (often due simply to physical indisposition) of most of his Kremlin associates, their eyes lackluster with age, Aliyev's blazing eyes bespoke of excitable temperament, which could be ascribed to his Middle Eastern origins. Moscow was abuzz with rumors about his amorous adventures; whatever their basis in reality, he was regarded as the only Politburo member capable of such a thing. Gorbachev was apparently also up to the mark, but he was under the thumb of his wife and never dared to indulge in amorous fun and games on the side. Aliyev's wife, Zafira, a very capable ophthalmologist, was gravely ill when she came to Moscow and died shortly thereafter.

At Kremlin receptions for foreign guests, Aliyev wittily fielded tricky questions and never seemed to be afraid of them. He often smiled and even laughed heartily—something that was new in the Kremlin, which in the eighties was coming more and more to resemble a hospital for the Party elite. He radiated vigor, enterprise, and initiative. Next to him, even the youngest members of the Politburo—Vorotnikov, Romanov, and Gorbachev—who didn't have his Caucasian temperament, lost their luster and looked older. Because of his self-confidence, his grasp of practical matters, and his physical appeal, Aliyev brought "masculine potential" into the Kremlin atmosphere, which had long been sexless. If there was anything that stopped Aliyev from officially taking over the post of prime minister after Tikhonov's resignation in the autumn of 1985, it was his Caucasian/Moslem origins. After all, even the Slav, Nikolai Ryzhkov, who before he became premier was identified in official biographical sketches as a Ukrainian, was obliged, once he had assumed that office, promptly to change his ethnic origin to "Russian."

Aliyev's father was a poor Shiite trader in Nakhichevan, a town on the Iranian border of the Republic of Azerbaijan. But his career, beginning in his teens, has been so completely Soviet as to wipe out any ethnic or religious differences. Despite his Middle Eastern name and appearance, he became a hundred percent cosmopolitan, as witnessed by the fact that Moscow entrusted him with the chairmanship of the Republic KGB, a post usually held by a Russian or a Ukrainian. (His predecessor as chief of Azerbaijan's secret police was Semyon Tsvigun, Brezhnev's brother-in-law, who before that had worked in the KGB in two other republics.)

Aliyev started working for the security organs in 1941, when he was not yet eighteen. Almost immediately, he was sent (along with the Red Army) into neighboring Iran to the city of Tabriz, where he worked in the ranks of radical separatists of the pro-Soviet Democratic Party of Iranian Azerbaijan. Their purpose was to help Stalin realize the traditional imperial dream: the annexation of northern Iran to Russia. Aliyev's familiarity with Moslem customs and his fluency in Middle Eastern languages—Farsi, Turkish, and Arabic, in addition to Azerbaijani—helped in his work in Tabriz and also a few years later in Turkey. It also came in handy much later, decades after Stalin's adventure in Iran had failed, when Aliyev, still serving as Party boss in Azerbaijan, became Andropov's secret consultant on the KGB's Middle Eastern policy, which involved matters ranging from the overthrow of the Shah of Iran, to the seizure by left-wing Iranian students of the American hostages in that country and later Soviet actions in the Middle East, to the occupation of Afghanistan.

Early in 1979, through Andropov's efforts, Aliyev even got a permanent apartment in Moscow, although his official residence permit was for Baku, and his official duties were there. But Brezhnev and his colleagues were still desperately resisting making yet another KGB man a member of the Politburo, since right at that time they were beginning to have trouble with Andropov himself. Neither Aliyev's proven abilities, nor his success in raising productivity in his republic, nor his endless flattery of Brezhnev helped his cause, while Andropov's sponsorship no doubt militated against his protégé rather than for him. The main reason for his exclusion from the Politburo, however, was that the Dnepropetrovsk mafia had certain knowledge of the unbridled cruelty Aliyev had shown in dealing with his enemies in his own part of the country.

Aliyev was a highly gifted man whose very long experience with the security organs had made him into a cynical, crafty, and ruthless plotter. As chief of the secret police in Azerbaijan, it took him only two years—using the pretext of an antigraft campaign—to overthrow the Party boss who had been named by the Kremlin to run the republic, and to take his place. By comparison, Andropov, who had helped Aliyev carry out his coup and even regarded it as a rehearsal for his own projected coup on the national scale, needed fifteen years to overthrow Brezhnev. (True, unlike Aliyev, Andropov had no helpers and sponsors, only enemies.)

In any case, the dwellers in the Kremlin feared Aliyev and kept him at a safe remove in his native republic. This was irksome to a man who for years had longed to make it into the Kremlin; Aliyev felt cramped in Azerbaijan—he was a politician of national, not just local, caliber. When he finally did make it to the capital under Andropov's reign, he rolled up his shirtsleeves and went to work with vigor such as had not been seen in the Kremlin for a long time. This was all the more necessary in that Andropov had spent much of his strength in his struggle for power; only a few months after his inauguration he began to fail physically.

Even judging only from information in the Soviet press, the scope of Aliyev's duties was extraordinarily broad, ranging from combating graft to making the trains run on time; from reforming "general" schools (computer courses were made obligatory in the upper grades) to overseeing Soviet policy in the Middle East. Thus, the day before Andropov's death, the Soviet papers announced an impending visit by Aliyev to Syria, the USSR's chief outpost in the Middle East.

As to the importance Andropov gave to that region, one may again judge from the Soviet press. It is generally thought that his last meeting with foreign officialdom was with the delegation of American senators that took place on August 18, 1983, two weeks before the

Korean airliner was shot down. Actually, six weeks later, on September 28, Andropov received Ali Nasser Mohammed al-Hassani, the president of South Yemen. But by that time he was already so ill that it was decided to publish no photographs of that meeting, merely an item about it, in order to avoid frightening Soviet citizens needlessly and stirring up new rumors abroad. The item duly appeared in the papers the next day. It is obvious that Andropov did not feel awkward in the presence of South Yemen's leader: the latter was his man, a Soviet puppet in the Middle East. The same goes for Hafez al-Assad, the president of Syria, whom the dying Andropov received at about the same time (probably even later) at his headquarters in the Kuntsevo Hospital. However, not so much as an item was published about this meeting. It was not made public until after Andropov's death, when Assad himself let slip a mention of that secret talk in his official message of condolence, which because of an oversight was printed in the Soviet papers. That message begins, "The close relations between us, the meetings we had, and Yu. V. Andropov's journey through life . . ." Yet during all the time that had elapsed since Brezhnev's funeral, the Soviet press had not published a single mention of a meeting between Andropov and Assad. And during Brezhnev's life, although the president of Syria had met with Brezhnev himself and with his ministers of foreign affairs and defense, he had not met with the KGB chairman.

What made Andropov keep his meeting with Assad secret? A year earlier, during dogfights over the Bekaa Valley in southern Lebanon, Syria had lost 104 MIGs, while Israel had not lost a single plane—a humiliating demonstration of the USSR's lag behind the United States in military technology. After forcing Syria to stop fighting, Israel attacked the PLO, which the KGB had not only assisted but had also used for purposes of international terrorism. Israel destroyed its potential for armed struggle and nullified its military significance. The Soviet Union could do nothing but look helplessly on as its client and proxy was vanquished. Surprisingly, the USSR permitted Syria to finish the job for Israel and to destroy the remnants of Arafat's Palestinian loyalists in Tripoli. In the struggle between its two clients, the Kremlin had taken the side of Syria, which was able to supply the Soviet Union with more effective agents than could the defeated Palestinians, whom the Kremlin had supported only out of self-interest. Andropov was more aware of the USSR's military weakness than any of the other Kremlin leaders, and he always staked more on the subversive activities of his agents. In shifting the KGB's headquarters from Dzerzhinsky Square to the Party headquarters on Red Square, he changed neither his principles nor his working habits; rather, in using a ramified network of international terrorists, the Soviet Union became virtually invulnerable. Working hand in glove, Soviet and Syrian state security agents found a replacement for the Palestinian terrorists: the Shiite terrorists, who became Middle Eastern kamikazes, blowing up embassies and barracks occupied by foreign soldiers, hijacking airliners, and seizing hostages.

Thus the Kremlin quickly and cheaply avenged its defeat in the war in Lebanon, bringing about the withdrawal from that country of the Americans and, a year later, of the Israelis, who although they had taken heavy losses in manpower had not been able to find a counterweight to the new tactic of the terrorists. According to Soviet sources that are reliable, although biased, in being hostile to Aliyev, it was he who conceived and initiated the replacement of Palestinian terrorists by Shias practicing the same trade.

Because of Andropov's death, Aliyev's visit to Syria was postponed for a month; it took place in March 1983 instead of February. (The last time a Politburo member had gone to Syria was in 1974, when it was Foreign Minister Andrei Gromyko.) After the death of Andropov, Middle Eastern affairs were shifted to the jurisdiction of the KGB, as were other areas of foreign policy concern: Aliyev also oversaw relations with Latin

America (keeping an especially sharp eye on Cuba, Nicaragua, and El Savador), and KGB Chairman Victor Chebrikov did the same with respect to the Warsaw Pact countries. The Ministry of Foreign Affairs now in fact served only for purposes of display, like so many posters put up in Western capitals from the Vatican to Washington. That policy must have suited Gromyko just fine: he had never been fond of "wet jobs" (as the KGB calls murders), countries along the empire's borders, or those of the Third World. This was all the more true in his old age. He and his wife, Lydia Dmitriyevna, preferred Western civilization. During their trips through Europe and America, they enjoyed the lunches and receptions arranged in their honor, and Lydia Dmitriyevna went on shopping sprees in department stores and fashion boutiques. What would they have done in Damascus, Managua, or Sofia? It is hardly likely that Gromyko was sorry even when he lost, within three months of Gorbachev's accession, the post of foreign minister. In exchange he was given the supreme (although ceremonial) post of president, which would now enable him to travel throughout the world with even greater pomp, as chief of state.

At the same time, the process of "KGB-izing" the Kremlin's foreign policy was completed. The man appointed as the new minister of foreign affairs was not a professional diplomat like Gromyko but a professional policeman and Andropov protégé, General Eduard Shevardnadze. Before becoming Party boss of Georgia, he had served there for seven years as chief of the regular police. Concomitantly with his appointment as foreign minister, he was brought into the Politburo, so that the number of top cops there was raised to three (the other two being Chebrikov and Aliyev) for the first time in Soviet history. This means that not only the foreign ministry but also all the other ruling bodies, including the supreme one, the Politburo, have been changed and have taken on more and more of a secret-police coloration. Even without Andropov, his loyal pupils, pursuant to his legacy, are carrying out his plan of transforming the bureaucratic empire into a KGB one.

All the world knows about the activities of the KGB outside the Soviet Union, where it does the same routine work of espionage, sabotage, disinformation, and so on, as its Western counterparts. In foreign countries its scope is limited, but at home in Russia it is almost absolute. Stalin, during all the time that he kept changing its official leadership—Yagoda was followed by Yezhov, and Yezhov by Beria—actually headed it up himself. Yet even he, so he said, acknowledged that its power was beyond his control. When Finnish Communist Otto Kuusinen came to Stalin about his son, who had been arrested, the great ruler, taking his extinct pipe out of his mouth, told him, "That's terrible. But what can I do with them? They've already put half of my relatives behind bars, and I'm powerless to save them."

That conversation actually took place. And here is a joke that was being told at the time when Andropov was chief of the KGB. At a session of the Politburo, Premier Kosygin whispered into Brezhnev's ear, "Listen, Lenya. Be on your guard with Andropov. They say he's a snitch."

That joke was not only witty but also prophetic. Kosygin's apprehensions proved to be very well founded, although Brezhnev did not heed his warning. Or else he did, but it was already too late.

The secret police is an organization that every Kremlin leader has had a vital need for, since without it his power wouldn't last for even a few days. Yet each of them has been deathly afraid of it, just like the other 270 million Soviet citizens.

During the Great Terror, Stalin in effect exchanged the post of Party leader for that of chief of the secret police. Making use of the latter, he completely destroyed the original top echelon of Bolshevik revolutionaries, called Lenin's Guard. Andropov took the reverse path, moving from the KGB chairmanship to the post of general secretary, but in actuality he remained the empire's top cop until the end of his days. He was of an age when it was too late to change his habits and his trade. Nor would it have been a good thing for him. It was thanks to them that he was able to seize supreme power in the country. During Brezhnev's sunset years, the very structure of power in the USSR had changed. The Committee of State Security once again broke loose from the control of the Party, which it was supposed to serve as its "trusty sword and shield,"* and turned its sword against the Party apparatus, including the top Kremlin echelon. In Andropov's hands the KGB became a potent weapon in the struggle for power.

The late seventies was a time of mysterious falls from grace and no less mysterious deaths in the Kremlin and its provincial branches. Kirill Mazurov and Andrei Kirilenko, who had been performing Brezhnev's duties in his absence, were expelled from the Politburo with no explanation. Similar was the case of Fyodor Kulakov, who had been universally regarded as Brezhnev's heir. Since he was the healthiest member of the Politburo, everyone was caught by surprise when his death was announced in a hastily issued bulletin. Another presumed heir, Grigori Romanov, was knocked out of the running by the obvious frame-up: the scandal about Catherine the Great's dinnerware. Petr Masherov, Party boss of Byelorussia, was killed in a highway accident, as were several other Brezhnevites, including the deputy commander of the KGB border troops, one of the Leningrad Party secretaries, and the prime minister of Georgia. (The prime minister of another republic, Kirgizia, was murdered—supposedly in a blood feud.) In the entire history of the Soviet ruling elite, there had never been such an epidemic of fatal automobile accidents. The death of Masherov, who was beginning to be seen as one of Brezhnev's heirs after Kulakov had perished, oc-

---

*Another tag for the political police, "the iron cohort of the Party," was in style in the twenties, but it is no longer used because the phrase was coined by Trotsky.

curred under particularly strange circumstances. His armored limousine crashed into two empty police vehicles blocking the road ahead of his motorcade. Finally, as the reader will remember, in January 1982, toward the very end of the Brezhnev era, his brother-in-law, General Tsvigun, first deputy chairman of the KGB, was found dead in his own office, shot in the head.

Thus, the KGB chief's rivals and enemies, one after another, were mysteriously put *hors de combat* until only one was left: Brezhnev himself. And Andropov could not fail to win the last battle; there was too great a difference in strength between the general secretary, an ornamental figure grown feeble in his old age, and the captain of his palace guard.

Andropov's accession to the Kremlin throne brought an end to the tripartite structure of power in which the Party, the government, and the secret police had worked together even while competing with one another. As very accurately described by George Orwell in *1984* and by Arthur Koestler in *Darkness at Noon,* the Party, assisted by the police, had put together and run the totalitarian state. Andropov led the "revolt of the machine" (the secret police) against its creator (the Party). Because of that, both novels are now obsolete. Neither reflects the new model of the Soviet empire proposed by Andropov and adopted by his heirs after that brief interim period, the Chernenko non-era.

The Andropov revolution showed that the core of the Soviet state is the secret police and that the Party itself is a mere appendix of the secret police.* The entire course of Russian history has led up to this; the secret police is the most impressive product of the Russians' political development. It's rather strange that a coup by that organization did not happen earlier. It was attempted twice earlier: once by Lavrenty Beria shortly after Stalin's death, and once by Alexander Shelepin in the

---

*Contrast the opinion John Barron offers in his book *KBG*: "The political controls are so strong and pervasive that the KGB will probably never break its leash and turn against its Party masters."

Brezhnev era. Both attempts failed by pure accident. In the first case the plotters were executed; in the second they were consigned to political disgrace.

Victor Mikhailovich Chebrikov, the present KGB chief, has a record of service in that organization even longer than Andropov's. He too joined "the organs" after doing Party work in Dnepropetrovsk. He was assigned to Andropov's staff as a deputy chief, but his real job was to spy on him, as other deputy chiefs from Brezhnev's Dnepropetrovsk mafia were doing. Toward the end of Brezhnev's life, however, Chebrikov sized up the situation and made a quick switch from the camp of his sponsor and landsman, Brezhnev, to that of his own immediate superior, Andropov, thereby saving his own skin. After the accession of Andropov, Chebrikov was rewarded for that switch: he was named chairman of the KGB—his boss's right-hand man, assigned to carry out especially complex, ticklish, and important secret missions.

While he was one of Andropov's deputies, Chebrikov occupied a niche in the structure of the state so supersecret that he felt it necessary to make himself mysterious. Thus, when dissidents were called in for interrogation, he introduced himself to them not as Chebrikov but as "Rebrikov." He usually conducted those interrogations in a low, even, unexpressive voice, never raising it or displaying his feelings, not even in response to answers given by the person under interrogation. Some of those who have met him have a distinct memory of his face: puffy and rough-hewn, as if formed from poured concrete. His expression was almost always haughty and contemptuous; the person he was interrogating would at first think the contempt was directed toward him, until he realized that it had become a permanent part of Chebrikov's face. Nor did Chebrikov's expression change when any of his aides came into his office. He would not give them so much as a glance or address a single word to them, confining himself to gestures and nods of the head. Later on, when he became top cop, he was known for having a stonier face than anyone who had held that position before him. Chebrikov is the model KGB bureaucrat: in him, that subspecies has evolved to a point of absolute perfection.

His sedentary occupation gave Chebrikov his sallow complexion, awkward bodily movements, painful hemorrhoids, and lumbago, for which he takes treatments at the same Krasnye Kamni sanitarium in the northern Caucasus where Andropov "took the cure." Today, Chebrikov uses the same cottage where Andropov once stayed; one might say he inherited it.

His whole appearance conveys the impression of something lifeless, congealed, or mechanical. He is rather tall and heavy-set and is oddly clumsy. When he turns in either direction, his whole body moves at once, much in the manner of a large, lumbering bear. That's exactly the nickname his aides use behind his back; when he calls them in for a meeting, they say, "The bear wants to see us in his office." At least, that was the case in 1977, when he was one of Andropov's deputies and we were still living in Moscow.

Although he was relatively young then (like Aliyev, he was born in 1923), he was already rather old-looking and evinced a curious fondness for old-fashioned clothes. He wore dark-blue uniformlike suits, quaint striped ties like those popular in the forties, and in winter a heavy, padded overcoat "of Stalin cut" with two hooks to fasten the collar. On his huge feet, rather like a bear's hind paws, his imported shoes looked as if they were orthopedic; his aides always tried to stay out of his way, "because," as one of them joked, "if he steps on one of *your* feet, it will be crushed."

Like Aliyev, Shevardnadze, and Fedorchuk (and Andropov in his day), he seldom appears in uniform: only at special conferences of military and KGB officers, where civilian clothes would be out of place on a man of high military rank. For example, he appeared in uniform at a grand ceremony held on April 19, 1984, in the

Kremlin, where Konstantin Chernenko awarded him a
marshal's gold star set with twenty-five diamonds. This
was a breach of a Kremlin tradition dating from right
after Stalin's death: until that day in 1984, the only chief
of secret police to wear a marshal's star in his button-
hole had been Lavrenty Beria, Stalin's accomplice in his
gory crimes.

It was, by the way, Chebrikov's third promotion in
only five months. In November 1983, he had been given
the rank of general of the army, and in late December,
only six weeks before Andropov's death, the Party gave
him a Christmas gift: he was named a candidate member of the Politburo. (His appointment as a full member
was announced six weeks after Gorbachev came to
power.) These upward leaps in Chebrikov's Party and
military career were not unusual. Andropov, in his
struggle against his chief enemy, time, had made haste
to promote his men. Chebrikov's rapid advancement
was matched by that of other Andropovites: Geidar
Aliyev, Grigori Romanov, Vitaly Vorotnikov, Mikhail
Gorbachev, Egor Ligachev, Nikolai Ryzhkov, and Vitaly Fedorchuk, who replaced the oldsters of Brezhnev's
graft-ridden mafia in what resembled an emergency action. But Chebrikov was the only one among the Kremlin elite who was allowed access to the dying Andropov
in Kuntsevo Hospital, although he was not yet a full
member of the Party's supreme ruling body, the Politburo.

According to some reports, Chebrikov masterminded
the murder of Semyon Tsvigun, who had been the KGB
chairman's sole first deputy, whereas Chebrikov was
just one deputy among several others. But we are inclined to think that those rumors arose long after the
fact and are grounded only on the fact that Chebrikov
gained more than anyone else except for Andropov himself from the death of his rival.

More reliable sources ascribe to Chebrikov an active
part in the KGB involvement in the attempt on the
Pope's life. This was indirectly confirmed by official

reports of visits by Chebrikov to Eastern European countries. In any case, in May 1983 he flew to Sofia on an urgent visit. (At the time, the Kremlin was making desperate efforts to cover its tracks in the Soviet-Bulgarian-Turkish plot against John Paul II.) A few months later, on November 25, 1983, he suddenly appeared in Warsaw, immediately after General Jaruzelski had steered through the Sejm (parliament) a law taking the Polish secret police out from under Kremlin control. The evident purpose of Chebrikov's visit was to put pressure on the Polish dictator, but he failed in his mission. In the summer of 1984, after Andropov's death, he made a more successful visit—to East Berlin, where he had a long talk with East German Premier Erich Honecker, for the obvious purpose of blocking rapprochement between the two Germanies. As a result of that "chat," Honecker's scheduled visit to Bonn was canceled.

For the KGB chairman to make trips openly, with press coverage, was unprecedented. Victor Chebrikov is now officially carrying out duties that earlier chiefs of the secret police fulfilled secretly. Although commanders in chief of the Warsaw Pact forces, ministers of foreign affairs, and CC secretaries had openly carried out similar missions in Eastern Europe, no KGB chairman had ever done so. This has little to do with Chebrikov personally; it reflects the marked enlargement of the KGB's role in governing the empire that was achieved by Andropov when he put the state security organs above all others, including the Party. In Moscow, people are joking that the CC is now a branch of the KGB. Another version has it that the Central Committee of the Communist Party of the Soviet Union, or CC CPSU, has been renamed the CC KGB. In any case, it was the KGB that, during the Chernenko non-era, kept that huge machine, the Soviet state, running without interruption. It became a collective regent under the feeble leaders, guaranteeing the continuity of the empire; it was its real, although still largely secret, government. Or perhaps that should be put somewhat differently: The KGB has replaced the government, the Party, and the ministry of foreign affairs, while of course continuing to control the armed forces. Behind the scenes, it is functioning with far greater effect than is apparent to outside observers of the Kremlin stage.

There is a joke telling of two policemen who are going to the birthday party of a third; they are discussing what kind of present to give him.

"Let's give him a book," one suggests.

To which the other replies, "He already has the book."

The KGB also has a book, one that has become its catechism; it is a regular bible for its members, from ordinary agents to chiefs of the rank of general. It is not Karl Marx's *Das Kapital* or Hitler's *Mein Kampf* or Machiavelli's *The Prince*. It was written long before them, at the turn of the sixth and fifth centuries B.C. Its author was the world's first military theorist, Sun U. Unlike Clausewitz, who regarded war as the continuation of politics by other means, the ancient Chinese theorist taught the ways in which one could defeat the enemy without waging war. Here are a few precepts taken at random:

"That person is skilled in military matters who defeats the enemy's army without fighting a battle."

"A victorious army wins the battle before going into it."

"The most important thing in war is to attack the enemy's strategy."

"I compel the enemy to take my strength for weakness, and my weakness for strength—striving at the same time to turn his strength into weakness."

Here is an example of how the precept to vanquish the enemy without fighting a battle was put into practice.

From time to time, the Soviet Union uses its armed forces to establish order in the countries along its border, as it did in Hungary in 1956 and in Czechoslovakia in 1968. However, in the Kremlin's satellite countries, separatist movements arise more often than it can use force against them. In the late seventies, such a movement sprang up in Bulgaria, a nation whose loyalty to its imperial overlord is somewhat exaggerated here in America. That movement, at once separatist and pro-Western, originated not at the bottom but at the top. It was associated with the name of Bulgarian leader Todor Zhivkov's daughter, Ludmila Zhivkova, who was an Oxford graduate, a member of the ruling Politburo, and one of Bulgaria's most influential leaders. Todor Zhivkov's closest friend, Premier Stanko Todorov, sided with Ludmila and supported her patriotic policy of independence. From the Kremlin's viewpoint, the situation was alarming and had to be brought under control "without going into battle." The KGB promptly did bring it under control with the help of its agents in Bulgaria.

Stanko Todorov was dismissed without prior notice and was replaced as premier by a Soviet puppet, Grisha Filipov, who was born in the Ukraine and was a graduate of Moscow University. Shortly afterward, in March 1981, the news media reported the death of thirty-eight-year-old Ludmila Zhivkova in an automobile accident, although in Bulgaria nobody doubts that she was poisoned on orders from Moscow. And Todor Zhivkov himself, shaken by the events in his country, disappeared from the political horizon for a long time. Thus, the Bulgarian crisis was nipped in the bud even before the world outside the Eastern bloc had heard of it.

The tragic and mysterious death of Ludmila Zhivkova came only two months before a Turkish terrorist, under the direction of Bulgarian agents, tried to assassinate Pope John Paul II and two and a half years after some equally mysterious incidents involving umbrellas. In the first of these 1978 incidents, Vladimir Kostov, a Bulgarian political émigré living in Paris, was seriously poisoned. Ten days later, another Bulgarian political émigré, Georgi Markov, died after a stranger had "inadvertently" jabbed him with the point of his umbrella in Waterloo Station in London. When he learned of his compatriot's death, Kostov, who by this time had recovered, went for a medical examination and X-rays. It turned out that he had been poisoned by a potent toxic substance contained in a miniaturized platinum ball about the size of a pinhead mounted in the tip of an umbrella. Chemical analysis revealed that the substance was ricin, which is extracted from castor oil. One ounce of it is enough to kill ninety thousand people. According to Western intelligence services, experiments with ricin are being conducted intensively in Hungary and Czechoslovakia. This is yet one more indication that in no other sphere, not in economic matters, nor even in military ones, has Eastern Europe reached as high a degree of integration and coordination as it has in the work of state security organs.

Later that same year, yet another Bulgarian political émigré, Vladimir Simeonov, perished in London, also under mysterious circumstances. When a journalist went to the Bulgarian Embassy in London to ask for a comment on all these strange incidents, he was refused admission. He was merely told, from behind a grille, that he had read too many novels by Agatha Christie.

All the foregoing incidents bear the signature of the Derzhavna Sigurnost, the Bulgarian secret police, which was described by writer Georgi Markov, who met his death at its hands, as "nothing more or less than the mighty arm of the KGB in our country." The Derzhavna Sigurnost was founded by the Soviet occupation authorities in 1944. The KGB put it partially in charge of "wet jobs." True, the murder of Markov and the attempt on the life of Kostov were done on its own initiative, but at the same time they served as good training for international actions ordered by the Soviet Union. In Bulgaria, the KGB had a man it could count on. The Sigurnost was headed up by Dimiter Stoyanov, who had studied at the Advanced Intelligence School in Moscow and worked for the KGB abroad. It was he who thought up the idea of using poisoned ballpoints in umbrellas. We might add that, according to some reports, Ludmila Zhivkova also died from poisoning.

Bulgaria was the KGB's base for experiments, and the Derzhavna Sigurnost was Moscow's trusty weapon no matter where—in Sofia, Beirut, or Rome. In Bulgaria, it was relatively easy for the KGB to follow the precept of its ancient Chinese counselor and win victory without fighting a battle. But an incomparably harder task faced the KGB in another Eastern European country: Poland.

5. The Kremlin's Hamlet Complex: What to Do or Not to Do About Poland?

AS WE HAVE already said, General Victor Chebrikov, the KGB chief, came back from Warsaw to Moscow in November 1983 with nothing. His urgent mission to Poland had been a complete failure. The law passed by the Sejm that centralized the commands of the regular police and the state security forces remained in force, and General Jaruzelski's closest aide, General Czeslaw Kiszczak, retained his post as minister of internal affairs even though he had refused to obey Kremlin directives and had insisted on the complete independence from Moscow of the troops and network of agents under his command. Thus, Poland became the second country in Eastern Europe, after Rumania, to get its secret police out from under the general command of the Warsaw Pact Forces.

For Jaruzelski, this was one more victory over the Kremlin, but it did not mean that he had settled the "Russian question" with finality. It meant merely that

he had put the settlement of the Russian empire's
"Polish question"—one of its most agonizing and vexing problems—at a still further remove and had made it
even more difficult.

Strange as it seems, it was easier for the Kremlin to
seize a new country than it was to keep a tight rein on
such an ungovernable satellite as Poland. On the eve of
1980, the Red Army had occupied Afghanistan, which
before then had been outside the Iron Curtain. Yet ten
months later, it came to a long and indecisive halt on the
border of Poland, although beginning in August 1980,
when the free trade unions of Solidarity had been
founded there, that nation had been irrepressibly moving farther away from the empire.

Kremlin leaders could find some consolation in analogies from history. Poland has always been the most
unruly of the Russian empire's subject nations. Russia
had lost Poland over and over again, but each time, by
force of arms, it had brought it back into its orbit. Since
its acquisition in 1795, there had not been a single Russian emperor—nor, after the Bolshevik Revolution, a
single Soviet *vozhd*—who had not run head on into the
Polish question. The way that painful problem was
dealt with did not depend upon who was ruling Russia
at the time; it was dictated by the interests of the empire
itself. The Polish uprising of 1831 was put down by Emperor Nicholas I, who had been so stern and cruel in
Russia as well that he was nicknamed "Nick the Big
Stick." Yet in 1863, his liberal son, Emperor Alexander
II, who two years before had abolished serfdom in his
own country, used no less cruelty in "pacifying" Poland. We find the same amazing consistency in our own
century. In 1920, Lenin, an internationalist and pragma-
tist, sent the newly formed Red Army into Poland to
take Warsaw by storm. Stalin had taken part in that
unsuccessful campaign as political commissar of the
Southwestern Army Group. On two later occasions, that
despot, chauvinist, and imperialist, as though wreaking
revenge for the failure of the 1920 campaign, "defini-

tively" put Poland into Russian hands. He did so just before World War II in the military pact with Hitler, and he did it again toward the war's end in the agreement with Roosevelt and Churchill at Yalta.

Definitively? A glance at the history of the Russo-Polish wars, which covers several centuries, includes several defeats that deeply injured Russian imperial vanity, from the capture of Moscow early in the seventeenth century to that of Kiev and Minsk and the Red Army's humiliating defeat near Warsaw in 1920, sometimes called "the miracle on the Vistula River." The cause of the national catastrophe in 1940 in the Katyn Forest, where over four thousand Polish officers who had retreated from the Germans were shot on orders from Stalin, was the Russians' traditional military fear of the Poles. The fear was aggravated by the personal experience of the Soviet tyrant, who never distinguished himself by great courage. One has only to recall how badly he panicked when he learned of Hitler's attack on Russia; months went by before he finally girded up his loins to resume the leadership of the country. And does not Stalin's twofold fear of Poland—his own, compounded by the traditional Russian dread—explain the Red Army's failure to help the Poles (actually, its betrayal of them) in August 1944?

The Warsaw uprising itself was the result of a carefully thought-out Soviet provocation. Two days before, a Soviet radio station had broadcast a call to arms to the inhabitants of Warsaw. "Poles, your hour of liberation is near! To arms! Seize the moment!" But once they responded to that call, Stalin not only refrained from ordering his own troops to cross the Vistula and help the Polish capital, which had been defending itself around the clock for sixty-three days, he even obstructed such aid from the other Allies. In letters to Churchill and Roosevelt, he called the insurgent patriots "a gang of criminals who have taken this gamble in Warsaw with the idea of seizing power." In 1940, he had seen to it that the flower of the Polish officer corps was destroyed by his own secret police. Now, in the summer of 1944, he saw to it that the rest of the Polish army was finished off in Warsaw by Hitler, thereby making it easier to transform postwar Poland into a Soviet satellite.

After the war, Katyn became a symbol and slogan for Polish Russophobia. When Khrushchev, in his unbridled crusade against the dead Stalin, wanted publicly to acknowledge Russian guilt for the Katyn tragedy, even Wladyslaw Gomulka, leader of the Polish "October Revolution" of 1956 (a polemical paraphrase of the Russian October Revolution of 1917), objected. He said that if such an acknowledgment were made, he would not be able to control anti-Russian emotions in his country. Even today, in both Russia and Poland, the Katyn massacre is officially ascribed to the Germans.

Of the Polish Communist leaders of the late thirties, Wladyslaw Gomulka was the only one to have survived. Just before the war, Stalin had dissolved the Polish Communist Party under the pretext that it had been infiltrated by enemy agents. "They are like an apple—red on the outside and white on the inside," Stalin had said of the Polish Communists at the time.* The leaders were summoned to Moscow, where they were all shot. Gomulka was spared only because at that juncture he was serving a seven-year sentence in a Polish prison for his communist activities; Stalin couldn't get his hands on him. But the despot had not forgotten him; in 1949 Gomulka was pulled out of the ranks of the postwar Polish Communists—Stalinists among whom Gomulka was indeed an odd bird—and imprisoned for "Titoism" and "nationalist deviation." But once again Gomulka was lucky: unlike other Eastern European Communists—Lazlo Raik of Hungary, Rudolph Slansky of Czechoslovakia, and Traicho Kostov of Bulgaria—he was not executed. In 1956, on the wave of de-Stalinization and the "thaw," he returned to power.

The first measures Gomulka took were to decentralize

*This terminology dates back to the Russian Civil War, when the Reds (the Bolsheviks) were fighting the Whites.

Poland's economic and political structure; relax censorship; abolish the *kolkhozes* (collective farms); and
liberalize the state's policy toward religion, ordering
(among other things) the release from prison of the Polish primate, Stefan Cardinal Wyszynski. Significantly,
he made radical changes in the army, so that it became
the chief guarantor of Polish independence. First and
foremost, he removed Marshal Konstantin Rokossovsky, the Soviet military governor, from his post as
minister of defense and expelled him from Poland. (It
was Rokossovsky, by the way, who, while in command
of the Soviet troops, had watched through field glasses
while the Germans destroyed insurgent Warsaw.) Gomulka carried out a major purge of the army, eliminating all Soviet generals and other officers in positions
of high command. They were replaced by Poles, including some "accomplices" of Wladyslaw Gomulka. The
new Polish leader had an urgent need for young army
cadres who were patriotic and faithful to the spirit
of reform. It was then that the thirty-three-year-old
Wojciech Jaruzelski was promoted to brigadier general
despite certain seeming blotches on his personal file.

His grandfather had been killed in the 1920 war
against the Russians; his mother was of Jewish origin;
and his father, Mieczyslaw, called Mietek, had perished
in a Soviet penal camp. Wojciech himself, a graduate of
the elite Jesuit lycée in Warsaw founded by the Marist
brothers, was exiled by the Russians to Siberia. There he
worked first as a miner in Karaganda, then as a lumber-
jack in the Altai Mountains. On the peaks of those
mountains, whose snowcaps were blinding, his eyelids
were burned and his vision impaired, so that he now has
to wear dark glasses.

True, a few years later, he had completed officers'
training school in Ryazan, southeast of Moscow, and he
had fought in General Zygmunt Berling's Second Polish
Infantry Division against the Germans, side-by-side
with Russian soldiers. But it is hardly likely that this was
simply an act of homage to the military tradition in the
Jaruzelski family. Rather, it was a deliberate and agon-

izing choice of the lesser of two evils, the kind of choice that Wojciech Jaruzelski would have to make more than once in the future. Although of those two evils he had chosen Russia, there were still things in his background that by Soviet standards were blotches. In the early Gomulka era, however, they were already regarded as merits; and taken all together, they served as a kind of guarantee of his decency and patriotism. It was in part thanks to them that Jaruzelski became the youngest general in the Polish army.

The sudden changes in Wojciech Jaruzelski's military and political career came at critical moments in his country's history. The first three of those moments were: Poland's liberation from the Germans, when the former Soviet prisoner became a Polish officer; the "October Spring" of 1956, when Gomulka revived the Poles' hopes, and Jaruzelski began his rapid rise in the Polish army; and the end of 1970, when the new leader, Edward Gierek, released Minister of Defense Wojciech Jaruzelski from house arrest. (He had been arrested for refusing to carry out a Party order to use troops to quell disorders in the port cities on the Baltic. He refused, with the words, "Polish soldiers are not going to fire on Polish workers!") A fourth such moment came in the early eighties on the wave of reform movements linked in one way or another to Solidarity, when the professional soldier was obliged to master a new specialty and become a politician.

The beginning of the most recent Polish revolution should be dated not at the time of the strikes in Gdansk, which led to the founding of Solidarity in the autumn of 1980, but at October 16, 1978. On that day, white smoke from the stove in the Vatican announced *urbi et orbi* the election of a new Roman Pontiff, Karol Cardinal Wojtyla from Krakow, who in his very first sermons in St. Peter's Square began calling for the political and religious independence of his country. By the fall of 1980, Poland was already deep in what poet Anna Kamienska called "a delirium of impossible possibilities." Or to quote Lenin's classic definition of a revolutionary situation, it was a period when no one was in power, "when the people at the bottom no longer want to live in the old way, and the people at the top are unable to." The government headed by Gierek had fallen; strikes and demonstrations were paralyzing the nation's economy; and the freedoms gained by Solidarity were degenerating into political anarchy that could not be controlled by anyone—not by Lech Walesa, and not by the Polish Church. Something exciting but dangerous was happening: the power was shifting directly from the Party bureaucrats' hands into those of the street mobs. It did not pass through any links in between because there were no democratic institutions in Poland.

The kind of simple, almost familiar, relations with democracy that, say, the United States or Holland has are totally lacking in Poland. In the past, freedom in that country often deteriorated into endless battles of words and political anarchy that were only brought to a halt by a dictatorship. There was even a time in the late seventeenth and early eighteenth centuries when the Sejm was incapable of passing a law because each deputy had a veto. That quaint institution, called the *liberum veto,* was Poland's own special contribution to democracy. No one else, quite naturally, ever used it, except for the UN Security Council, which, because each of its permanent members has a veto, has become an impotent body of no significance. It was owing chiefly to the Poles' unwillingness to place even reasonable limits on their liberties, to bring them within the framework of a constitutional democracy and give up some of their rights in favor of at least a few duties, that Poland lost its independence at the end of the eighteenth century. (Naturally, there were other causes as well, both internal and external.) The brief period of Polish independence between the two world wars was marked by a coup d'état in 1926 and the establishment of a military dictatorship called the *Sanacja* by Jozef Pilsudski, a former socialist.

General Jaruzelski knew what anarchy would lead to. He knew it not only from Polish history but also from

current international events. In an interview with Walter
Cronkite, he referred to the political chaos then spreading through Iran. He was careful, however, not to mention that his country and Iran had in common not only
street anarchy but also religious fanaticism. Certainly
the Church in Poland is more than a church; it is the
nucleus of Polish nationalism and its banner. It is a
counterweight to pressure from occupying forces and
has more than once helped the Poles to survive as a nation. But at the same time, it has shut that nation off
from Western civilization. For example, the Poles' bitter struggle for the display of the crucifix in public
schools comes from their failure to understand the difference in function between church and state. If their
politico-religious instincts were given totally free play,
the result might well be not a democratic state of the
Western type at all but a theocracy like that of the
Ayatollah Khomeini's Iran. Thus, General Jaruzelski's
grave apprehensions were well founded.

There was also an economic factor that was impossible to ignore; it is illustrated by a joke originating at that
time, in the early eighties. Pope John Paul II asks God
whether he would live to see the day when the Polish
economy emerged from its crisis, and God replies sor-
rowfully, "No, and neither will I."

Paradoxically, the five hundred days of long-awaited
freedom—from the Gdansk strikes in August 1980 to
the military coup d'état in December 1981—not only
failed to help Poland cope with its political and, especially, its economic problems, but actually aggravated
them. Its debt to the West rose even higher, to $27
billion; its exports fell off; coal production in Silesia
dropped sharply; shortages of food and other necessities
worsened; the rate of crime rose catastrophically; and
each day saw an increase in Poland's vulnerability to
seemingly inevitable Soviet aggression.

In the Kremlin at the time, the question as to whether
to settle the Polish crisis by military means became more
and more urgent. Threats that the Soviet Union would

intervene and put an end to the "counterrevolution" streamed from Moscow one after another. But the Poles were not frightened by words or hints, and the Kremlin couldn't make up its mind to use force. What really frustrated the Kremlin was the resolute warning issued by General Jaruzelski on the night of December 4, 1980: In the event of a Soviet incursion, he would order the Polish troops to fight. Two years later, a Polish diplomat told us about that ultimatum; what he said was unofficially confirmed by a Polish journalist close to the present regime. But even without such confidential information, one could arrive at that same conclusion by a process of elimination. Neither Western public opinion, nor American sanctions, or threats from Pope John Paul II were frightening to the Kremlin. Or if they were frightening, they were less so than the threat of the empire's disintegration. In December 1980, when the Soviet troops were put on top combat alert, their determined advance was stopped by the same kind of thing that had stopped them twenty-four years before, in October 1956, when Wladyslaw Gomulka, in response to Khrushchev's threats, said that Poland would take up arms against the Soviet Union. To try to take Poland "with slight losses," as had been done with Hungary and Czechoslovakia, would be futile because the Poles would have stopped at no sacrifice in resisting the neighbor who had offended them and whom they had hated for several centuries.

The Poles tell a remarkable joke in this connection about a genie whom a Pole had let out of a bottle. He promised to carry out any three wishes his new master might make. "I want the Chinese to attack Poland," the Pole said. The genie carried out his order and waited for the next one. "I want the Chinese to attack Poland," the Pole said again. And his third wish was the same. When he had carried out all of his liberator's wishes, the astounded genie asked what sense there was in having his own country destroyed three times over. The Pole said with satisfaction, "In order to reach Poland and then get back home, the Chinese had to cross Russia six times.''

After exhausting all methods of blackmailing and frightening Poland, and at the same time having decided not to intervene militarily in its affairs, Moscow decided to rely more on its own secret agents than on its troops. It resolved to lop off the spiritual head of the Polish revolution by means of a carefully planned and camouflaged terrorist act. The Polish question, which up to then had been the responsibility of military and Party leaders in Moscow, was put into the hands of Andropov's KGB.

That is why the next round of the fight for Poland was fought in St. Peter's Square in Rome. There, on May 13, 1981, Mehmet Ali Agca, a Turkish terrorist from a fascist organization known as The Gray Wolves, fired several shots at the Polish Pope, John Paul II.*

To return to the matter of Karol Wojtyla's election to the pontifical throne, it is significant that right after it, Special Service #1 of the KGB's First Main Administration, then headed up by Victor Chebrikov, drew up a special report on how the new Pope had been elected by the Curia. Chebrikov and his aides concluded that three Poles had played leading roles in that process: Zbigniew Brzezinski, President Jimmy Carter's national security adviser; John Cardinal Krol of Philadelphia; and Stefan Cardinal Wyszynski, Primate of Poland. All three, according to Soviet information, were Russophobes and raging anti-Sovietchiks. It was an obvious plot, and its ultimate aim was to tear Poland out of Moscow's grasp. And subsequent events—the Pope's triumphal visit to his homeland, the founding of Solidarity, and its support by the Poles' spiritual leader, now in the Vatican —confirmed, in the view of Andropov and Chebrikov, the correctness of the information, conclusions, prognoses, and recommendations contained in the report. (A

---

*As for the reconstruction of the KGB plot against John Paul II, we have omitted it in this book because it may be found in our book on Andropov.

copy of that curious document was later pilfered by foreign intelligence services.)

In the spring of 1983, when Andropov was already the Soviet ruler and Chebrikov KGB chief, the newspaper *Zycie Warszawy (Warsaw Life)*, citing its Washington correspondent as the source, reprinted from a leftist Madrid paper a "top secret memorandum" from Zbigniew Brezezinski to President Carter detailing the operation for the election of a Polish Pope, the destabilization of Poland, and bringing it "from the communist camp into the capitalist one." Not only that memorandum's content and style but its itinerary (one typical of Moscow's disinformation tactics: from a leftwing Madrid paper through Washington to a Polish paper) betrays the hand of the KGB, which concocted and distributed that forgery. The aim was no doubt to neutralize increasing suspicions that the KGB was implicated in the attempt on the Pope's life. One month later, for the same purpose, Victor Chebrikov made an emergency trip to Sofia to work out a joint Soviet-Bulgarian plan for refuting the claim that those two nations had ties with the Turkish terrorist, who had been trained in Palestinian camps in the Middle East.

Even more important than the falsity of the "memorandum," however, was the fact that in order to make it more plausible, the KGB had supplied it with its own version of the Pope's election under the covert guidance of Brzezinski, whose purpose was subversive anti-Soviet activity. This means that Moscow believed in that version not only in 1978, when the new Pope was elected, but in 1981, when the attempt was made on his life, and still later, in 1983, when the KGB chairman went to Bulgaria, and his ghostwriters concocted the forgery under the pseudonym "Zbigniew Brzezinski." And the Kremlin still believes it, having no doubts about it whatsoever.

But instead of refuting claims of "Bulgaro-Turkish" links with the KGB in the attempted assassination of the Pope, that forgery indirectly confirmed them. It thereby revealed Moscow's alarm at his election and his role as instigator of the events in Poland, and especially in regard to Russia's Enemy Number One, concealed in the background, which had set all this Polish machinery in motion and was continuing to operate that machinery from beyond the seas—the United States.

The attempt on the Pope's life created a worldwide sensation, but it must have made its strongest impression on the Kremlin, on Andropov's associates and rivals in the Politburo. Although the Pope remained alive, this failure of Andropov's in the international arena—one of his worst—became one of his greatest victories on the home front. In the Kremlin, experience, intuition, and fear sufficed to make plain what in Rome and Washington it took a long, thoroughgoing investigation to discover. The truth was grasped all the more quickly in Moscow because, as the reader will remember, at this very time an epidemic of mysterious deaths had broken out in the Kremlin itself and in its provincial branches. "Suicides," "automobile accidents," and "family vendettas" followed one upon another and ceased (all at once) only after Andropov's death.

The Soviet secret police have at their disposal a wide variety of means that can be used in combating both internal and external enemies. But after the execution of Beria, heads of that organization employed those means with great moderation, requesting the Politburo's authorization of their use in each individual case. Now, however, the KGB chief himself was a member of the Politburo, the first top cop since Beria to be a member, and with the exception of Mikhail Gorbachev and Andrei Gromyko, his relations with the others were conflictual. It was not merely that he deemed it unnecessary to request authorization from the Politburo; he even thought it superfluous to inform that supreme imperial organ of actions he planned to take, since he knew in advance that he would not get approval for the riskiest of them. Brezhnev, whose presence at the head of the state was merely ceremonial, was not let in on the Vatican scheme by Andropov—naturally. Because judging from his very cautious policy in the past, if he had known of it in advance he never would have approved it. All the other Kremlin gerontocrats, too, were presented with a *fait accompli*.

The panic in the Kremlin was no less than that in the Vatican. For example, we have accurate information from a member of Andrei Kirilenko's apparatus as to how shaken Kirilenko, the number-two man in the Kremlin, was when he learned of the attempted assassination. None of them could have cared less about Pope John Paul II; each of them was thinking only of himself and his total defenselessness before the KGB chief, that enigmatic man with the fleeting smile on his thin lips and the nearsighted eyes behind the thick lenses of his imported glasses. None of them had any more doubts as to what kind of a man had wormed his way into their ranks. From their viewpoint, this was a revival of Stalinism, with intrigues, perfidy, murders, and fear. Thus, the shots fired at the Pope, which, thanks to a miracle and the skill of Italian surgeons, did not prove to be fatal, did prove fateful for the Kremlin elders. Beginning on May 13, 1981, Stalinist fear returned to the Kremlin.

But although Andropov gained more power in the Kremlin thanks to the sensational incident in St. Peter's Square, he had not made one inch of progress in settling the Polish crisis. Indeed, he had been set back, because the attempt on the life of the Polish Pope had given even greater resolve to another Pole, General Jaruzelski. The general realized that there were people in Moscow who would stop at nothing to pacify Poland—if not by means of the regular army, then by means of regular subversive activity—and that their moves had to be forestalled at any price. And so, on the night of December 13, 1981, when Soviet threats were at their most feverish and it was no longer possible to distinguish between blackmail and reality, after sealing off Poland's borders with the USSR and its satellites, General Jaruzelski carried out a coup d'état.

"It is very regrettable that in such cases human nature is obliged to resort to force. But on the other hand, it cannot be denied that this is the highest tribute to truth and justice." Those words of José Ortega y Gasset are fully applicable to the Polish general. In paying the highest tribute to truth and justice, he saved his country from a Soviet invasion. He did something for Poland that neither the two Eastern European schismatics, Imre Nagy of Hungary and Alexander Dubcek of Czechoslovakia, nor their conformist successors, Janos Kadar and Gustav Husak, had been able to do for their countries. In close fighting, General Jaruzelski had held out against the Kremlin and won the victory.

The army, headed by General Jaruzelski, had seized power only after it had become convinced that Solidarity could not carry out its promised program of reforms without jeopardizing the very existence of Poland. Solidarity had played an interim role politically, as in a brief second act. It had managed to topple the old government, but had not proved capable of succeeding it. In destroying the Party's prestige, Solidarity had cleared the army's way to power. By the military coup d'état of December 13, 1981, the army assumed responsibility for the fate of the republic: the Polish revolution had passed from the hands of the workers into those of the military. After playing leading roles in the preceding act of the Polish drama, Lech Walesa and his comrades retired to the wings. He had inscribed his name in Polish history, but it is hardly likely that he will again play much of a role in it.

Such is the nature of revolutions, one of their traits that might be called international. As a revolution develops, it follows a zigzag pattern, reversing its course and destroying its original model en route. Like a gigantic pendulum, it swings from anarchy to the eternal antithesis in that process: dictatorship.

Nineteen months after it had been established, martial law was lifted, although the military did not restore power to the country's previous leaders, the Communists. True, Jaruzelski has a Party card; but it is no more than a facade turned toward a suspicious Mecca: Moscow. (It should be remembered that Poland's prewar dictator, Marshal Pilsudski, was also officially a socialist.) Although Jaruzelski sacrificed several kinds of freedom gained by Solidarity in order to save the independence of Poland, that country remains the freest in Eastern Europe. It is a country with antigovernment demonstrations, privately owned farms, and an independent church that is partly in opposition to the government. Its workers have the official right to strike, and its ordinary citizens can travel abroad almost without restrictions. Jaruzelski's merits are even recognized by opponents he has vanquished; one of the former leaders of Solidarity, Janus Snushkevicz, has fittingly called the present regime "totalitarianism with a human face." We all know the result produced by the "socialism with a human face" of Alexander Dubcek and his co-authors of the Prague Spring. Can it be that "totalitarianism with a human face" is more reliable, and more justified historically, in opposing the Soviet Union?

One can hardly compare Wojciech Jaruzelski with Western political leaders, who do not have to cope with tasks as complex, demanding, and mortally dangerous as he does, or, for that matter, Poland itself with countries that are independent of the Soviet Union. Poland is the nearest Western neighbor of the USSR and is a member of the Warsaw Pact bloc, which the USSR heads up. Moreover, Poland's present leader should not be blamed for its dependence on the Kremlin but rather Roosevelt and Churchill, who four decades ago lost Poland to Stalin, their opponent in the Yalta games. Unfortunately, it is for that very reason that all we can do now is view Jaruzelski's Poland in an Eastern European context. Yet that angle of vision reveals how sharply Poland differs from other Soviet satellites, which is recognized even by the general's opposition, the Church and Solidarity.

Even more important for Jaruzelski was Pope John

Paul II's recognition of his government. In the course of his second religious pilgrimage to his motherland in the summer of 1983, the Pope showed himself to be not so much a pilgrim as a wise politician, making a choice—a very hard one, in his position—between patriotic rhetoric and patriotic pragmatism, between romantic posturing and responsible behavior. After two secret meetings with the general, the Pontiff gave Jaruzelski his full support. Their mutual understanding was a profoundly moral act, yet it provoked charges of immorality on the part of John Paul II. We are living in a world of inside-out, behind-the-looking-glass concepts, one in which even Lewis Carroll and his Alice would have lost their way.

In that world behind the looking glass, one of America's most insightful journalists, William Safire, has called Jaruzelski "a Russian puppet"; U.S. Secretary of Defense Caspar Weinberger has said he is "a Russian general in a Polish uniform"; and it seems that in the White House, Poland itself has been called "an Auschwitz." To top it all off, President Reagan, in an off-mike remark, called the Polish military government "a bunch of no-good lousy bums" and refused to meet with Jaruzelski when he came to the United States in the fall of 1985. Thus, American political ignorance is, without realizing it, giving Poland a strong push back toward the Moscow camp. E.T.A. Hoffman wrote a story about a wicked and ugly man called Little Zaches who, by a wave of a fairy wand, appeared to everyone to be a noble and handsome fellow. It looks as if fate has played the opposite kind of trick on the present leader of Poland: whatever he does, everyone takes it to be evil and him to be a villain. It is time to take an unbiased look at the man and give him his due.

The sad paradox of Poland should be recalled—its unfortunate proximity to Russia. With its Western orientation, Poland would prefer to be under the political, economic, and military protection of the West, rather than remain dependent on the Russian empire. Dependence on the USSR is economically unreliable, ideologically alien, and politically and historically humiliating. The question is: Is the West ready, if necessary, to provide protection? (A completely neutral and independent status—like that of Austria or, in the worst case, Finland—would be hardly possible for Poland; just as it is impossible for an iron filing placed between two opposite poles of magnetic field to remain "unaligned.") Jaruzelski clearheadedly weighed the potential of both interested parties; the strength of the Soviet will to keep Poland within the empire's sphere of gravity and the strength of the Western will to break Poland loose from it. Both of those forces had already, on several occasions, shown just how strong they were, most clearly at the time of the Hungarian revolution of 1956 and of the Prague Spring in 1968. Both times the Soviet Union showed that its will to keep what it had plundered was stronger than the West's will to take it back from the plunderer and right the historical injustice. So all Poland could do, as before, was to rely on itself; otherwise it would have suffered the fate of its national hero, Prince Jozef Poniatowski.

In 1811, Prince Poniatowski, a pretender to the Polish throne, wrote to Napoleon asking for help against the Russians. Napoleon replied, "I would be glad to help you with all my strength, but you are too far from me, and too close to Russia. Whatever anyone does, it will end up with her conquering you. Not only that, but she will conquer all of Europe."

During the French campaign in Russia, Prince Poniatowski commanded the Polish Corps in Napoleon's Grand Army. On October 19, 1813, during the Battle of the Nations near Leipzig, when the retreating French had burned behind them a bridge over the Elster, Poniatowski and his corps were left in the rear guard on the east bank. Pressed hard by Russian troops, he waited in vain for help from the French. Then, badly wounded, he tried to swim the river, but he drowned. In 1831, the same year the great Russian poet Pushkin wrote his jingoistic dithyramb to the Russian troops who had savagely put down a Polish uprising, the French poet Béranger remembered Prince Poniatowski and honored him with an inspired poem, comparing his fate with the tragic one of his native land, which once again had waited in vain for help from the West.

Poland's national icon is painted in the somber tones of tragedy and martyrdom; the Poles even take pride in the country's martyr's halo, calling themselves "the nation of Christ." But there is an element of hurt, wounded pride, humiliation, and helplessness in that very pride of the Poles. Behind its facade, national complexes are hidden. If it had not been for Wojciech Jaruzelski, Poland would have again suffered the fate of Prince Poniatowski: it would have written yet another heroic page in its history, perhaps the most heroic of all. It is to Jaruzelski's credit that he made it impossible for his country to play its traditional role of heroic sacrifice. Too much Polish blood had already been spilled.

In welcoming the Pope to Belvedere Palace in Warsaw eighteen months after the coup d'état, Jaruzelski very accurately characterized the patriotic mission he had performed. "It is said that Poland suffers. But who put in the scales of the enormity of human suffering, torment and tears which have been successfully avoided? We do not fear the judgment of posterity. It will be just—certainly more balanced than many of the contemporary assessments."

Like Israel, Poland has to defend its right to exist, a problem that most other countries do not have to face. Thus, in making his tragic choice between Poland's independence and its freedom (some of which he later restored to its citizens), and in transforming the country into an armed camp on a full wartime footing in case of aggression from without, Jaruzelski deprived the Kremlin of any choice, for a time putting to an end its Hamletesque doubts and internal debates. In Belvedere Palace, Jaruzelski reminded his compatriot of the words of another Polish national hero, Tadeusz Kosciuszko: "Sometimes we must sacrifice much in order to save all."

The Soviet Union had let slip by the moment when it could have attacked its neighbor with a chance of easy success, because Wojciech Jaruzelski's Poland was better prepared for defense than the anarchic Poland of Lech Walesa had been. To attack Poland after the coup would have meant, for Russia, beginning a war whose duration and outcome were both unknown quantities. Under these circumstances, the only thing the Kremlin could do was play a double game. On the one hand, it put a good face on a bad situation. Thus, in February 1983, Jaruzelski was given a firm handshake by the man he had beat to the punch and outplayed, Yuri Andropov. In May 1984, Konstantin Chernenko pinned the Order of Lenin to his lapel.* And in April 1985, at the Warsaw airport, he was kissed on both cheeks by Mikhail Gorbachev, who is renewing the Brezhnev tradition of embracing foreign leaders when welcoming them and seeing them off.

On the other hand, behind the scenes the USSR is playing a second game: the KGB, under Victor Chebrikov, is continuing secret subversive activities against unruly Poland.

The failed attempt to assassinate the Pope in Rome in 1981 did not discourage the KGB. Rather, it merely led to a geographic shift in terrorist actions: the Russians realized that it was easier and less dangerous to act against the Poles in Poland itself than outside its borders. Moreover, Moscow now figured that its Polish Enemy Number One was neither the leader of Solidarity nor the head of the Vatican but the leader of Poland,

*The awarding of this decoration to Jaruzelski on the occasion of his sixtieth birthday was interpreted in the West as Kremlin approval of his policies, whereas in fact it was a sign that he was out of favor. Jaruzelski and President Nicolae Ceausescu of Romania, who has followed an independent foreign policy, are the only Eastern European leaders who have not been given the highest imperial award: the Gold Medal of a Hero of the Soviet Union.

that maverick in the Warsaw Pact camp. In the West, there were also those who surmised what was what, from Willy Brandt to François Mitterrand. Helmut Schmidt, the former chancellor of West Germany, said that Jaruzelski was "not a man whom Moscow had installed. They didn't like him, they didn't trust him, and deep in his heart he utterly disliked the Russians."

Nonetheless, the KGB did not decide to try to eliminate Jaruzelski. For the time being, that was not within its power. But it was within its power to set up a Polish fifth column, a terrorist organization that, functioning underground and camouflaged by police uniforms, would provoke disorders in Poland. The disorders in turn would lead to the downfall of the Kremlin's *bête noire*, the general, which would bring the pro-Soviet Polish communists back into power and Poland itself back under Soviet tutelage. Such is the present plot against Poland by the KGB, whose agents are vigorously putting it into effect.

In 1983–84, a wave of mysterious murders passed through Poland. Grzegorz Przemik, the nineteen-year-old son of a widely known dissident Polish poet, Barbara Sadowski, died after being beaten in a police station. Andrzej Grzegorz Gasiewski, a former Solidarity activist, was taken into custody by the police after he attended Pope John Paul II's open-air mass in the Warsaw soccer stadium. Several days later, his body was found on a railroad embankment in the suburbs. Jan Samsonovicz, another Solidarity activist, was found hanged from a wall in the Gdansk shipyard, where the free trade unions were born in August 1980. And finally there was Father Jerzy Popieluszko, known throughout the country for his antigovernment sermons. His savage murder in the autumn of 1984 shook all of Poland, and Jaruzelski more than anyone else. It is hard to imagine a more serious act of provocation against the general, except perhaps the murder of Lech Walesa, whom the government—taking such a possibility into account—is carefully guarding by ostensibly tailing him.

Jaruzelski condemned this act of political gangsterism in very strong language, and he took vigorous and effective steps to catch the murderers. Naturally, they turned out to be functionaries of the Ministry of Internal Affairs, headed by an army general, Czeslow Kiszczak, a man loyal to Jaruzelski, but not to Moscow! Most likely, the aim of the provocation was to compromise both patriots at once, to stir up disorders in the country, and to weaken or bring down Jaruzelski's government. That was precisely the way the terrorist act was interpreted even by his opponents, such as Lech Walesa and Jozef Cardinal Glemp. But once again the Kremlin's calculations went awry: in Poland the Kremlin's intentions were surmised at all levels, from the government to the popular, and the Poles were not taken in by the provocation.

Incidentally, these tragic events clearly refute a notion that, although superficial and oversimplified, is commonly held in the United States, namely, that the Jaruzelski government and its opposition, the Church and the former leaders of Solidarity, are still the only main characters in the Polish conflict. Alas, there is still another main character on the political stage in Poland, one whose interests coincide neither with the government's nor with those of the opposition. In any case, at the trial of Father Popieluszko's murderers—which was unprecedented in contemporary Eastern Europe—the most intriguing defendant was the instigator of the murder, a state security colonel named Adam Petrushka. It was he who was sentenced to twenty-five years in prison and not the gangsters who had committed the crime with their own hands. But no one in Poland doubted that the origins of the plot reached up even higher. The least doubtful of all, Jaruzelski, after Father Popieluszko's murder put the Ministry of Internal Affairs under his personal supervision, taking those duties out of the hands of State Security General Mireslaw Milewski, who as a CC secretary and Politburo member had been overseeing that ministry and who was known for his harsh views and his ties with Moscow. A few months later, when Jaruzelski had obtained proof that General Milewski was the liaison between the hired killers and their Kremlin employers, Milewski was expelled from the Politburo, the Secretariat, and the Central Committee. (Interestingly, this took place only two weeks after Mikhail Gorbachev and Wojciech Jaruzelski had embraced at the Warsaw airport.) It became evident that the KGB's terrorist activities against the most freedom-loving and independent of the Eastern European countries had not been halted with the arrest of a few Turks and one Bulgarian in Rome.

Who is next in this fatal line?

6. The Origin of the Kremlin Mafias: Why There Are No Jews, Women, Muscovites, or Military Men in the Politburo

UP TO THE TIME of Wojciech Jaruzelski's military coup, the KGB had its own man in the Polish Politburo: General Mieczyslaw Moczar, the former minister of internal affairs. After the student disorders of 1968, he had managed, under the supervision, and perhaps the direction, of Moscow advisers, to drive the last Jews who had miraculously survived the Nazi holocaust out of Poland. But the fact that, when this had been done, there were virtually no Jews left in Poland did not prevent the dogmatic Kremlin leaders from declaring that it was Zionists and only Zionists who were to blame for the workers' riots of the eighties and for the founding of Solidarity. Actually, of course, Solidarity was strictly a Polish creation in all respects, including that of membership: out of its ten million members, there were at most a few dozen Jews. Nonetheless, Poland was flooded with anti-Semitic pamphlets, articles, leaflets, and graffiti instigated from Moscow, although they were signed by the chauvinistic Polish Grünwald group, which had close ties with Moczar. This anti-Semitism in the absence of Jews—a phenomenon with no parallel in world history—had been predicted by Sartre when he said, "If there weren't any Jews, the anti-Semites would invent them."

Equally astounding, however, was the fact that after General Jaruzelski's "Eighteenth Brumaire," the anti-Semitic attacks by Moscow and the Polish "Muscovites" did not cease but rather were intensified, although the supposedly Zionist Solidarity had been banned and the Jews in Poland could be counted on the fingers of one hand. That tiny group, however—and this was what counted—included not only a few Solidarity advisers but Jaruzelski himself, who was regarded by the Kremlinites as a pure-blooded Jew. (Our only information is that his mother was Jewish.)

Jaruzelski has, in fact, confirmed the Kremlin's worst suspicions on that score by his own behavior. He has tolerated no manifestations of anti-Semitism; his country is the only one among Moscow's satellites to have reestablished diplomatic ties with Israel; Jaruzelski's government has funded the restoration of monuments to Jewish culture in Poland; and on the anniversary of the uprising in the Warsaw ghetto, the Polish Army awarded military honors to those who perished while taking part in it. He has also taken on several Jewish aides and has expelled almost all the anti-Semites from the leadership, including General Moczar, who was not even included in the rather large membership of the ruling Military Council that was formed after the coup. He was expelled from the Politburo, although he did remain the Party's inspector general. One day, acting on orders from the KGB, he appeared at a Politburo session where he took a file out of his attaché case and began to read a document charging General Jaruzelski with corruption.

The allegation was that Jaruzelski had acquired for himself a luxurious villa at 5 Ikar Street, in the southern part of Warsaw. It was worth 1,690,052 zlotys, but he had paid only 373,052 zlotys for it—the price of a small apartment. It was a stupid, totally unfounded charge: Jaruzelski lives in a two-bedroom apartment that is much more modest, for example, than Lech Walesa's. General Moczar was playing for high stakes: he was counting on Moscow's promised help in overthrowing Wojciech Jaruzelski. But Moscow didn't help enough even to defend its own agent. This was Moczar's last power play; after it failed, he disappeared from political life in Poland. And finally in the fall of 1985 Jaruzelski expelled from the Politburo and government the last Muscovite anti-Semite, Stefan Olszowski, former foreign minister.

With respect to anti-Semitism, a burning issue in the Kremlin, the very laws and analogies it brings into play in its theater of the absurd are interesting. If the Prague Spring was a provocation by the Zionists—and the Soviet leadership has no doubt at all about that—it follows that the Zionists are to blame for any other ferment in Eastern Europe. By the eighties, "Zionism" had become for Moscow a universal scapegoat. A survey of the Soviet press over the past few years yields some really staggering finds. Among those labeled "Zionists" are Zbigniew Brzezinski, Jimmy Carter, Ronald Reagan, Caspar Weinberger, Anwar Sadat, Leon Trotsky, and many others, up to and including Adolf Hitler, whom the Zionists "brought to power" and so "facilitated the maximum annihilation of their fellow-Jews in order, afterward, to exploit their victimization to their own benefit."

Nonsense? If so, it is by no means an isolated instance. *Izvestia* and *New Times* magazine will tell you that the Zionists bear direct responsibility for the assassinations of Indira Gandhi and Gamal Nasser, even though the prime minister of India was cut down by Sikh terrorists and the Egyptian president died a natural death. *Pravda* "revealed" to its readers that Israeli soldiers disemboweled a pregnant Arab woman—an "incident" earlier reported by the trade-union paper *Trud (Labor),* which cited the Israeli paper *Ha'aretz* as its source, although *Ha'aretz* had never printed anything of the kind. In the year 1984 alone, the periodical press of Moscow, Leningrad, and the republics printed 2,824 anti-Zionist articles, or an average of eight per day. Over that same period, the number of articles on Afghanistan, the countries of the Far East, and those of Eastern Europe averaged one per day; and those about the Iraqi-Iranian war, to one every two or three days. Given such a massive propaganda attack on its own people, it is quite possible that the Kremlin was above all trying to convince itself and came to believe in its own propaganda.

Unlike Nazi Germany, whose campaign against the Jews was fought openly, without the use of trickery or verbal camouflage, the Soviet Union has never officially acknowledged that its anti-Semitism is just that. Rather, in accord with the rules of "Newspeak" laid down by Orwell in *1984*, Soviet anti-Semitism has been disguised by euphemisms. Today it is called "the struggle against Zionism"; in the first few years after World War II it was "the struggle against the cosmopolites"; and before the war it was called "the struggle against the Trotskyites,"* as if to confirm the well-known prediction that the Bronsteins (Trotsky's actual last name) would have to pay the bill for Trotsky. "The question of my Jewishness did not take on importance until the beginning of my political harassment," Trotsky himself wrote. "Anti-Semitism raised its head at the same time as anti-Trotskyism."

Stalin, though, had become an anti-Semite long before, most likely as a reaction to the disproportionate part taken by Jews in Russian political life (by no means

*Another synonymous phrase very common in Soviet propaganda is "the struggle against the Masons," who in the USSR are considered identical to the Jews.

merely among the Bolsheviks but across the whole prerevolutionary spectrum, except for such extreme rightwing organizations as the pogromist "Black Hundred").

Still and all, neither the twenties nor the thirties can be called periods of State anti-Semitism: there were many Jews among Stalin's victims, but there were also many Jews among the butchers. The Party holocaust that he set up and carried out was international. Not until after the war did anti-Semitism become the basic orientation of Stalin's domestic policy. The campaigns he then launched—the one against the "rootless cosmopolites," the "struggle against the Zionists," and, toward the very end of the Stalin era, the so-called Doctors' Plot (in which Jewish physicians were arrested on medieval-type charges of having murdered, or having tried to murder, Kremlin leaders on instructions of an international Zionist center)—would ultimately have led to a "final solution" of the Jewish problem in Russia if Stalin had not died during the preparations for it.

Earlier, however, Stalin had been dealt some unexpected blows from a most unlikely direction. First Yakov, his son by his first wife, married a Jewess. (When Yakov was taken prisoner by the Germans, Stalin ordered her arrest.) But Yakov was never an object of paternal affection as was Svetlana, Stalin's beloved daughter. It was a real shock for her father when agents brought him secret reports of her affair with journalist Alexci Kapler. Kapler was arrested, and Stalin, giving Svetlana a slap, shouted at her, "Couldn't you have found yourself a Russian?" Shortly afterward, Svetlana married another Jew. Stalin had the man's father imprisoned. Of the husband himself, Stalin said to Svetlana, "The Zionists planted him with you as a spy."

Stalin left a heritage of anti-Semitism to succeeding generations of Kremlin leaders, and it cannot be said that they declined it. To the contrary, they have put it to shameless and large-scale use, in both theory and practice—especially in recent years—up to and including attempts in the Soviet press to justify prerevolutionary pogroms. (Now that those pogroms have been vindicated, can their revival be far behind?)

However, we are interested here not so much in the scope of official anti-Semitism in the USSR as in the odd forms it assumes in the Kremlin.

For example: What are Jews called there? Jews? Kikes? Zionists? No, in Kremlin "table talk" neither their real names, nor offensive epithets, nor euphemistic pseudonyms are used. As we were told by a person who frequents the Kremlin and its branches—who was formerly "our man in Tripoli" and now teaches at the KGB's international school for intelligence agents near Moscow—in the CC, the KGB, and the ministry of foreign affairs, Jews are called, aloofly and diffidently, "they," thereby stressing "their" alien nature and the distance between "them" and "us." Here are a few bits of dialogue that our acquaintance heard there, which we wrote down just as he told them to us. (He himself talked about them as something amusing in an absurdist vein.)

"Once again 'they're' cooking up something in the White House behind the president's back."

"If it weren't for 'them,' we'd have no trouble reaching agreement with America. But 'they're' interfering. It's part of 'their' overall plot."

"The situation in the U.S. today is like the one we had here after the Revolution, when 'they' grabbed all the key posts in the country. Whatever office you stick your nose into, all you see is 'them,'—only 'them,' and nobody else. And the fact that today there aren't any of 'them' in top posts here is a reaction to 'their' domination in the twenties. It's a healthy anti-Semitism, so to speak, coming from the instinct of self-preservation."

Of course, none of the Soviet top leaders since Stalin has manifested his pathological hatred of Jews. Under Khrushchev, the level of official anti-Semitism dropped sharply. He himself, to be sure, was not altogether unblemished by prejudice, but he did not give rein to it.

As for Brezhnev, he was ashamed of Victoria Petrovna* Brezhneva's relatives: he snubbed and avoided his Jewish in-laws and even barred them from the Brezhnevs' apartment on Kutuzov Prospekt. But this could hardly be ascribed to anti-Semitism on his part: it was owing, rather, to a fear of his rivals in the Politburo. And as a matter of fact, later on, when the Kremlin power struggle was in its decisive phase, Andropov's agents widely circulated information about Victoria Brezhneva's Jewish parentage, saying that Jewish emigration had been permitted in the period of détente because of her influence over her husband. In underground leaflets, Brezhnev was called "Zionist Number One" and his Politburo "a den of Jews." For Andropov, any weapon would serve in a power struggle, including anti-Semitism. (He himself, however, was too cynical to be a mad-dog anti-Semite.)

As for Mikhail Gorbachev, he cut his political teeth by taking an active part in the anti-Semitic campaigns at Moscow University in the last years of Stalin's life; we shall have occasion to shed light on this stage of his career in greater detail later. At the moment, it would be premature to examine just how deeply the lessons in Stalinist anti-Semitism that he got at the time took root in him or how they are affecting him now that he is the top Party leader. One thing worth mentioning, however, is that Gorbachev, on a certain fairly recent occasion, was heard to say, apropos of "them," the familiar saying: "What is bred in the bone, comes out in the flesh." (Literally: "No matter how well you feed a wolf, he keeps looking back toward the woods.") He reportedly said that in 1981 after Georgi Arbatov, the Kremlin "Americanologist," was elected to the CC. Arbatov's Jewishness is an open secret. Up until 1969, in his internal passport he was identified by "nationality" (race) as "Jewish." But he somehow managed to exchange it for a new one in which he is identified as "Russian."

*Her father's name was not really Petr but Pinkus, a Jewish name Russianized into Petr.

Whom is Arbatov or those who gave him the revised passport trying to deceive? Or was this done (as so much else has been done) because of the Kremlin's apprehensions vis-à-vis the Party masses? After all, every time the CC holds a congress, a list of its members is published giving each one's age, "nationality," and other information of that kind. Yet even though Arbatov has shuffled off his Jewish "skin," many people are of the opinion that his "discarded" origins will obstruct his further advancement. In the view of Gorbachev and his colleagues, Arbatov is a wolf still looking back toward the woods, although he has long been as loyal as a dog to his Kremlin masters.

It is especially in his approach to the Jewish question that Gorbachev, who was born thirteen years after the Bolshevik Revolution, and whose mother—and only—tongue is Soviet Newspeak, has achieved in that language a virtuosity that none of his predecessors attained. Replying to questions from French journalists, he described (without so much as a blink of the eye) the "Jewish paradise" in the USSR:

> I would be glad to hear of Jews enjoying anywhere such political and other rights as they have in our country. The Jewish population, who account for 0.69 percent of the entire population of our country, are represented in its political and cultural life on a scale of at least ten to twenty percent. Most of them are the well-known leaders of our country.

Gorbachev's accurate knowledge of the figure "0.69 percent," down to two decimal points, stands out sharply against the background of that tapestry of cynical lies. It was not by chance that the new Soviet leader mentioned that statistic. It often figures in Kremlin discussions as an argument against the disproportionate number of Jews in Soviet science and culture (but by no means in Soviet politics). In order to convey some notion as to just what measures the Kremlin is taking to achieve greater "harmony" in this respect, it suffices to mention the fact that in the last fifteen years, the number of Jewish students enrolled at institutions of higher learning in the USSR has been halved.

As in earlier days, the level of anti-Semitism is a kind of barometric reading, at once an indicator and the result of the general political climate of the country. Any sudden rise in the reading has usually coincided with a very reactionary period of crisis in Russian history. But this is true not just for Russian history; Georgi Fedotov, the well-known philosopher, wrote, "Whenever a nation wants to break violently all the ties binding it to the rest of humankind, it begins by finding some Jews and wreaking vengeance on them."

It would be premature to say that about the Russian people, the nation as a whole, but it is not too early to say it about that "nation" that rules the empire from the Kremlin. It is breaking its ties with the rest of humankind with unbridled passion, taking an ever-more-suspicious attitude toward Jews. So there is no reason to wonder why there are no Jews in the Kremlin: in the Politburo, in the CC Secretariat, or in the KGB apparatus.

There are no women in the Kremlin either; the "weaker sex" is no less discriminated against than are members of the "untrustworthy" ethnic group. During May Day parades, when the mass of participants, flaunting flags and banners, march through Red Square "with a joyous, springing step" (as the Soviet newspaper reporters are fond of putting it), the people are favored with benevolent waves of the hand by the Politburo members—the military and civilian representatives of the regime—standing on the rostrum atop Lenin's Mausoleum. It is a strictly male conclave: not a single woman is included. Four times a year, when Soviet citizens open *Pravda* and eagerly scan the entire centerfold showing photographs of the members of the USSR Council of Ministers, they usually don't find a single female face among the 117 shown there. There is not one woman among the ten national secretaries of the Party CC or among the 181 Party bosses of the Soviet republics and big provinces. The special Kremlin Cemetery in Red Square, where former members of the Soviet government lie buried (as well as the American communist John Reed) is an almost exclusively male necropolis. With rare exceptions, no urn containing the ashes of a Soviet woman prominent in the affairs of state was ever placed, to the strains of a funeral march and the booming of an artillery salute, in the columbarium in the Kremlin Wall. An exception was Lenin's wife, Nadezhda Krupskaya.

In short, Soviet women, who are officially the most emancipated in the whole world, in no way take part in the nation's political leadership. They are represented only in the Soviet parliament, which in fact serves as a facade and passes no important laws. This sex discrimination on the part of the regime is not so much unjust as bizarre if we bear in mind that in the USSR women account for more than half the labor force and constitute fifty-five percent of the population and sixty-three percent of the inhabitants having a higher education. Not only that, but despite the marked increase during the past decade in the number of women who are Party members (today one-third of the members are women), their number in the CC has markedly dropped. Soviet propagandists often point with pride to the fact that the Soviet Union was the first country to proclaim full equality between males and females. But up to now, male predominance in the management of the country has been tacit but unmistakable. As Khrushchev once remarked in disgruntlement, "It turns out that it is the men who do the administering, and the women who do the work."

Khrushchev decided to break the male monopoly in the Kremlin and bring a woman into the Politburo. The woman in question, Ekaterina Furtseva, was a loyal supporter of Khrushchev, and her Party background

was irreproachable from the Soviet point of view. She
had been a loom operator, then had served as a Party
worker and State official, with gradual advancement
from the provinces to Moscow. Her constant glumness
and air of dissatisfaction fitted right in with the habitual
facial expressions of the other Politburo members, yet
she encountered evident hostility, both from her Politburo colleagues and from the other members of the CC
Secretariat (who plainly found it hard to bear the presence of a woman in their male milieu). Furtseva did not
take part in all the Politburo sessions, and she never had
any real power or noticeable political influence.

Her gradual loss of favor in the Kremlin was accompanied by a quasi-official wave of criticism for
her incompetence on the job, female capriciousness,
"moodiness," money-grubbing instincts, and proclivity
for luxurious living. At least half those charges could
have been brought, with at least as much justification,
against the other members of the Politburo. It was
simply that the strictly male top leadership was ridding
its ranks of a foreign element, a woman. And that in-
bred aggressiveness, which ultimately brought about
Furtseva's removal from the Politburo, for no apparent
reason, in her fourth year there, was solidly supported
by the populace, with its deeply ingrained male chauvinism.

The thrust of many well-known derisive sayings is
that a woman should be taken off any job that involves
heavy responsibilities and demands a practical approach: "A job is one thing, and a woman's another."
"A hen isn't a bird, and a woman's not a real person."
"I thought I saw two people coming this way, but it was
only a man and a woman." Such being the common
man's view of these things, Furtseva was the butt of a
good many salacious stories and out-and-out dirty jokes
(more than her share, as compared with the other Politburo members). They didn't die down when, after being
removed from the Politburo and the Secretariat, she became minister of culture. Indeed, they continued right

up until her suicide in 1974, after a severe reprimand (by no means the first) from Brezhnev.

Although in becoming minister of culture, Furtseva suffered a marked loss of status within the Party hierarchy—so much that some foreign observers figured she "had almost vanished from the scene for good"—she once again had entered a "for men only" zone. In the Soviet Union, there is a tacit understanding (a "gentlemen's agreement") that no woman should hold ministerial rank. During her term of service in the Ministry of Culture there was a constant flow of scandalous stories, slanders, and "spicy" jokes making good use of a theme that was an old favorite, her sexual forwardness, even when Furtseva was already more than sixty years old.

And so Khrushchev's experiment ended, like most of his bold innovations, as a total fiasco. Since then, not a single female hand has waved from the rostrum on Lenin's Mausoleum to the exultant crowd below on national holidays.

During the Khrushchev era, Valentina Tereshkova, Cosmonaut Number Six, became the first woman to travel in space. These days it is easier to put a woman into space than into the Politburo. To do the latter would violate the traditions and customs of an elite men's club in the USSR, a place where (at any rate, up until the time of Chernenko) members could freely use strong swear words and pound their fists on the table; where during long sessions they drank not mineral water but vodka and the marvelous cognac distilled in Armenia, and smoke so much that the air is veritable London fog; where it was quite all right to belch or fart and trade lip-smacking jokes—not political ones but dirty stories in the vein of locker-room humor; where it was the jocular custom for one member to ask another how bad his "piles" are—hemorrhoids being the classic affliction of statesmen; where in Brezhnev's day it was a common practice to arm wrestle with the general secretary. Naturally, no member would ever have dared to vanquish Brezhnev, who could count, among his victories, one over President Nixon in Air Force One as they were flying from Washington to California during the 1973 summit. When Gorbachev was brought into that august body, Brezhnev desired to match his own strength against that of "the youngest cadre." Gorbachev, in his accommodating way, did not use his full strength, which, according to the recollections of people from Stavropol, is considerable. Hence it is still not known whether Brezhnev actually was the strongest man in the Politburo, or whether everyone simply yielded to him.

A female colleague would have been out of place at such Politburo sessions.

United by the power they share, Politburo members are disposed to strengthen their close male bonds not only on the job but during their leisure time. Some eighty-five miles northeast of Moscow, there is an extensive (130 square miles) hunting preserve, Zavidovo, the Politburo's private property. It is staffed by foresters in green uniforms, huntsmen, whippers-in, and an entire army of guards, and it is provided with a pack of hounds and all kinds of hunting gear. Along the edge of that beautiful wildwood are comfortable hunting lodges. There is an ornate two-story villa of the Swiss-chalet type belonging to the general secretary, with an Olympic-size swimming pool, a gymnasium, and a private movie theater. Riding in their official custom-made ZIL limousines at speeds well beyond those permitted to mere mortals (ninety miles an hour or more), the Politburo members come to the Zavidovo Preserve eager to gratify their passion for hunting far away from their wives and families or any other hindrance. For some inexplicable reason, most of the top Soviet elite, from Lenin, Trotsky, Bukharin, Voroshilov, and Beria to Khrushchev, Gromyko, Brezhnev, Chernenko, and Gorbachev, have been possessed by that passion. Andropov was the only exception, no doubt because he was near-sighted and in general physically unfit for sports.

In Brezhnev's day, even Politburo sessions were sometimes shifted to Zavidovo, where after work the members could hunt wild game in the regal manner. Mounted whippers-in and their borzois and beaters drove the quarry from cover directly "under the guns" of the Politburo members who, dressed in their green hunters' outfits, had grown more and more excited as the sounds of the "chase" came closer and closer. In the evening, they all gathered in the reception room on the ground floor of the general secretary's villa, with its many low easy chairs, huge carpet, and low table laid out with choice appetizers and silver goblets of vodka, all made cozy by the crackling of logs burning in the huge fireplace, where it was so pleasant after a stressful day to trade stories about past and present hunting feats. Then, before retiring for the night, they would watch a cowboy movie in Brezhnev's private movie theater.

The high-ranking members of the government did not hunt only in Zavidovo. Their ardor for hunting drove them from one place to another through the abundant wilderness preserves of the Soviet Union. They shot a great variety of wild fowl and game animals: wood grouse, dabchicks, hares, foxes, moose, wild boars, bears, and especially wild ducks. Duck hunting was the favorite pastime of both Lenin and Gorbachev, who avidly pursued it on the Manych Lakes in his native Stavropol Territory. Sometimes they arranged special competitions to see who could kill the most game. The dwellers on the Kremlin Olympus were not always satisfied with the regular game preserves or forests, mountains, and lakes that they usually frequented; they sometimes set up their own "proving grounds" for hunting. Dmitri Polyansky, a member of both Khrushchev's and Brezhnev's Politburos, enclosed a huge tract of state-owned woodland southeast of Moscow, making it his own private tract. He stocked it with foxes, deer, and bears.

In view of the all-consuming passion for hunting of

most members of the Soviet government, one can't help
wondering what role the bloodthirsty, brutal pursuit of
hunting plays in the nation's foreign and domestic
policies. In any case, there can be no question that it
serves as an outlet for the kind of political extremism,
ambition, revanchism, and crude masculine strength
that it would be dangerous for them to vent openly, as
in bourgeois parliamentary life, because of their close
working bonds and the vigilant watch each keeps on the
others.

And of course in that wilderness of dense forests,
flood plains, and marshlands, with the barking of the
hounds, the grunting and wheezing of the quarry
brought to bay, and the roar of gunfire, when the
hunters' thirst for blood is at fever pitch, the presence
of a female colleague among the Kremlin Party and
military leaders—like some kind of Party Amazon—is
something quite unimaginable.

But not only ethnic and sexist discrimination blocks
the way of those aspiring to get into the Kremlin, the
Politburo, and the CC Secretariat—into the sanctum
sanctorum of the Soviet regime. There is also a more
specific and devious kind of discrimination: that against
Muscovites. The Politburo does not include a single person who was born in the capital or who began his
political career there. This applies to all the top leaders
of the Soviet Union: Lenin was from the Volga region,
Stalin from Georgia, Khrushchev and Brezhnev from
the Ukraine, Chernenko from Siberia, and Andropov
from the provincial southern part of Russia, as is Gorbachev. Although it is located in the very center of
Moscow, the Kremlin is by Moscow standards insuf-
ferably provincial. The elite of the Soviet government
consists chiefly of people who grew up, got their education, and made their Party careers "far, far away from
Moscow," as is said in a well-known song. According to
a count taken by Jerry Hough of the Brookings Institution, as of 1980, out of sixteen top officials in the
ministries and the Central Committee apparatus born

after 1925, only one was born in Moscow; one was born in another of the ten largest cities, two in one of the hundred largest cities, four in small towns, and eight in villages.

Muscovites are barred from the Politburo because the Kremlin leaders fear that people who have strong and longtime connections in the capital would have an adequate power base there for plots and coups. Preference is given to provincial nouveaux riches who have not had time to build a broad network of influential Moscow acquaintances in the various sectors of the central power, from the Party sector to the military and KGB milieux, and depend completely upon the *vozhd* (chief) as godfather. The latter—be he Stalin, Khrushchev, Brezhnev, Andropov, or Gorbachev—begins as soon as he becomes general secretary to insure himself against any possible plot or palace coup, such as the one by which he himself has just come to power. He builds around himself a solid defense perimeter, consisting of "his people," that is, his own protégés, whom he trusts and who have a vassal's dependence on him.

Thus, Kremlin mafias are created: a Caucasian one under Stalin, a Ukrainian one under Khrushchev, and, even more specifically local, a Dnepropetrovsk one under Brezhnev. Khrushchev began to build his personal political base in 1957, immediately after his attempted overthrow by a majority in the CC Presidium (as the Politburo was then called). In the chief centers of power throughout the country, which oversee the Party apparatus, the KGB, and the armed forces, he placed "his own Ukrainians," people who had begun their careers in the Ukraine under him when he was first secretary there. Those persons, his closest associates whom he trusted and who were personally obligated to him for their rise in the Soviet hierarchy, constituted the foundations of his might. In Moscow, the predominance of the Ukrainian element among the high Party apparatchiks was called "the Ukrainian occupation."

Khrushchev had spent almost as much time in high

Party positions in the Ukraine as in the most important Party posts in Moscow (including that of the city's Party boss), where he had also put together his own group of trusty lieutenants. But he preferred to fill the key positions in the State and Party apparatus with Ukrainians, people without connections or patrons or sponsors in the capital except himself.

In the case of Brezhnev, however, his preference for "locals" in consolidating his power led to a unique geographic narrowing of the selection of cadres, to a "Dnepropetrovsk anomaly" in the Kremlin. Remembering his own betrayal of Khrushchev, Brezhnev decided, in putting his own group in place on the main avenues to power, to recruit his people on the basis of maximum loyalty, personal devotion to himself, and reliability. Unlike the people who got on the Khrushchev bandwagon, all of whom had been his closest associates in Party work, the Brezhnev team consisted for the most part of friends from his childhood, adolescence, and early manhood, his school and college (institute) classmates, and his close and more distant relatives, the majority of whom he had become acquainted with, and in some cases had grown close to, in Dnepropetrovsk.

Brezhnev was so enamored of the idea of drawing Party cadres from Dnepropetrovsk, which he considered the only real smithy for the forging of political skills, that even the young, postwar generation of apparatchiks from that city gradually migrated to Moscow, where they got appointments to ministerial posts, to the CC to beef up the contingent of Dnepropetrovians already there, or as Party bosses of the Soviet provinces. There was even a real danger that the number of Party and State cadres in Dnepropetrovsk itself would be totally depleted. Under Brezhnev, high-ranking apparatchiks were given virtually lifelong tenure; and at Party congresses there were almost no personnel shifts on the Kremlin Olympus, except for two cases of emergency when Dnepropetrovians, both aged men, were put in top slots, Chernenko in 1978 and Tikhonov in 1979.

Thus the entire post-Brezhnev generation of Party apparatchiks and government officials from other cities of
the Soviet Union, including all the ill-starred Muscovites, was stricken from political life.

After strengthening his power base with the help of
his far-flung Dnepropetrovsk network and plugging up
all the holes and tunnels through which his "one-man
management" of the country could have been under-
mined, Brezhnev could "reign lying on his side" in the
full sense of the phrase, enjoying everything that, as
Macbeth said, "should accompany old age, as honor,
love, obedience, troops of friends." He could, that is,
until his own captain of the palace guard, KGB chief
Andropov, began very successfully to weaken that massive but poorly designed system of fortifications around
Brezhnev's throne, wielding a weapon that has been
used at all times and in all places for eliminating one's
political opponents: the charge of corruption—something to which the entire Dnepropetrovsk mafia (along
with its *capo di tutti capi,* Brezhnev) was vulnerable.

When Andropov became the top leader and began to
consolidate his own power, he used a procedure different from Brezhnev's. He had only one landsman,
Gorbachev, in the Politburo, and he used, for the most
part, professional criteria in putting his own mafia
together, choosing KGB men or Party and military men
with close ties to the KGB. Although he had worked in
Moscow in various important posts for about twenty-
five years, he also did not make a single Muscovite
either a full or even a candidate member of the Politburo or of the Secretariat. His Kremlin entourage contrasted sharply with Brezhnev's; it included one man
from Kiev (Fedorchuk), one from Baku (Aliyev), one
from Siberia (Ligachev), one from the Urals (Ryzhkov),
one from Leningrad (Romanov), and one from Stavropol (Gorbachev). All were untainted by Moscow corruption, had not yet put down roots in the capital, and did
not have connections there: they were political loners
fully dependent upon their protector, a good guarantee

that they would not plot against him. A skillful intriguer and plotter himself, the moribund Andropov saw to it that what he himself had done to Brezhnev would not happen to him.

As for Gorbachev, even before he became the leader of the Soviet Union, he had prudently begun to seek out for his own apparatus people he had known back in Stavropol and had quietly built the nucleus of a future Stavropol mafia. It was not the easiest thing in the world to do, since provincial Stavropol, with its basically agricultural orientation, was a meager source of cadres as compared with Brezhnev's source, the industrial city Dnepropetrovsk. Yet as a national CC secretary and hence overseer of the Party apparatus and cadres as a whole, Gorbachev had the best of opportunities to get the right jobs for his people. In a short time, some of his Stavropolians showed up in the CC apparatus: Nikolai Kruchina, Benjamin Afonin, Alexander Budyka, and Alexander Vedernikov. And when Gorbachev, having become general secretary, had to pack the Politburo in short order—its ranks had been thinned out by the deaths of gerontocrats—he did not violate the time-honored ban against Muscovites. Among the four new appointees to the Politburo and the three new national CC secretaries, there was not a single man from the capital by the end of 1985. Moreover, after the removal of Victor Grishin from the Politburo for his opposition to Gorbachev's appointment as general secretary, Boris Yeltsin from the Urals, who had been in the capital only a few months, was named the new Moscow party boss.

Although the absence of Jews in the Politburo is "in the nature of things," that of women understandable, and that of Muscovites explainable, the fact that there are no professional military men in the governing body of a superpower armed to the teeth and living under the laws of a military camp in wartime must strike the outside observer as puzzling and hard to believe. (For that matter, only 5 percent of the 470 full and candidate members of the CC are military men!) It must be especially puzzling in view of all the talk about the growing role of the military in the Soviet leadership that is spread about in the West and enlivened in times of international crisis or when there is a change of guard in the Kremlin. When the Red Army invaded Afghanistan in 1979; when a Soviet missile knocked down a Korean airliner in 1983; and eighteen months later (with Gorbachev already in power), when an American officer, Arthur Nicholson, was shot and killed by a Soviet sentry in East Germany—each of these deeds was promptly interpreted in a way that saved face for the Kremlin, namely, as the actions of trigger-happy military men acting contrary to the Kremlin's will, and as showing that the armed forces were squeezing out the Party leadership. Even Andropov's takeover of the Kremlin was ascribed to his longtime alliance with Minister of Defense Ustinov; the KGB coup was camouflaged as something more understandable, a military coup d'état.

Regardless of who circulated those rumors or what their authors' purpose was, their model is more Western than Russian. And it is Western in a broader, political sense, not in a narrowly geographic one. It can be found not only in such historical cases as General Bonaparte's Eighteenth Brumaire but also in present-day eighteenth Brumaires in Greece, Chile, Pakistan, Argentina, Turkey, Poland, or the Sudan, where the army has political power. In the Soviet Union, power has been taken from the army by the secret police, whose agents permeate the armed forces from top to bottom. It is not surprising that in all the sixty-eight years of Soviet history, there has not been a single attempt at a military coup d'état: not by Marshal Zhukov (although he was cashiered by Khrushchev for "Bonapartism"); not by Marshal Tukhachevsky (although he was executed as a plotter during the Great Terror, the charge was a false one); not even by Leon Trotsky, the builder and favorite of the Red Army, when Stalin began to squeeze him out of the Soviet leadership immediately after Lenin's death. On the other hand, a secret-police coup *has* been carried out in Russia—by Andropov. Andropov's was not the first such coup attempted; it was the first one that succeeded.

Throughout Soviet history, the Kremlin has kept its marshals and generals at a respectful distance from the centers of power. Every attempt by the military to shrink that distance has been nipped in the bud and punished with all the harshness of the repressive practices current in the USSR at the time: by execution in Stalin's day, and by disgrace under his successors—even if the attempt was a figment of the Kremlin leaders' imagination.

For instance, Mikhail Frunze was for only ten months, from January to November 1925, at one and the same time chairman of the Revolutionary Military Council and people's commissar for military and naval affairs. His appointment to those two top posts of the military establishment was a result of the power struggle between Stalin and Trotsky; Frunze had replaced Trotsky as leader of the Red Army. An able military commander, Frunze carried out a housecleaning in the armed forces, abolishing the institution of Party overseers or political commissars (Stalin restored that institution in the summer of 1937), dissolving the guerrilla (partisan) bands of the Civil War period, and rebuilding the armed forces chiefly on the basis of former tsarist officers and new draftees. In creating a professional army, he took it out from under the Kremlin's control. This gave Stalin a very bad fright, but since those were not yet days of overt political terror, he had to resort to the covert variety.

In October 1925, after Frunze had fully recovered from an acute stomach ulcer, Stalin suddenly showed great solicitude for his health and insisted that he have an operation. He entrusted the conduct of it to Grigori Kanner, his aide for "wet jobs," and Pogosyanets, a Kremlin doctor. The perfectly healthy Frunze died right on the operating table; his wife, convinced that he had been murdered there, committed suicide. Following the fresh tracks of the murder, writer Boris Pilnyak wrote a novella called *The Tale of the Unextinguished Moon,* which through an oversight was published the next year in the magazine *Novy Mir.* Although neither Stalin nor Frunze was mentioned by name in the novella, the magazine was subjected to blistering criticism for printing it. In 1937, the author was arrested and executed. Also executed that year was the person who had reliably reported the subject matter to Pilnyak, Marshal Tukhachevsky, whose fate was shared by seven other Soviet commanders.

All but a few of the remaining Soviet commanders were executed a year later. In that gigantic meat grinder, thirty thousand officers of the Red Army were annihilated. They included all fifteen of the army commanders, sixty out of sixty-seven divisional commanders, three out of five of the first Soviet marshals, fourteen out of sixteen generals of the army, and all ten full admirals of the Soviet fleet. Thus, on the eve of World War II, the Red Army was beheaded, which was one reason for its lightninglike and tragic defeats by the Germans during the first months of the war. Stalin's fear of his own military leaders had been greater than his fear of Hitler.

The fate of the commanders who remained alive was also unenviable. General Konstantin Rokossovsky, a divisional commander who during the war became a marshal and hero and afterward minister of defense (actually military governor) of Poland, went, in 1938, through all the hell of Soviet prisons. His torturers knocked out nine of his teeth, broke three of his ribs, and smashed his toes with hammers. He was sentenced to death, put in a cell on death row, and twice led out to be shot by a firing squad. One night, along with others sentenced to death, he was taken into the woods and made to stand at the edge of a large, freshly dug grave. A squad of soldiers fired at them when the command was given, and the generals standing to the left and right of Rokossovsky fell into the grave. A blank had been fired at Rokossovsky.

Marshal Zhukov, the "Soviet Eisenhower," fell into disgrace twice. The first time was in the Stalin era, right after the victory over Germany, in which he played a leading role. The second was in the Khrushchev period, in October 1957, six months after Zhukov, with a sudden use of force, had prevented Khrushchev's overthrow, when it already looked inevitable: a majority of the Politburo, headed up by the Stalinist Molotov, had come out against the anti-Stalinist Khrushchev. That was one of the rare cases when the army played a political role in Kremlin life, and it was the last such case. After having made use of Marshal Zhukov at that very critical moment in his own career, Khrushchev made haste to get rid of him; for in strengthening his own political influence, Khrushchev's confederate had become a dangerous rival.

After removing Zhukov from his post as minister of defense and expelling him from the Politburo, the prudent Khrushchev did not bring into that body the next minister of defense, Marshal Malinovsky—nor did Brezhnev, although Malinovsky held his ministerial post for a whole ten years (1957 to 1967). Marshal Grechko was minister of defense for almost as long a time, but he didn't become a Politburo member until he was seventy, a few years before his death, when it was already known in the Kremlin that he was terminally ill. After his death in 1976, the Kremlin took an altogether unusual step and named a civilian minister of defense: Dmitri Ustinov. So that he might be invested with military authority, Ustinov was promptly awarded the title of marshal, although this was patently honorary and formalistic and in no way altered the fact that the new defense minister was quintessentially a civilian.

That same year, Brezhnev also became a marshal, and a year later he was proclaimed supreme commander in chief. At a conference on military theory held in the autumn of 1977, in order to explain that concentration of Party, civil, and military power in the hands of one political administration, adduced, on the one hand, the "creative development of the Leninist principle of the unity of political and military leadership'' and on the other the experience of the World War II period, when Stalin was at once the nation's military, Party, and government leader. There was a basic difference, however, because on this occasion a civilian was being named military leader of the country in peacetime.

The same thing happened with the next three Kremlin leaders, Andropov, Chernenko, and Gorbachev, each of whom was proclaimed supreme commander in chief automatically, right after being appointed to the top Party post. Yet the very practice of naming civilian leaders to the nation's top military position was so strange that each time it had to be justified anew, Leninist principles were cited less and less, and Stalin's experience more and more. But the absence of military men in the Politburo and the presence of civilians in the top military positions of defense minister and supreme commander in chief can really be explained by only one thing. The Kremlin partocrats traditionally fear the military, and the chiefs of the secret police perceive the military as a dangerous rival.

After the cashiering of Marshal Zhukov, the Kremlin prudently removed all army contingents from Moscow. The only forces now stationed in the capital are those of the KGB and the regular police. That is one more reason why the army cannot play a big role in a Kremlin power struggle: any challenge from it would mean war against both types of police forces, and it is hardly likely that any high military command would ever make such a decision. The army has reconciled itself to the pecking order established by the Kremlin, in which it has a subordinate status.

Yet this does not rule out any and all attempts to violate the status quo on the part of ambitious individual military men if they are supported by someone in the Kremlin, and if that support is facilitated by the political situation that has developed there.

Such a favorable situation arose during the period of the decentralization and fragmentation of power under

Chernenko, when the aged and ailing Ustinov's functions as minister of defense were actually being performed by the ambitious and resolute Marshal Nikolai
Ogarkov, chief of the general staff. The functions of the
politically impotent Chernenko were then being shared
(as the reader will remember) by Mikhail Gorbachev
and Grigori Romanov, the two CC secretaries in the
Politburo.

After their duel at Andropov's coffin, a kind of calm
settled over the Kremlin power struggle during a few
months in the spring and summer months of 1984. Gorbachev, with his aversion to friction and conflict, went
so far as to try to arrange a kind of ceasefire with
Romanov; this modus vivendi even took open forms of
expression. Gorbachev emphasized it by chatting with
Romanov at various public ceremonies, by seeing him
off at Sheremetyevo Airport when he left for a trip
abroad (one in April to Finland and one in May to
Czechoslovakia), by meeting him at the same airport
when he returned, and in general by trying for a personal détente between them, although one can be sure
Gorbachev had no intention of retreating.

The power struggle entered its decisive phase in the
autumn of 1984. While the eyes of the world were glued
to the Kremlin stage, where after a two-month absence
the terminally ill Chernenko, assisted by doctors and
aides, was making his last ceremonial appearances, the
real action of the Kremlin show was, as usual, taking
place offstage. But what was unusual this time was that
a very rare opportunity opened up—one that, sad to
say, no one took advantage of—to peek into the Soviet
empire's holy of holies, not on the sly and not by way of
secret sources, rumors, guesswork, conjectures, and
hypotheses, but through the prism of the official press.
Judging from it, here is how the autumnal act of the
Kremlin drama unfolded.

In early September, when Konstantin Chernenko had
once again come back from a close brush with death,
Grigori Romanov went off to Ethiopia. His purpose,

however, was not at all to help save its people from starvation. Officially, it was to attend a congress of the newly founded Communist Party of Ethiopia in Addis Ababa. But unofficially it was to strengthen, with weapons and advisers, the pro-Soviet regime there. This time Gorbachev neither saw Romanov off on his trip nor met him on his return, just as, later, Romanov did not see Gorbachev off on his trip to Hungary or the one to Great Britain or meet him at the airport on his return. The diplomatic ceasefire between them had been broken off.

It should be remembered here that many big shakeups in the Soviet leadership have taken place while certain Kremlin dwellers were away. The plot against Beria sprang up when he was in East Germany. Khrushchev removed Marshal Zhukov from his post as defense minister when the marshal was on a hunting expedition with Marshal Tito on the Yugoslav island of Brioni in the Adriatic. Khrushchev himself was overthrown while he was vacationing in Pitsunda at his Caucasian dacha on the shore of the Black Sea. The earlier, unsuccessful plot against him, in 1957, had been mounted while he was in Finland.

The same kind of thing happened this time. While Grigori Romanov was in Ethiopia, his supporter, Marshal Nikolai Ogarkov, chief of the general staff and de facto defense minister, was removed from office.

Besides being closely related in the official pecking order—Romanov, a CC secretary, was overseeing the nation's armed forces and was hence Ogarkov's immediate superior—the two had close ideological ties. In two articles that ran counter to the official Party line— one of them published in the magazine *Kommunist* and the other in the armed forces newspaper *Red Star*— Marshal Ogarkov had come out as an advocate of a nuclear first strike and of a Soviet "Star Wars" program. In addition, at his notorious press conference in the autumn of 1983 he claimed that there was complete justification for the destruction of the Korean airliner and warned that the same thing would happen to anyone who in the future violated the sacred Soviet borders. In exchange for Ogarkov's support, Romanov demanded that the Politburo officially approve Minister of Defense Ustinov's retirement (he was already ill) and the appointment of Ogarkov to succeed him. In early September, the feeling among high-ranking military officers in Moscow was that this transition was inevitable, and they expected it from one day to the next. So the cashiering of Marshal Ogarkov came as a surprise to everyone, including Ogarkov himself, and produced a shock effect among the Party-military elite. The evening edition of *Izvestia,* carrying an item saying that Ogarkov, still in his capacity as chief of the general staff, had seen off a Finnish military delegation, was put on sale at Moscow newsstands at the same time that a radio broadcast reported his removal from that post without giving any reason for it.

Ogarkov's demotion in September was not due to personal animosity against him but was the result of Kremlin cloakroom intrigues against Romanov, who upon his return from Ethiopia suddenly dropped from sight. He failed to show up at any of those Kremlin ceremonies where his presence was *de rigueur,* such as that for the conferring of awards upon Konstantin Chernenko held on September 27, or the same kind of ceremony for Victor Grishin held on October 4. Both of these ceremonies were covered in detail by the Soviet mass media: the first on radio and TV reports and in accounts, with photos, published on the front page of every Soviet newspaper. The listing of those who take part in such ceremonies is routine in the papers, but on TV it was done for the first time in that medium's coverage of the presentation of awards to Chernenko. The announcer read off a long list of the names of the twenty-seven Party and government officials who took part, not counting the general secretary and Ustinov, who presented the awards and who stayed at his post of defense minister until just a few months before his death. That long list, from which the name of Grigori Romanov was missing, was a graphic demonstration of his defeat by Gorbachev. And the ceremony provided other proofs of the same thing. For instance, standing next to Chernenko, on his left, and smiling triumphantly, was Mikhail Gorbachev. (A week later, when awards were presented to Grishin, Gorbachev was again standing next to Chernenko, but this time on his right.) Another astonishing thing was the very fact that, in what was almost an isolated case in Kremlin history, Chernenko was given the awards out of turn: Kremlin leaders usually get them on round-numbered days, but this was Chernenko's seventy-third birthday.

In his acceptance speech, Chernenko made a slip of the tongue and said something that can be understood only in the context of that phase in the Kremlin power struggle we are describing here: "I accept this award in the most crucial—and, frankly speaking, very difficult—period in my more than fifty years of work in the ranks of the CPSU."

It is hardly likely that Chernenko was talking about the state of his own health: that kind of thing simply isn't done in the Kremlin. Nor could he have been referring to the state of affairs in Russia. In the course of his more than fifty years of Party work, Chernenko had lived through incomparably more dramatic events: collectivization, famine, the Great Terror, the war with Finland, the war with Germany, the death of Stalin, the anti-Stalinist Twentieth Party Congress, the overthrow of Khrushchev, Andropov's coup, and others too many to count. And now, outwardly at any rate, a certain calm had descended over life in the empire. In the empire, yes, but not in the Kremlin. That is why that strange Chernenko remark could only have referred to the Kremlin power struggle, in which he had taken Gorbachev's side. That was the reason for his receiving these out-of-turn awards, the gold medal of a Hero of Socialist Labor and the Order of Lenin.

In Moscow at the time, rumors that were most likely

being floated by supporters of Gorbachev had it that Ogarkov's dismissal and that of Romanov (expected to take place soon) were measures taken to counter an attempt by them to carry out a coup.

The outcome of the Kremlin struggle seemed already to have been decided, along with the unenviable fate of both "plotters." A special plenum of the CC had been scheduled for October, one at which, as Kremlin officials openly told Western journalists, important personnel shifts were to be effected. In other words, Gorbachev's victory was to be officially confirmed, and Romanov was to be expelled from the Politburo and the Secretariat. Victor Afanasyev, editor-in-chief of *Pravda,* got ahead of the game and expressed his fealty to the victor. In an interview with Japanese correspondents, he even went so far as to call Gorbachev the "second secretary general"—a position that doesn't exist either in the Party rules or in Soviet political reality. Within a few days, however, Afanasyev had to eat his words, disavowing them publicly, because in mid-October events took a completely unexpected turn.

Ten days before the opening of the special Party plenum, the disgraced Marshal Ogarkov, to everyone's amazement, headed up a Soviet military delegation to East Berlin, where he was personally received as a VIP by Erich Honecker, the East German leader. This event was a lead story in the TV news broadcasts and was given front-page treatment (with photos) in *Neues Deutschland,* although with no mention of the Soviet marshal's official post. *That* was reported the next day, and it was a most unusual post, in that formerly it had existed only in wartime: commander in chief of Soviet forces in the entire European theater of operations, from the Urals to Berlin.

Marshal Ogarkov's rehabilitation after his fall from grace had been arranged with considerable tact so as not to sow discord among those in the upper echelons of the military establishment, where Ogarkov's former deputy, Marshal Sergei Akhromeyev, had already been appointed chief of the general staff.

The most interesting thing, however, was that the creation of Ogarkov's new post had been announced not in Berlin and not in Moscow but in Helsinki, and that it had been announced by none other than Grigori Romanov, who had come to Finland on an official visit. It was evident that at this stage of the power struggle, Romanov had reversed his earlier disadvantage and had got the upper hand over his rival by means of behind-the-scenes maneuvering. At that same time, Minister of Defense Dmitri Ustinov, who along with Chernenko had approved Ogarkov's dismissal and who had taken Gorbachev's side against Romanov, fell ill and no longer appeared in public.

The Party plenum that had been announced earlier was held exactly at the scheduled time; for purely organizational reasons, cancellation of it would have been impossible, since delegates were coming to it from all corners of the vast Soviet empire. But instead of being a political triumph for Mikhail Gorbachev, the plenum confined its agenda to a few hours' discussion of Soviet agriculture, a crisis that had become permanent and did not require a special plenum. Gorbachev, who was in charge of agriculture, did not give a speech; his plan for innovations was not considered, and his name was not even mentioned in the reports.

At a routine Kremlin awards ceremony shown on the evening TV program and reported with front-page photographs in all Soviet newspapers the next morning, Gorbachev, although present, was relegated to the very edge of the group, while in the middle, among a few remaining gerontocrats, stood Romanov. Within a few days, the Soviet press, radio and TV began to feature Romanov's experience as a leader in managing the industry of Leningrad as an example to be emulated.

By contrast, Gorbachev's junket to Great Britain just before Christmas was given scant coverage by the Soviet mass media (unlike its Western counterparts). Moreover, the TV cameras had filmed the British hosts and not their Russian guests. In the newspapers, where accounts of the junket were published on the fourth page out of six, not a single photo of Gorbachev appeared. Also, one astounding detail: although during the first few days of his trip the headlines of the stories had read GORBACHEV'S VISIT TO GREAT BRITAIN, during the last three days they were depersonalized into THE SOVIET DELEGATION'S VISIT TO GREAT BRITAIN. This was obviously the Kremlin's response to the Western press's announcement that Gorbachev was "the crown prince," "the second-ranking secretary," and "number two in the Politburo." The Kremlin has habitually taken a very suspicious attitude toward predictions, and especially praises, coming from enemies. The Western myth about Gorbachev, born of wishful thinking, was a windfall not for him but for his rival, Romanov.

Romanov managed to strengthen his position even more thanks to Gorbachev's absence from Moscow at a crucial moment in the power struggle. Because of Minister of Defense Ustinov's death and the illness of Chernenko, the political balance in the Kremlin was upset. When Gorbachev learned of the latest events in Moscow, he cut short his visit to Britain and promptly flew back to Moscow. The man appointed as the new defense minister was Marshal Sergei Sokolov, a military bureaucrat who, moreover, was seventy-three years old and ailing (one more bit of evidence showing how the Kremlin "mistreats" the military, fearing them and keeping them at a good arm's length from power). A few months later, Sokolov became a candidate member of the Politburo; but even if he ultimately manages to become a full member, it will be nothing more than an honorary title, since by that time he won't be any younger or healthier.

Grigori Romanov was named chairman of the committee in charge of arrangements for Ustinov's funeral. When it was held on December 24, 1984, it was Romanov, in the absence of Chernenko, who headed up the Politburo members as they stood on the rostrum atop Lenin's Mausoleum and throughout the ceremonies. All the Soviet radio and TV networks broadcasted from Red Square for more than an hour, and the newspapers gave their front pages entirely over to the ceremonies, stressing Romanov's role in them, as if they had been specially arranged in his honor and for his political benefit.

As for Gorbachev, he stayed on the sidelines and didn't even speak at the graveside of his "old friend," as he had called Ustinov at a press conference in Edinburgh before his departure from Britain. All he could do at that symbolic funeral in Red Square was to be an observer at his rival's political triumph.

If the British had made haste to inaugurate Gorbachev, Romanov was also making haste, rehearsing at Ustinov's funeral in Red Square his role as the new Soviet leader. Neither of the pretenders had a stable, decisive edge over the other: by turns, each kept outstripping the other. If Chernenko had died in September, his successor would have been Gorbachev; if he had died in December, while Gorbachev was in Britain, it would have been Romanov. There were still, however, ten weeks remaining before the death of Konstantin Chernenko, to whose position both Romanov and Gorbachev had laid claim, plenty of time for a new Kremlin intrigue.

7. The King Is Dead, Long Live the King!

AT THIS POINT we must turn briefly from Kremlinology to gerontology, where we shall find no conundrums, mysteries, or wrong predictions, just facts and figures. The dwellers in the Kremlin paradise enjoy a longevity a full fifteen years greater than that of their male subjects, thanks to their high standard of living, their huge service staffs, their posh dachas in the countryside near Moscow, in the Caucasus, in the Crimea, and on the Baltic, and the very best of medical care. Nonetheless, they have not yet managed to win the final victory over death. That is why certain patterns governing their transition to the next world merit the closest scrutiny.

It is not only the age at which the Kremlin Olympians leave this life that is interesting but precisely when—in what season of the year—they do it. In this they display an astounding unanimity. So as not to stray far afield, let us take only the eighties as an example. The former Soviet premier, Alexei Kosygin, died in December 1981

at seventy-six. The chief Party ideologue, Mikhail Suslov, died in January 1982 at seventy-nine. Brezhnev died
in November 1982, and former Soviet President Nikolai
Podgorny died two months later at seventy-nine. Andropov died in February 1984, several months short of
his seventieth birthday, and Marshal Ustinov in December 1984 at seventy-six. If we add two historical examples—the death of Lenin in January 1924 and the death
of Stalin in early March 1953—the picture becomes
clear even to a person not equipped with a knowledge of
Kremlinology. The Russian winter is the season the
Kremlin leaders have chosen for their deaths. Or, to put
it more precisely, it is the season death has chosen for its
raids on the Kremlin. Moreover, if we look at a pheno-
logical calendar, we see that on the days of the deaths
—and even the funerals—of the comrades mentioned
above, from Lenin to Ustinov, the cold was especially
severe, even by Russian standards.

One can find several objective and by no means mystical reasons for this tendency in the Kremlin way of life
and death: the long Russian winters, outbreaks of winter epidemics, the susceptibility of old people to colds
and pneumonia, the risk of hypothermia, and so on.

Taking all this into account—along with the record-
breaking age and worsening health of the top Soviet
leaders at the time—we predicted right after Marshal
Ustinov's death in a newspaper article titled "The
Kremlin: The Winter of Their Discontent" that death
would visit the Kremlin at least one more time that
winter. For at the age that had then been reached by the
Kremlin gerontocrats, death becomes an infectious disease. Moreover, they had to walk through a freezing
Moscow behind the coffin of their "precursor," and
then stand shivering on top of Lenin's Mausoleum during the funeral ceremonies in Red Square. It was precisely because of that mortal danger that Konstantin
Chernenko, who already was barely alive, did not appear at the funeral of his associate and friend Marshal
Ustinov. But would that help him to live through the

season that causes the Kremlin leaders the greatest anxiety? It was with that rather rhetorical question that we concluded our prediction. We do not take credit for the fact that it proved right. We mention it, rather, because that melancholy and solemn ceremony was repeated so regularly that it had become a parody of itself.

For the three last Soviet leaders, old age was not an easy time, because each of them had to keep on performing the functions of chief of state until his last days. Andropov did so in the full sense of the word, and although Brezhnev and Chernenko fulfilled only ceremonial functions, in their moribund condition that required almost heroic efforts. Hence it may even be said that while the Kremlin gerontocrats have a longevity fifteen years greater than that of their male subjects, their old age is burdensome and joyless. One paradox of the Soviet system is that after providing for the ruling elite a standard of living that is luxurious by Russian standards, toward the end of their lives it shows them its other face, merciless and inhuman. This is not experienced by other citizens of the USSR, who enjoy well-earned rest and peace in their old age. Kremlin leaders never enjoy those things.

What happened to Konstantin Chernenko showed this paradox in its purest form, because the fate of his two predecessors was, after all, distorted by subjective circumstances. In the last years of Brezhnev's life, his work schedule had been deliberately overloaded by his impatient rival and heir, who wearied of waiting for his death and decided to hasten the denouement. Ruthless toward his predecessor, Andropov was the same toward himself, running the empire from his deathbed and spending his last strength on it. (In Russia, it is said that people like him "burn themselves out on the job.") But it was the system itself that was merciless toward Chernenko. He had no impatient heir who was nudging him toward the grave; and he himself had no big plans for restructuring the declining empire, not even ordinary zeal for work. Yet the system didn't allow even him to die in peace, and undoubtedly it hastened his end.

The event that precipitated his death is notable for its insignificance.

A conference among the leaders of the Warsaw Pact countries had been scheduled for mid-January 1985—an urgent one for the Kremlin because in recent years the sheep of the Eastern European flock, in the absence of any real supervision by their shepherd, had begun to stray, one by one. First Romania, then Poland, and then both East Germany and Hungary had begun to display unhealthful inclinations to wander off on their own. At the very last minute, however, this long-over-due conference was canceled because of Chernenko's illness. But what was not called off was his purely ceremonial participation in the purely ceremonial elections to a purely ceremonial parliament—which, moreover, was not even the Soviet parliament but merely that of one of the USSR's fifteen republics, the Russian Republic. No one dared cancel it for fear of violating protocol established once and for all time. In view of Chernenko's terminal illness, there could be no question of his really taking part in the elections. But in order to put on a show for the hundreds of millions of TV viewers in the vast Soviet empire and far beyond its boundaries, his aides had to drag the dying old man from his hospital bed, put a suit on him, drape a tie around his neck and knot it, set him on his feet, and take him to a movie-set polling place with a stage-prop ballot box into which the dazed Chernenko, after mumbling something unintelligible, put a ballot.

Such is the Soviet tradition: The people must see their ruler vote.

Not only that, but a few days later Chernenko was shown again on Soviet television, this time accepting the congratulations of "the workers" on his election as a deputy to the Russian parliament. Perceptive TV viewers noticed, however, that although there had been a lapse of four days between the first and second acts of this drama starring Chernenko, with supposedly different settings for each (the polling place for the first act, and Chernenko's office in the Kremlin for the second), the sets were exactly the same: the same pink walls, the same distinctively patterned white curtains, the same oriental rug, and the same crowd of "workers" headed by the Moscow Party boss, Victor Grishin, talking to Chernenko with explanatory gestures and encouraging him as one would a toddler learning how to walk. It was obvious that both scenes had been shot in the same place at the same time, although it was not clear just when, on election day or on a day when the invalid felt slightly better. In both, it was plain to see how hard it was for Chernenko to bear up under all these theatrics; one felt sorry for him, as one would for any dying man forced to pretend that he was fully alive and in good health.

Chernenko died on March 10, 1985, two weeks after he had been compelled to play the role of a healthy, functioning leader of the Soviet Union.

It would be useless to look for the nameless, untalented director of those scenes, which produced an impression the opposite of what was intended. The very system of Kremlin power that had raised a mediocre Party functionary to the heights had cast him down after showing the whole world how physically pathetic he really was.

However, if we focus not on the bizarre power system, which is unlike anything else in the world, but on the individuals who exercise that power, we find things that, while no less incongruous, are more understandable.

The seventy-year-old Party boss of the capital, Victor Grishin, was shown along with Chernenko in both of those TV clips. Two days before the elections, Grishin presided over a meeting at which Chernenko's speech to the "voters" was read. In each case, the Soviet mass media especially emphasized Grishin's participation; many people both in the Soviet Union and abroad decided that he would be the next interim, compromise "king of the hill" after Chernenko. Actually, he was more of an understudy, to be called upon if once again neither Romanov nor Gorbachev managed to prevail in their prolonged battle for power.

Grishin never was one of the main performers. Thus, in the second half of January 1985, even though the power struggle was raging fiercely, Grishin went to Warsaw at the head of a Soviet delegation, which would obviously have been careless on the part of a real claimant. By contrast, Mikhail Gorbachev, having learned from his bitter experience of the visit to England, wasn't taking any risks. He canceled a scheduled trip to Paris to attend a congress of the French Communist Party, notwithstanding his and his wife's fondness for that kind of foreign junket.

On election day, February 24, when Soviet television was about to put on its show with Chernenko in the leading role, unsuspecting foreign correspondents were invited to the polling place in the House of Architects where Chernenko usually voted. Instead of Chernenko, however, it was Gorbachev who appeared, accompanied by his wife, his daughter Irina, and his granddaughter Oksana. Gorbachev handed his ballot to the five-year-old Oksana and helped her put it in the slot in the ballot box. When the photojournalists, touched by this tender scene, asked him to repeat it, he spread his hands in a gesture of helplessness, smiled, and said, "You can only vote once."

On that evening's TV news, however, Chernenko was shown "voting" and not a word was said about the voting Gorbachev family. This would have no particular importance and would not even be worth mentioning if the foreign correspondents had just chanced to drop in at the House of Architects that day and had just chanced to catch the Gorbachevs there. But such was not the case: they had been invited there and, although they were not told in advance whom they would see, they had hoped it would be Chernenko. But he was being filmed elsewhere, in their absence, by better masters of photomontage than they; and the surprise was deliberately arranged for them at the House of Architects.

Usually, unofficial photo sessions are organized by the KGB through some of its trusted people like Victor Louis, a KGB "salesman" who, under the guise of a foreign correspondent, occasionally supplies the Western press with items on Kremlin dwellers, Andrei Sakharov, Svetlana Alliluyeva, Solzhenitsyn, and other Soviet stars of the first magnitude of worldwide importance. This time, however, representatives of the world press were officially invited for an unofficial meeting with Gorbachev, not by Victor Louis, but by the ministry of foreign affairs. And that fact, as well as the lack of even a mention of Gorbachev on the Soviet evening TV news, meant that the combat between Gorbachev and Romanov was still going on although Minister of Foreign Affairs Andrei Gromyko had already taken a clearcut position on it. The same could not be said of KGB Chairman Victor Chebrikov, who, having taken a wait-and-see position, had refused to make his people available for setting up that meeting, so that Gromyko had to use his own, direct channels—something that was new and conflicted with the usual practice.

How to explain such resolve on the part of the minister of foreign affairs and such irresoluteness at the same time on the part of the chief of secret police?

Before answering that question, let us be precise on one point, in order to avoid using hindsight and reconstructing past events in the light of their present consequences. For the first time, the predictions of the Western Kremlinologists proved to be right—the number-two man in the Kremlin became, after his predecessor's death, the number-one man. In the West, Gorbachev's inauguration as the seventh Soviet leader came several months before his official inauguration in his own country. Yet, as we have seen, all the time that the heralds in the free world were predicting his certain victory, Gorbachev's shares on the Western market were not only higher but more stable than they were on the Kremlin market. The conflict between the minister of foreign affairs on the one hand and the KGB and the mass media on the other shows that at most ten days before Chernenko's death, the question as to who would succeed him had still not been finally settled.

The ambivalence of Victor Chebrikov on the eve of Chernenko's death was not at all due to his irresoluteness but rather to his own plans and ambition. And the fact that the KGB chairman ultimately did support Gorbachev can be ascribed to two things. First, his decision was based on a clear-headed calculation: Gorbachev, actually more bustling and excitable than truly vigorous, would be easier to control than the self-confident, haughty Romanov. Second, Chebrikov's support was the result of a trade: in exchange for it, the KGB got two more slots in the Politburo and full control over the empire's foreign affairs.

According to some reports, Romanov proved less willing to make a deal and, apprehensive that it might weaken his prospective one-man rule, made fewer concessions to the KGB—which in the final analysis cost him considerably more. Fearful of giving up a part, he lost the whole. He not only lost the game to Gorbachev, but he was even stripped of those posts he had held: membership in the Politburo and in the Secretariat. Officially, he was retired from both positions at his own request, "for reasons of poor health," in the idiom of Soviet-style Newspeak. This is patent nonsense, especially when one considers that Brezhnev, Andropov, and Chernenko, despite ailing health, held the empire's top post until they went to their graves.

And even though the real truth about Romanov's disgrace was an open secret—it was plain for everyone to see that he had lost the power struggle—his enemies still spread the rumor that he had become a hopeless drunk. That smear had become a standard weapon in combating him, from the incident at his daughter's wedding to his allegedly drunken behavior at a reception in neighboring Finland during Chernenko's interregnum. According to recent reports from Moscow, Romanov has forcibly been confined in a hospital for alcoholics. This is a frame-up. Having made the personal acquaintance of Romanov, we hasten to assure the reader that drunkenness was one vice he certainly did not have, however many others he may possess.

As for Romanov's fall, with hindsight it showed clearly how close he had come to the top of the Kremlin hill. The fatal mistake that spelled his defeat was that, in relying on Marshal Ogarkov, he overestimated the role of the armed forces and at the same time underestimated the KGB. As a brief footnote to the jousting between Romanov and Gorbachev that we have been following, we add that their personality differences had no great political importance, especially in view of the KGB's strengthened position in the Kremlin.

Gorbachev was declared general secretary with unprecedented rapidity—only four hours after the announcement of Chernenko's death; the Soviet newspapers for the first time published a photo of a dead ruler on the second page, while his successor's photo, biographical sketch, and inaugural speech appeared on the front page. But this does not in any way prove that Gorbachev's election had taken place before Chernenko's death. Quite the contrary; the decision was made so quickly as to present Gorbachev's enemies and rivals with a *fait accompli,* to make that decision irrevocable except by means of a countercoup.

The designation of Gorbachev was the result of a palace coup, however bloodless and on whatever small a scale. And that was in an old Kremlin tradition, since every Soviet leader came to power through a coup: Lenin, Stalin, Khrushchev, Brezhnev, Andropov, Chernenko ("the oldsters' countercoup"), and finally Gorbachev. On the eve of Chernenko's death, there were at least three plots in the Kremlin: Gorbachev's, Romanov's, and that of Grishin, who was fronting for the old guard. Gorbachev's supporters simply beat his op-

ponents to the punch. And Gorbachev himself, as he
had in most things all during his life up to then, played
rather an auxiliary role in the Gorbachev plot. The
main, decisive role was played by the godfather, Minister of Foreign Affairs Andrei Gromyko.

For the first time in his life, that old Kremlin wolf was
a kingmaker, and he coped brilliantly with that duty,
which he had assigned to himself. He did not conceal
the fact that he was on Gorbachev's side in the plot:
Gromyko had made the nominating speech at the CC
plenum, and he did not use a prepared text. It was an
impassioned speech, with personal and polemical over-
tones. At whom were his arguments directed? Whom
was he trying to win over? Who, at that plenum, had to
be convinced that the choice made by Gromyko personally was the correct one? If anyone, acting alone,
chose Gorbachev as leader of the country, it was Gromyko himself; he put down any and all objections with
his authority as a Kremlin old-timer.

After all, he had taken part in the Yalta conference
along with Stalin, Roosevelt, and Churchill, and was the
only participant in that historic meeting who was still
alive and politically active. For almost three decades he
had had a big hand in making the empire's foreign
policy. He had begun his career in the late thirties and
rose rapidly, thanks to Stalin's gigantic purges of the
Party, which had entirely destroyed the Leninist school
of new Soviet diplomacy and replaced it with his own
Stalinist school. Gromyko has always remained loyal to
it, covertly during the Khrushchev era and more and
more openly later on. Thus, in the summer of 1984,
he took the initiative in the political rehabilitation of
his former chief, the ninety-four-year-old Vyacheslav
Molotov, who had been one of Stalin's closest accomplices in his bloody crimes. Molotov had been expelled
from the Party in 1962 during the period of Khrushchev's de-Stalinization. His restoration to membership,
in 1984, came during the onset of re-Stalinization.

To restore Party membership to a very old and now-harmless criminal, even though it was seen by some in the Soviet Union as an omen of another Stalinist era, was one thing. But for one person to put a new leader on the Kremlin throne by the force of his own will, taking on himself all responsibility for the choice, was another. What dictated that choice? Concern for the empire's future? A notion of what a Soviet leader should be? Or in putting his money on Gorbachev—and we must not forget that Gromyko did not have a wide choice—was he guided by more personal interests? Was he taking revenge for past humiliations (especially under Khrushchev, whose rating of him was very low) and making sure, with the help of an obedient and grateful protégé, that he would enjoy tranquillity and high esteem in his old age? We have no unequivocal answers to that question. It is quite possible that, among other things, in making the case for Gorbachev, Gromyko was convincing himself that the choice he had made was the correct one.

We shall not recite all the compliments with which Gromyko embellished his panegyric to Gorbachev but instead point to its emotional, personal nature. Gromyko constantly brought in his own experience: "I can personally confirm this." "By virtue of my own duties. . . ." "This may be clearer to me than to some other comrades." Since throughout his long career, Gromyko's "own duties" had been confined to foreign affairs (his Party comrades had often objected that his speeches were lacking in ideology), the first criteria used in choosing a general secretary were likewise related to foreign affairs.

Surprisingly, those foreign affairs criteria were being applied to a man who had spent the greater part of his life in his own part of the country dealing with matters of agriculture. His entire experience with foreign countries amounted to no more than a few trips abroad in very recent years, most of them for purposes of pleasure rather than business. And Gromyko himself knew that very well. There is good reason why, immediately after Gorbachev's inauguration, the former "took over the guidance" of his protégé in international matters, especially those having to do with his image abroad. This went so far as to include choosing the old-fashioned fedora that Gorbachev wore when he arrived at Geneva for the summit talks. It was the same style of hat that the young Gromyko had favored in the forties, when he was Soviet ambassador to the United States and the United Nations. And according to Arkady Shevchenko, in the seventies, on the occasion of one of Gromyko's sporadic visits to America, he sent the staffers at the Soviet Mission in New York on a search all over the city for that kind of hat. Finally, one was found in the storeroom of a little shop. And now, acting on the advice of his conservative tutor, the young Soviet leader, when he met Ronald Reagan, theatrically swept off his black fedora, amazing millions of Western TV watchers with his (actually, Gromyko's) old-fashioned taste.

Gromyko's speech at the CC plenum testified to his own limitations; given the economic, ideological, and demographic decline in which the Soviet Union now finds itself, domestic affairs are the most urgent. But Gromyko had never in his life dealt with them, and as a narrow specialist, he wasn't much interested in them. As he said, "We live in a world in which, figuratively speaking, various telescopes are aimed at the Soviet Union, and there are not a few of them, big and small, from close up and from a distance. They watch, just waiting for some sort of crack to appear in the Soviet leadership. The unanimous opinion of the Politburo is this: Once again we, the Central Committee and the Politburo, will not give our political enemies satisfaction on that count."

The stability of the power that Gorbachev was handed by the minister of foreign affairs—in itself, a most unusual thing in Kremlin practice—is another question. A power struggle in the Kremlin is not necessarily brought to an end by the death of one ruler and the accession of another. Indeed, sometimes it only begins at that point. It is odd that, counter to tradition, Gromyko's panegyric to Gorbachev was not published in a single Soviet newspaper but only in a special bulletin, and a week later at that.

And there are still other facts indicating that the power struggle is not yet over. For instance, while the military are still being kept at a respectful distance from the Kremlin (at an even greater remove than it was during the tenures of Brezhnev, Andropov, and Chernenko), the empire's secret government, the KGB, is not only continuing to function at full capacity but is also strengthening its position. This is even manifest in certain ways: The Politburo does not include a single military officer, but it does include three KGB generals in civilian clothes—KGB Chairman Victor Chebrikov, First Deputy Premier Geidar Aliyev, and Foreign Minister Eduard Shevardnadze—more than there are CC secretaries, headed by Gorbachev. Even under Stalin, there were fewer representatives of the secret police in that supreme ruling body of the empire.

Thus the KGB has now taken over the Council of Ministers and the Foreign Ministry, not to mention the Ministry of Internal Affairs, whose upper echelon includes many generals from the Committee of State Security, and the armed forces, which are completely controlled by the secret police. That organization is now busy consolidating its position in the Politburo.

That it is doing so explains why, unlike Brezhnev, Andropov, or Chernenko, Gorbachev did not manage to add the supreme State title to his supreme Party one. The honorary post of president was conferred upon Andrei Gromyko, which for purposes of ceremony elevated him to the very summit of the State pyramid and guarantees him a magnificent funeral in Red Square and a burial plot behind Lenin's Mausoleum instead of a niche in the Kremlin wall. In other words, he went up the down staircase. Gromyko's token promotion left vacant the post of foreign minister—a key post in the

Kremlin power structure. The KGB has promptly taken it over by putting in one of its own people, Eduard Shevardnadze, despite the fact that he had no previous diplomatic experience and was making a fabulous leap from his Caucasian province right into the world arena. (Incidentally, he is the first Georgian in the Kremlin for thirty-two years, since Stalin's death and the execution of Beria.)

As a result of this realignment, Gorbachev was prevented from concentrating too much power in his own hands by assuming yet another post. Likewise, six months later, when the eighty-year-old Tikhonov was sent into retirement, the vacated post somehow did not go to Gorbachev. (It is worth remembering that three other Party leaders—Lenin, Stalin, and Khrushchev—had held the post of premier.) This has guaranteed that the empire's leadership will continue to be collegial, with the scales steadily tipping in favor of the KGB as compared to the other Kremlin contingents: the gerontocrats who are fading from the scene and the new generation of partocrats, like National Secretary Egor Ligachev and Premier Nikolai Ryzhkov, who are also closely tied to the security organs and were protégés of Yuri Andropov. In general, since Andropov's death no Kremlin appointment has been made that would have run counter to his will, as if he were secretly continuing to rule the Kremlin from his grave.

It is simply wrong to say that Gorbachev is putting together a Kremlin team out of his own people. Except for a small group of Stavropolians in the CC apparatus, all the newcomers to the Kremlin are, like Gorbachev himself, Andropov's people—his liege men and protégés. They owe their careers not to Gorbachev but to Andropov. They remain loyal to their mentor, and the new general secretary is regarded as, at most, first among equals.

Any unsteady step that Gorbachev takes may cost him his power. Moreover, precisely the men upon whom he relies in holding that power are potentially the most dangerous to him, if not right now, then in a few years, when their own ambitious plans will have ripened. The troika of KGB generals in the Politburo—each a plotter of proven skill—would be sufficient to constitute the nucleus of a conspiracy if Gorbachev were to go against its will and act of his own volition, if he has any.

Indeed, the complex maneuver (almost like one in chess) that resulted in Gromyko's promotion-demotion, in the KGB's seizing control of the ministry of foreign affairs, and in the restricting of Gorbachev's power, was engineered by Victor Chebrikov and Geidar Aliyev, according to a reliable source. While Gorbachev was busy wreaking vengeance on his former rival, Romanov, and making his grand debut working the crowds in Moscow, Leningrad, and the Ukraine, receiving foreign visitors and making junkets abroad, his Kremlin colleagues were maneuvering offstage, limiting his power and increasing their own.

One move in that direction was the release of a film about Yuri Andropov in the summer of 1985, both at movie houses and on TV. It emphasized his fifteen years of service with "the organs"; it was a eulogistic melodrama that included Andropov's philosophical and love poems, plus interviews with his wife, Tatyana Filippovna, and his children, Igor (then ambassador to Greece) and Irina (now editor of the magazine *Musical Life*). Andropov was the only Soviet leader since Lenin about whom a movie was made after his death. Not only did the film officially reinforce the popular legend about him, it took attention away from Gorbachev, who was not even mentioned in it. According to its director, Oleg Uralov, it was first screened at a session of the Politburo. Although Geidar Aliyev, Victor Chebrikov, and Vitaly Vorotnikov praised it, Gorbachev alone had no comment to make.

Exercising power in the Kremlin is like walking a tightrope or walking on thin ice over deep water in early winter. It demands great skill and is very risky. That is why, fond as we are of making predictions, we are not going to say that Gorbachev is young enough to rule Russia into the next century. More than age is involved here, and often it is not involved at all. So we shall do no fortune telling about the immediate future.

The will of Andrei Gromyko alone is not a strong enough base for Gorbachev's power. And then, Gromyko is not immortal; he is almost seventy-seven. He is Gorbachev's fourth mentor, after Suslov, Kulakov, and Andropov, but he is the oldest mentor Gorbachev has had, and his political career is on the wane. The day will soon come when Gorbachev, for the first time in his life, will be left without sponsors—all alone with the Kremlin, the country, and the world.

8. Meet Mikhail Gorbachev

> Comrades, this man has a nice smile,
> but he's got iron teeth.
>
> —ANDREI GROMYKO'S speech
> at Gorbachev's inauguration

His Political Debut at Moscow University

ALL OFFICIAL BIOGRAPHIES of Soviet leaders are falsified to one degree or another. The most striking example of this is the case of Stalin, who proclaimed himself Lenin's closest comrade in arms and a revolutionary second only to him, whereas Lenin's real comrades in arms and the true revolutionaries—from Trotsky, Bukharin, Zinoviev, and Kamenev to others on down the line—were physically destroyed by Stalin; the very mention of their names was prohibited under penalty of death. Not only were histories of the Bolshevik Party and of Russia in the twentieth century rewritten, but in photographs and newsreels of the post-revolutionary years, Lenin's closest aides standing next to him were, as Stalin's accursed enemies, cropped out. Even in anthology pieces by the major Soviet poet Mayakovsky dealing with the Revolution, lines mentioning former leaders of the Revolution who had become personae non grata were deleted and replaced by doggerel hastily scribbled by editors with no regard for rhyme, rhythm, or the poet's style. In group snapshots, photographers made Stalin look taller than all the others, and his face was retouched so that none of the mere mortals in the USSR would know that the deified despot was not only short but had a pockmarked face and a withered arm.

After he died and was even condemned some time later by his successor, Khrushchev, for his bloody crimes, some of his heritage was disowned; but the tradition of falsifying the biographies of top Soviet leaders persisted. Khrushchev himself took credit for taking an active part in the Revolution, in which he played only a walk-on role, if he played any at all. On the other hand, *hush* was the word when it came to his truly active role in the Great Terror of the thirties, when he was viceroy of the Ukraine. His successors, Brezhnev and Andropov, who had been too young to play any part in the Revolution, were credited with fighting in the Great Patriotic War (as World War II is called in Russia), although neither of them was ever in combat.

Andropov, after having served for fifteen years as head of the secret police, floated (with the help of his henchmen) a rumor about himself as a liberal, Westernizer, and intellectual once he had come to power. Judging from the international press, he brought if off very well. Even the nominal and interim ruler Chernenko managed to conceal, in official biographies of himself, the fact that during the Great Terror of 1937 he had voluntarily taken part in the so-called bloody weddings in Dnepropetrovsk.

It might seem that Lenin was an exception to this

rule, but alas, such is not the case. His Soviet biographers still carefully conceal a "stain" in his origins: the fact that his mother, Mariya Aleksandrovna Blank, was the daughter of a German Jew.

We both remember an incident from our childhood, which may strike the Western reader as a joke, but is not only a slice of Soviet life but is astonishingly typical of it. Once every year, when we were attending grade school, we would be taken on a group excursion to an ethnographic museum with an exhibit that featured a huge multicolored carpet woven by peasant craftsmen. Covering an entire wall and called *Friendship Forever,* the tapestry depicted a ceremonial reception at which Chinese leaders, headed by Mao Zedong, met with their Soviet counterparts, headed by Stalin. That carpet was amazing because it underwent transformation even more fantastic than those undergone by the picture of Dorian Gray: every year the number of Chinese increased as the number of Russians decreased. The first one to be rewoven into a Chinese was Lavrenti Beria, Stalin's closest accomplice in his bloody crimes, after Beria was executed in the basement of the Lubyanka, the same infamous prison where he had tortured political prisoners. After Khrushchev had carried out his countercoup in 1957 and expelled Molotov, Malenkov, and Kaganovich from the Politburo, the size of the Soviet delegation shrank even more, and another three Chinese appeared. Not long afterward, it was ascertained that the anti-Khrushchev faction included a few more people, and they too were replaced by Chinese in the carpet. We were convinced that every time the newspapers published a report of a new exposure, peasant craftsmen would come from somewhere deep in the countryside and, working like gnomes, reweave overnight the Russians fallen out of favor into slanty-eyed Chinese. Finally, when the Soviet press began to criticize Stalin openly, we hurried on our own to the museum for a look at the "magic carpet," hoping to see Khrushchev as the sole Russian on it, with anonymous, yellow-faced Chinese crowding in on him from all sides. But alas, we got there too late; the carpet had been removed from the exhibit and replaced by a notice reading, "For Restoration." It was never put up again; the Kremlin soon quarreled with China, and Khrushchev was overthrown. Apparently, there are some limits, if not to the art of falsification, then to the art of reweaving.

If Russian history itself is the property of the Kremlin rulers, who dole it out to the people in modest amounts according to the needs of the moment, they regard their own biographies as being their personal property in an even greater degree, and revamp them any way they like. Not only are biographies treated in this way; the same thing applies to photographs. As we have said, Stalin's photographs made him look taller than he was and removed his pockmarks. Again, not only Brezhnev, during his declining years, but Andropov and Chernenko, throughout their brief reigns, were made to seem in glowing health, although in fact each of the three at the time in question already had one foot in the grave. As for the present Soviet leader, those who do the retouching for the Soviet newspapers, newsreels, and TV have their work cut out for them—and cutting out is literally what they have to do. Everywhere in the world except in the Soviet Union it is known that Gorbachev has a large birthmark to the right of his bald pate. A few smaller but very noticeable marks run from it down one side of his forehead right to his eyebrows. That would be a serious drawback if he wanted to make a career as an actor in Hollywood, but obviously it didn't hinder him from reaching the top of the Kremlin hill. Nonetheless, in all official photographs of Gorbachev—from the huge ones that are displayed on holidays on the streets and public squares of the Soviet Union to the one that appeared on the front pages of all the Soviet newspapers the day he was named general secretary of the Communist Party—that distinctive birthmark is missing. No ordinary Soviet citizen even suspects that it exists. How does one explain this? Chalk it up to the Kremlin's habit of lying even when there is not the slightest need for it —lying unconsciously, as a matter of tradition or momentum? Are they afraid of damaging Gorbachev in the eyes of the public, of offending the people's notion of what, aesthetically, a great leader should appear to be: impressive, confident, without any visible physical defects on those parts of his body exposed to view?

But the official photographs of Gorbachev, which have until recently only rarely been published or put on public display, are one thing. It is quite another thing today, when the Soviet mass media must regularly show him live in the glare of klieg lights as he goes about his public business receiving foreign dignitaries in Moscow, traveling abroad, speaking at meetings, and so on. What to do in that case?

The way out found by the Soviet propagandists might seem original had it not been borrowed from an old Near Eastern parable. According to the parable, a long time ago, in the Near East, there lived an all-powerful caliph who was blind in one eye. That caliph decided to invite three court painters to his palace so that each of them could do his portrait. He warned them that although he would pay a rich reward for a good portrait, he would cut off the head of a painter who did a bad one.

The first artist painted him as he actually was, blind in one eye; he was promptly killed for lacking respect for the sovereign.

The second portrayed the caliph as having good vision in both eyes; he was executed for lying.

The award was won by the third, who painted the caliph in profile with his good eye showing.

In the Soviet Union, in any group photograph, Gorbachev is shown from the left, in profile, or in three-quarter view, so that his birthmark—which might compromise him in the eyes of the Soviet people—is not noticeable. Soviet photographers and cameramen are forbidden to shoot him from the right. We know this from fellow-journalists in Moscow, but it is also obvious from his pictures on TV and in newspapers. But when Gorbachev appears on the speakers' platform atop Lenin's Mausoleum, or at Sheremetyevo Airport, with a hat or Persian lamb cap pulled down low over his brow, photographers and cameramen are free to take pictures from any direction.

Naturally, if this kind of manipulation and misrepresentation is possible in photos and documentaries, it is still easier, technically and otherwise, to practice in the biographies of Kremlin leaders published in Soviet newspapers and encyclopedias. But although it is easy to detect visual falsification, detecting lies in print is much harder. And yet Gorbachev's official biography begins with a lie, and that lie has spread, without any great difficulties, from the Soviet press into the world press, precisely because it was hard for people to suspect any fakery at such an early point in his life.

One can understand why Stalin and Khrushchev colored their own life stories with tall tales or revolutionary activity, and why Brezhnev and Andropov used invented military exploits to the same end. It is also understandable why Chernenko wanted to conceal the terrorist period in his own life. But why did Gorbachev stick on to his own biography the story that before entering Moscow University Law School in 1950 he had worked as an assistant combine operator in his native *stanitsa* (large Cossack village) of Privolnoye in the Stavropol Territory? This information is carried in all the official biographies of Gorbachev in the national press, some of which even specify the years during which he did this kind of work: from 1946 to 1950, that is, from the ages of fifteen to nineteen.

But in the Stavropol papers, which don't reach the Moscow public (not to mention newspaper readers abroad), the story is quite different. There it says that Mikhail Gorbachev went directly from high school to the university and worked as an assistant combine operator on the *kolkhoz* only in the summer and during vacations, either to earn extra money or by way of compulsory on-the-job experience. The latter kind of work usually lasts no more than a month and is a mere formality. The provincial papers in Gorbachev's own part of the country, where facts about local life are much harder to conceal than they are in Moscow, went on writing about the temporary, seasonal nature of Gorbachev's work when he was already living in Moscow as a CC secretary and a member of the Politburo. (One example: *Stavropolskaya pravda,* February 6, 1979.)

What made Gorbachev credit himself with four years of work experience? A work record was helpful in getting accepted by a university, especially by a prestigious law school. But in 1950 there was not yet such huge competition—almost insurmountable by mere mortals —for acceptance by colleges (institutes) as was introduced in the mid-fifties. The doors of virtually all the country's institutions of higher learning were open to Gorbachev because of his ethnic (Russian) and social (peasant) origins. But one incident in his life history was carefully masked by the fictive work period between his graduation from high school and his enrollment at the university.

In the Soviet Union, a child starts school at the age of seven and graduates exactly ten years later at age seventeen. But Gorbachev, who entered the university right after high school, graduated from the latter at the age of nineteen. True, he might have had to repeat two grades because of low marks or ill health, but nothing in that required concealment or faking the record. What Gorbachev so carefully concealed when he was in Moscow was that for two years he didn't attend school at all. There was no place where he could, because the years in question were 1942 and 1943, when the Stavropol Territory was occupied by Hitler's troops and the German staff was headquartered in his native village of Privolnoye. This had to be concealed because in Stalin's time, all those who lived in occupied zones were automatically regarded as politically unreliable—in the best

case; in the worst, they were classified as collaborators
and accomplices of the enemy. Sometimes entire peoples were so classified, such as the Crimean Tatars, who
were all declared to be traitors and shipped off to Central Asia and Siberia. Half of them perished en route.
(Their civil rights still have not been restored, and they
are forbidden to return to their homeland under penalty
of imprisonment.) Another example, in the Stavropol
Territory itself, is the Karachay, or Sunni Muslims,
whose autonomous region was abolished by Stalin.
They were forcibly deported within the USSR for treason—an unfounded charge all the more groundless in
that most of them were either serving in the Red Army
or fighting against the Germans as guerrillas. But who
then bothered to check into that? Indeed, who would
have checked into what the teenaged Misha Gorbachev,
who took no part in any guerrilla movement, was doing
in German-occupied territory at the time? That is why
such a stain on his personal history—however pre-
posterous it may seem—was much more dangerous for
his future career than the birthmark on his head, which
was not even noticeable in his youth since he didn't go
bald until later. With that stain, it would have been
virtually impossible to begin his career in Moscow.
When he padded his questionnaire, he was telling a
"life-saving lie." His two dropout years from school
vanished, and he was spared being interrogated by the
university personnel department (a branch of the secret
police) as to what he was doing at the time in territory
occupied by the Nazis. Thanks to that innocent and
quite-justified falsification, he entered Moscow University Law School with no trouble; then, in effect, his
political career began.

   It is interesting, though, how one lie brings another in
its wake. In the biographical sketch of Gorbachev,
which prefaces the collection of his speeches published
in the United States, it is mentioned that in 1949, in
recognition of his youthful feats of labor in the kolkhoz
fields, he was given one of the highest Soviet awards:

the Red Banner of Labor. The case is so unusual that it should have been prominently reported not only by the Stavropol papers but by the entire Soviet press. Alas, a very thorough search through the papers for that period has yielded nothing. The labor heroism of the adolescent Misha Gorbachev is an invention of the Soviet propagandists—one undoubtedly made with his knowledge. (The story is such an unlikely one that it is not told in the official biographical sketches of Gorbachev published for Soviet consumption.) The only information we were able to find was that both Gorbachev's grandfather, Andrei, and his father, Sergei, were active participants in the kolkhoz movement, his grandfather being the organizer and chairman of one of the first collective farms in the Stavropol Territory. So that farming in the Soviet, kolkhoz manner is traditional in the Gorbachev family, although when Mikhail Gorbachev entered Moscow University, he tried to break with that tradition and follow a more promising career.

We can, with relative ease, reconstruct the five years —1950 to 1955—that Gorbachev spent at Moscow University. Three, and perhaps more, of his former classmates at the law school now live in Western Europe: a Czech, Zdenek Mlynar, and two Russians, Friedrich Neznansky and Lev Yudovich. Also, at our request, interviews with two of his former classmates have been conducted in the Soviet Union. Here, to be sure, one must allow for Mnemosyne's caprices—after all, more than three decades have gone by since then—and for the possibility of personal or political bias in these accounts. Hence, we mention only traits that are mentioned in several accounts. For example, all those who knew Gorbachev at the university agree that at first the other students made fun of him. They laughed at his insufferable provincial manners, his deplorable ignorance, and at his Ukrainian accent, with the particular "g" sound and the way he misplaced the stress in certain words. His pronunciation still has these defects.

Gorbachev was the Komsomol organizer in his own

department. As early as his sophomore year, he joined the Party, and soon he became a member of the Party committee of the entire university, which included both professors and students. He made close contacts with the instructors and secretaries of the Party's Krasnopresnensky District Committee, hoping they would help set him up in the capital. "He was one of the boys with his colleagues, and he played up incredibly to those in authority," recalls his former fellow-student Lev Yudovich, who now teaches Soviet studies at the U.S. Army Russian Institute in West Germany. "It was obvious he realized that Party political activity would get him further than his studies would."

As an out-of-town student, Gorbachev lived in a university dormitory on Stromynka Street, which under Peter the Great had been the barracks of the famous Preobrazhensky Regiment and to which extra floors had been added after the Revolution. About ten thousand students lived in that one dormitory. Each room was occupied by from seven to fifteen persons; on each floor, where several hundred students lived, there was one communal toilet with washbowls and one communal kitchen; in the courtyard there was one communal Russian bathhouse. The majority of the students were war veterans who had brought to the university a fondness for hard drinking acquired at the front. As Zdenek Mlynar recalls, they would drink on any occasion: a birthday or other family celebration, a national holiday, or simply because they had got hold of some money for vodka. The young Czech was at first amazed by the Russian norm: a full glass would be tossed off in one gulp, and only after that would the serious drinking begin.

Judging from the accounts of former students at the law school, Gorbachev at first took part in these bouts, but he usually drank only a little. This set him rather apart from his comrades. One of his roommates recalls that many of them even wondered if he wasn't an informer. That suspicion was based on the fact that, the day after each of several drunken conversations on political subjects, many of the young men were called into the dean's office for interrogation. One of his classmates recalls, "We all got drunk as lords and didn't remember a single thing the next day. He alone remained sober as a judge through the whole evening and remembered everything. Our suspicions grew stronger when we were sent out to serve internships. Some went here, some went there: to courtrooms, to the prosecutor's office, to prisons for regular criminals. But Misha chose the Lubyanka. That was in those very years when it was full of political prisoners, and the devil only knows what was done there! At that point, we stopped having doubts and tried to make sure he wasn't around when we had our parties. Otherwise it would have been too costly—and dangerous. And he himself, after he had joined the Party and made his connections at the Lubyanka, began to avoid us and stopped studying: he was beginning another career."

The bull sessions during those evenings were more than frank. One Russian saying is a kind of warning: "What the sober man has on his mind, the drunken one has on his tongue." Nor were those evening sessions among the students limited to talk. A photo of Stalin was of course hung in each room of the dormitory; Zdenek Mlynar remembers that when the vodka was put on the table, the photo was turned face to the wall. Glued to the back of it was an indecent picture from prerevolutionary times. "We closed the doors, but for several hours we opened our souls. And my neighbors, throwing off all hypocrisy, began in slurred speech to say something more intelligent."

It is important to note that a Soviet law school (and this was especially true in the Stalin era) is not like the law schools of American or European universities. Zdenek Mlynar, who later became one of the leaders of the Prague Spring but in the early fifties was a confirmed Stalinist, was a classmate of Mikhail Gorbachev's during the entire five years at the law school.

They lived in the same dormitories, went to the same seminars, and were well acquainted. Today, after expulsion from the Party and forced emigration from Czechoslovakia, he lives and works in Vienna. Here is what he has to say.

It was only later, at one of the stages in my emancipation from the vicious circle of the Stalinist faith, that I came to realize that the courses at the Moscow University Law School had nothing to do with the study of law and its role in human society. Soviet jurisprudence—not only in Stalin's time but still today—recognizes only one criterion of justice. 'Just' is what the State (more precisely, those governmental organs formally invested with the appropriate power) regards as justice. . . .

The law schools of Soviet universities do not teach the students to think in the categories of law. They train 'specialists in jurisprudence,' who must memorize what the regime prescribes in this or that case, what action to take in this or that circumstance, and what is prohibited. . . .

During the five years I spent in order to become a 'specialist in jurisprudence'—viz., a qualified (by Soviet standards) bureaucrat—I had an opportunity to find out what is permitted in various areas of Soviet life, and what is forbidden.

Unfortunately, the false jurisprudence was only a part—and perhaps the most innocent part—of what was learned by the students at the Moscow State University. Mlynar remembers the strictly Stalinist atmosphere of denunciations and brainwashing that prevailed in the law school. "In the hotbed atmosphere in which the young Party elite then attended college in Moscow, there arose a tendency to look for 'wreckers' in our own hotbed, and we could accuse only one another." For Soviet students, however, as compared with those like Mlynar from Eastern Europe, the field of activity was

considerably broader: they could also inform on their
teachers.

In the last stage of Stalin's State terror, law school
seemed the most promising route for the careerists;
those who entered it could count on getting a job with
the secret police, which was then headed by Stalin's
closest henchman, Lavrenty Beria. (And that's how the
law students were regarded officially: as young replacements.) Judging from the recollections of his
classmates, such was indeed the aspiration of young
Misha Gorbachev, the nineteen-year-old from the
Stavropol countryside, when he chose to go to law
school.

Then, in the last convulsions of the Stalin era, the
aged tyrant launched his campaign against "rootless
cosmopolites and Zionists." This anti-Semitic campaign
was planned on a very broad scale, that of the whole
empire, including its East European provinces. The
campaign against the "cosmopolites" was carried out
under the banner of the exposure (or, as was said then,
the "disclosure of pseudonyms") of Jews and their expulsion from the universities, from scientific societies,
from literature, and from art. This included those who
had inwardly completely suppressed their Jewishness
and stood for the full assimilation of Jews into Russian
culture. One such was Pasternak, who said, "I have
Jewish blood, but nothing is more alien to me than
Jewish nationalism. Perhaps only Great Russian chauvinism." Just such deniers of everything Jewish in themselves were most tragically traumatized by this State-
sponsored Great Russian chauvinism—which is what, in
essence, the "struggle against the cosmopolites" became.

During those hideous years, Pasternak wrote to his
cousin, Olga Freidenberg, in Leningrad, "What, then, in
the last analysis, am I worth if the obstacle of blood and
origins has remained insurmountable (the only thing
that had to be overcome) and can mean something, if
only in a nuance? And, really, what kind of a preten-

tious nonentity am I, if I end up with a mere coterie-popularity among Jewish intellectuals of the most hounded and unhappy kind?''

More important to us today, however, than the complaint of a confused genius who couldn't manage to distance himself from his own people is a reply from his sister, who was a specialist in ancient Greek poetry and a professor of classical languages at Leningrad University. Here is how she describes the situation in a letter to Pasternak.

Moral and mental pogroms have swept through all the cities of long-bodied Russia like a plague.

The people of the spiritual professions have lost their faith in logic and hope. The most recent campaign, in its entirety, had the aim of provoking concussion of the brain, vomiting, and dizziness. Those persons with Jewish names who pursue cultural activities are being morally lynched.

The setting of the pogroms carried out in our department is something worth seeing. Groups of students scurry about, and rummage through the writings of Jewish professors. They eavesdrop on private conversations, and whisper in corners. They go about their hurried business before our eyes.

Jews are no longer being given an education. They are not accepted either by universities or by graduate schools.

The university has been destroyed. All of the most important professors have been dismissed. The murder of the remnants of the intelligentsia goes on uninterruptedly. . . .

The campaign against the ''cosmopolites''—and, a bit later, against the ''Zionists''—at Moscow University was waged even more ruthlessly than at Leningrad University, since it was closely observed by its secret instigator, Stalin, and its invisible general, Mikhail Suslov, who in 1948 became the Party's top ideologue. The Kremlin demanded that all the university's purge operations be carried out by the teachers, graduate students, and undergraduates themselves. Although officially it was directed by aging historian Arkady Lavrovich Sidorov, the young people at the university brought a hunter's eagerness to the pogromlike campaign that was animated more by the enthusiasm of careerism than by fanatical belief. In general, the era of revolutionary fanaticism had been left far behind, somewhere in the early twenties. Now, vigorous participation in exposing the "cosmopolites," and "Zionists," "enemies of the people," and "agents of imperialism" guaranteed the exposers lucrative places in the sun of the Stalin epoch. For some reason, it was just at the time of its decline, a few years before Stalin's death, that his epoch seemed destined to last forever. Not only its hangmen but also its victims could see no light at the end of that terribly long, dark tunnel; they didn't believe it could *have* any end. As for the careerist students who exposed the old professors and their own comrades —people like Gorbachev—they had been born in the Stalin era and had never known any other. They were convinced it would last forever, that there would never again be different times. It was rather like the Germans' belief in the thousand-year Reich, if not even stronger. So that when people say today that Gorbachev belongs to the post-Stalin generation, they are forgetting that his youth coincided with the death agonies of the Stalin era and was lastingly seared by it; that it left an indelible mark on his soul.

Lev Yudovich recalls that in 1952, when Gorbachev joined the Party, the atmosphere at the university was "strictly Stalinist, some fellow-students disliking Gorbachev because he had actively supported Stalin's 'anticosmopolitan' (anti-Semitic) policies, and because he took a hard line during discussions of people's personal affairs." At Komsomol and later at Party meetings, that gung-ho Stalinist "exposed" professors and students of Jewish origin and demanded their expulsion from the university.

Historian Alexander Nekrich recalls:

The atmosphere at such meetings was very reminiscent of a bullring where a bullfight (or people-fight!) was going on. The scent of blood intensified the thirst for it. . . . The sight of the hapless, frightened, and penitent victims further stimulated those giving them a working-over. . . . In the law school the punishment was dealt out strictly on the principle of (Jewish) ethnicity. Academician I. Trainin, Professors A. A. Gertsenson, I. D. Levin, E. A. Fleishits, and M. L. Shifman were anathematized. . . . The campaign against the cosmopolites at Moscow University spelled their destruction not only morally but physically. . . . Moral destruction is a prelude to the physical kind.

Gorbachev also looked into the personnel files of other students and professors of non-Jewish origin and exposed as "enemies of the people" those who, from his point of view, were lacking in Stalinist orthodoxy. In that urban, university milieu, the young man from the country—or, as they liked to say then, "from the plow" —represented the common people and always managed to profit from his social and ethnic background, exposing the people's enemies in its name. One of his classmates recalls, "He was really the plague of the law school. We feared Misha like the devil himself. When he walked by, everybody stopped talking."

In early 1953, the witch hunt was renewed with even greater intensity when the infamous Doctors' Plot, allegedly to murder Kremlin leaders, was mounted. The majority of the doctors arrested were Jews.

Ready at hand was an appeal from prominent figures in culture and science who were of Jewish origin calling for the resettlement of the Jews from industrial centers to remote eastern regions to give them an opportunity to reform "by means of doing useful physical work and getting to know the land." Dmitri Chesnokov, a member of the Presidium of the CC, wrote a brochure explaining the necessity of deporting the Jews. A huge number of copies were printed, to be distributed when the signal was given.

With the deportation of the Jews imminent, barracks were hurriedly put up in Siberia, on the banks of the Yenisei, and in the Far East near the Chinese border. Boxcars were already waiting at railroad stations. It was reported to Stalin that, by the beginning of the trial of the "murderers in white smocks," only enough barracks for two hundred thousand persons would be finished, although there were more than two million Jews in the Soviet Union at the time. Stalin, it is said, merely grinned and, removing his extinguished pipe from his mouth, said, "So much the better!"

The great moment in the political career of the young Stalinist Mikhail Gorbachev was drawing near. Then something happened that has since been called "Jewish luck" but was in fact also good luck for tens of millions of non-Jews. For Gorbachev and those like him, however, it was bad luck, the collapse of all their hopes. On March 5, 1953, Joseph Vissarionovich Stalin died.

According to Gorbachev's classmates, Stalin's death was a tragic experience for him, and he sobbed at the funeral, where he was almost crushed to death by the crowd. (Hundreds *were* crushed to death.) Today it is hard to say whether it was real grief for the dead leader on the part of a naïve provincial or the despair of a young careerist whose ambitious plans had suddenly fallen into ruins.

Gorbachev's only consolation was his family life: he married a classmate, Raisa Titarenko, two years younger than he, who lived in the same dormitory. She, too, was from the provinces and had quickly started a political career. She had joined the Party in 1952 and became the Komsomol organizer in the philosophy department, where she specialized in Marxism-Leninism. (At the time, it was called Marxism-Leninism-Stalinism. But after Khrushchev's exposure of Stalin's crimes, the last part of that jawbreaking three-word phrase was dropped.)

Especially after the Gorbachevs' triumphal visit to England just before Christmas in 1984, the world press not only compared Raisa Maximovna Gorbacheva to such Western stars as Jacqueline Onassis but also called her a philosopher, or a person with an education in philosophy. She herself contributed to that image. While visiting the Shakespeare Theatre in Stratford-on-Avon, she was asked by reporters if she wanted to recite anything and she replied coquettishly, "I'm a doctor of philosophy, so anything I might say would be extremely boring."

But then, what could she have recited? In the philosophy department of Soviet universities, they don't read Plato, Aristotle, Spinoza, Kant, Schopenhauer, Nietzsche, or Kierkegaard; the three last-named are strictly banned in the USSR; they are not published and are scarcely mentioned. In the days when she was a student, what they chiefly read were the works of Stalin himself, plus the anonymously written (partly by Stalin) *History of the Party,* which actually bore no relation to the real history of the Party and was a falsification from beginning to end. In those days, even many works by Marx, Engels, and Lenin were banned; reading, say, Lenin's "testament," with its not-very-flattering comments on Stalin, was tantamount to treason. The young "scholars" didn't so much study the works of Stalin as learn them by rote so that later on they could pound them into the heads of succeeding generations. Thus, about the only thing that Raisa Gorbacheva could have quoted from memory at Stratford-on-Avon would have been something she had learned by heart from the works of Stalin when she was at the university. It is known that learning something in one's youth is like engraving it in granite, whereas what we learn in our old age is written on sand.

In 1954, a year after Stalin's death and a year before the Gorbachevs graduated, a new Moscow University building in the Lenin Hills was opened with great pomp. Compared with the former barracks, it must have seemed like one of the tsars' palaces. The Gorbachevs were given a small room of their own in the new dormitory, and their last year at the university must have been a happy time for them—in their private lives, but not in their political careers.

For when, after Stalin's death, a political "thaw" set in and the prisons disgorged those political prisoners who by a miracle had survived, and when Khrushchev adopted a policy of de-Stalinizing the empire, Gorbachev's former contacts were of no further help to him. Instead, they compromised him, as did his eagerness to expose "enemies of the people" at the law school. When he graduated from the university in 1955, he could not set himself up in Moscow. He had to go back to his own part of the country, along with the pregnant Raisa, and there start again from scratch. De-Stalinization had confused him and pulled the rug out from under his feet. For him, it was a real political catastrophe.

Down Home in Stavropol Again

The Stavropol Territory is a remote province of the empire to which the faint sounds of political and cultural events in Moscow are wafted—if they reach there at all—only after a long delay and with curious distortions. There, in the eyes of the locals, the Party's first secretary—the "boss" of the huge territory, who was governor-general, tsar, and God wrapped in one—stood far higher than the leaders of the whole country. Stavropol had its own elite and lower orders. Because of the paucity of opportunities there, the only way to make a career was through flattery, sycophancy, servant-master loyalty, or out-and-out bribery of superiors: all that old bag of tricks—servility toward rank, obsequiousness, and kickbacks—immortalized in classical Russian literature, for example, in Gogol's *The Inspector General*. After Moscow, with its intense, pulsating life, and especially after a year spent in the new university dormitory in the Lenin Hills, where the living conditions were splendid even by the standards of the capital, life in the steppes of the province must have been depressingly dreary to Mikhail and Raisa Gorbachev. Yet here they spent twenty-three straight years—a good third of a human lifetime.

Not only that, but Gorbachev had to begin at the very bottom of the provincial hierarchy, as assistant head of the propaganda section of the Komsomol's territorial committee. Never before had a graduate of Moscow University, with three years in the Party to his credit, had to take such a low position, one that usually served as a launching pad for provincial careerists who lacked not only a Moscow education but any higher education at all.

It was enough to drive a person to desperation, to make one "howl like a wolf," as Raisa Gorbacheva later said of their first years in Stavropol. The only thing that brightened their life then was the birth of their daughter, Irina, shortly after their arrival.

Gradually, however, the winds stirred up by the new political weather reached that remote province of the Soviet world, carrying not faint, distorted sounds but incontrovertible directives from above. In late February 1956, several months after the Gorbachevs had arrived in Stavropol, a delegation of local Communists returned from the Twentieth Party Congress, at which Khrushchev, before fifteen hundred delegates from all parts of the country, had made an off-the-record speech exposing Stalin's crimes. By March, his secret speech was already being discussed at closed Party conferences in Stavropol, which the Gorbachevs attended.

By that time, Mikhail had climbed one rung higher on the career ladder and was chairman of the Komsomol's city committee. Before 1960, his "upward mobility" was strictly mechanical: he simply moved into posts left vacant as those ahead of him moved up. All that was demanded of him was that he carry out orders implicitly and please his immediate superior, something that he plainly did well and that came in handy later in the Kremlin.

But in 1960, when Fyodor Kulakov was sent from Moscow to become leader of the Stavropol Territory, Gorbachev's career took a sharp turn upward. Kulakov was an outstanding maverick among Soviet politicians: independent, intelligent, he was a man of great intellectual scope, with his own ideas for sweeping economic and political reforms in Russia. He had turned up in Stavropol through a whim of Khrushchev's, who used the area as a kind of "Siberia" for members of the Kremlin elite who had fallen from grace. (Former Soviet premier Marshal Bulganin and Nikolai Belyayev, a former member of the CC Presidium, had also served there.) In Moscow, Kulakov had been a minister of the Russian Republic, and whatever the reason for his exile to Stavropol, it did not involve ideological disagreement with Khrushchev. Kulakov himself was of the Khrushchevian mold, not a bureaucrat but a worker, with a sharp sense of personal responsibility for the dire situation of agriculture; like Khrushchev, he recognized the urgent need for radical changes in its management. Hence, it is not surprising that, unlike other "exiles" in Stavropol, Kulakov did not regard his post in the south as the end of his career, and did not mope about it. To the contrary, he knew and liked the job very much, being a real agricultural expert with broad and varied experience as a professional agronomer, and tackled it vigorously, and even with inspiration. He knew how to take risks and loved doing it, always experimenting and trying to dismantle the obsolete, wasteful *kolkhoz* (collective) system—a brainchild of Stalin's. He achieved remarkable successes in all four years he served as first secretary of the Stavropol Territory. Under him, Stavropol shook with a fever of new projects, technical innovations, and fervor for work as it never had before Kulakov and never did after him.

At first, he did not take any special notice of Gorbachev among the young Stavropol apparatchiks. The modest and businesslike Gorbachev, who is not given to gross flattery, did not at first glance attract the notice of any of the influential men who later became his patrons, not of Kulakov, Suslov, Andropov, nor Gromyko. Not until two years after he had come to Stavropol did Kulakov pull Gorbachev out of the Komsomol swamp in which he had plainly got stuck (even in terms of age: the cutoff point for a Komsomol member is 26, and Gorbachev was 31), and brought him into the very center of economic restructuring. A year later, Kulakov rated Gorbachev's qualifications highly enough to put him in charge of the territory's entire agricultural system. What the energetic, hard-driving Kulakov liked in Gorbachev was his youth and his university education, which gave him an advantage over the uncultivated provincial apparatchiks. But most important was his readiness to become totally absorbed in new ideas—of which Kulakov had an abundance, and Gorbachev not a single one.

Gorbachev was the ideal student and follower of a teacher, mentor, and guide who took all responsibility and initiative on himself. By nature, Gorbachev was dutiful in fulfilling assignments. He was an obliging subordinate, although his eagerness to oblige was not obtrusive or blatant. He had mastered the art of pleasing superiors to the fullest, and in a perfectly straightforward way; when he was "other-directed" and hence relieved of responsibility and risk, he could display vigor and even, within safe limits, initiative.

According to a former reporter for *Stavropolskaya pravda,* Kulakov set up a demanding work schedule for the entire Stavropol Party apparatus. He himself got up at six every morning and promptly set off in his Volga, or in his Gazik (a kind of Jeep made at the Gorky Automobile Plant) if he had to use bad roads, on exhausting trips to "production sites." It might be to one of the sites where irrigation canals were being constructed in the dry steppe, which he himself had introduced on a broad scale, using the latest technology. Or it might be to fields of sugar beets. They were his agricultural hobby, and he got high yields by using select fertilizers, insecticides, and integrated mechanization.

Everywhere he went, he took Gorbachev with him, his right-hand man. After his make-work with the Komsomol, Gorbachev gave his all to his training period with Kulakov. Within the boundaries of Stavropol Territory, Kulakov liked to do what Khrushchev was fond of doing all over the country: make on-the-spot checks to see how his instructions were being carried out. Since he himself couldn't go everywhere, he would send Gorbachev to check up on the widely varied branches of agriculture. This fieldwork under his boss taught Gorbachev more than the Stavropol Agricultural Institute did, from which he needed a diploma for his career. (Like almost all the local Party officials, he didn't really take any courses there at all. The director of the institute formally presented a diploma to him at the offices of the Party city committee in 1967, after Gorbachev was already its secretary.)

With disdain for the strict, established principles of the "ideological management" of agriculture, Kulakov put part of the kolkhoz land at the disposal of special teams of six to twelve persons, either individuals or families, for a period of several years. Without any planning or instructions from central authority, they themselves were to work the land and sow and reap the crops; their pay would be based directly on the size of the harvest. These small production teams regarded the kolkhoz land they had rented as their private plots, and got as much as they could out of them. The harvest they reaped usually amounted to several times the kolkhoz norms, so their pay was several times higher than that of kolkhoz members. Most important, however—and this is the dream of any agricultural manager—the labor productivity of those experimental teams was in some periods six times higher than the kolkhoz indexes.

But further introduction of individual teams into the kolkhoz system was undermining its ideological foundations, which had been inviolable since the Stalin era. The team reform was essentially a compromise between kolkhoz management, which nipped initiative in the bud, and private farming Western-style, which ran counter to the very concept of socialist property and which in the USSR had long been banned. Ultimately, the team initiative would lead to a capitalist variant, show that the entire kolkhoz system was absolutely counterproductive, and cast it aside en route. So the new system provoked violent opposition, both from local Party bosses and from the agriculture commissars in Moscow, whose comfortable existence would have been rendered superfluous if it had been extended throughout the country. After the overthrow of Khrushchev, the team initiative was abandoned and the kolkhoz system took over again completely.

During Kulakov's administration of the Stavropol Territory, Gorbachev got the reputation as a specialist in agriculture that has followed him right up to his enthronement in the Kremlin. But he never has actually been a bona fide, highly skilled specialist in either agronomy or technology; it was his boss who was both those things. When Kulakov left Stavropol and went back to Moscow, where he became one of the pretenders to the Kremlin throne, he taught agronomy at a research institute there. And during his tenure in Stavropol, he had found the time to write some meaty, polemical articles, which were published in Moscow scientific journals. They were incomparably superior to the banal, superficial student's exercises in agricultural journalism that Gorbachev published from time to time in *Stavropolskaya pravda*.

Nonetheless, during that period of continuous reforms, under Kulakov's guidance Mikhail Gorbachev evolved in matters of ideology from an orthodox Stalinist (such as he had been at Moscow University) into a Khrushchev-type reformer (more accurately, a "little

Kulakov"). This would help him move up the career ladder during the unpredictable Khrushchev era, but Gorbachev could not have known that the energetic and tireless reformer and shaker of the system would be unexpectedly forced into retirement "owing to his advanced age and the state of his health," as the reason for Khrushchev's retirement was officially formulated.

Actually, the plot that led to Khrushchev's downfall (at the hands of his former allies) was hatched in the Stavropol Territory when Kulakov was first secretary there. It was instigated by Suslov, a former Stavropol Party boss, and the plotters included Brezhnev, Shelepin, and Marshal Malinovsky. In the fall of 1964, they were vacationing in the Teberda Preserve in the Stavropol Territory, and Kulakov was playing host to them. Although Kulakov was also a member of the plot, he was not an ideological opponent of Khrushchev; he supported the reformist spirit of the administration. But in time he was driven to desperation by some of Khrushchev's hare-brained schemes for economic revival, which Kulakov was required to put into practice, knowing that they were disastrous for the economy. Moreover, Khrushchev had deprived him of political prospects by shipping him off to Stavropol. So his guests from the Kremlin placed complete trust in Kulakov, since he had been among the victims of Khrushchev's high-handedness, and they took his support of the plot for granted. With Khrushchev gone, Kulakov might be able to get back to Moscow, the center of power.

That is precisely what happened. Only two months after Khrushchev's fall, Kulakov was called from his Stavropol fiefdom to the capital to work as the CC secretary in charge of Soviet agriculture. And so he was able to undo the damage done to his government career four years earlier, and renew his reformist activities, in which he achieved great success.

Now Mikhail Gorbachev had an influential sponsor in Moscow. Kulakov had not forgotten his capable assistant from Stavropol, and he met with him at congresses of agricultural managers in the capital and tried in every way to help him rise to the summit of power in the province.

It seems worthwhile to mention here a curious, if perhaps trivial, phenomenon of psychology. Individuals built on the grand scale—independent thinkers with high ambitions who on their own, through their own efforts and abilities, have traveled that road fraught with hardships *per aspera ad astra*—like to keep on tap a compliant, imitative student who blindly, and sometimes even with some inspiration, copies their own achievements. On the other hand, they cannot bear authoritative, ''contrary'' people who march to the sound of a different drummer. Before Kulakov came to Stavropol, Gorbachev's progress in his career was steady but slow, like the tortoise in the race with the hare. After Kulakov had taken his political revenge, however, and had been shifted almost overnight to the very nucleus of Kremlin power, the Politburo, Gorbachev moved swiftly upward, and by 1970 he had realized what was then his greatest ambition. He became first secretary of the Stavropol Territory, the sole master of a huge domain about the size of Austria, or of Denmark and Switzerland taken together, whose economic importance was considerable.

Once he was in his new position and accountable only to Moscow, however, Gorbachev's performance was perfunctory. In no way did he distinguish himself from the many other Party apparatchiks on the provincial committee level, scattered throughout the whole nation. Unlike Kulakov, who had felt fenced in in Stavropol, Gorbachev found his own part of the country spacious enough for his purposes. And the fact that his ego had been dealt a crushing blow in Moscow during his student years had made him something of a Muscophobe. Given his notion of what a career was, he had reached the peak, and his chief strategic concern was to hang on to what he had. He probably never even dreamed of getting to Moscow, because he had no good reason to do so. He was one of 181 provincial Party bosses—not the worst of them, but not the best by a long shot, in terms of economic indices. On those regular occasions when he supplied bottles of top-quality *narzan** from the Stavropol mineral springs for the conference tables in the Kremlin, it could not have entered his mind that he himself would one day be sitting there enjoying equal rights with the others around the table, and would ultimately preside over them.

But hanging on to his position was not all that simple. In 1972, during his tenure as first secretary, the harvest in the Stavropol Territory was catastrophically poor. He reported to Moscow that an early drought was the cause, but in fact it was due to his lack of efficiency and his bureaucratic complacency. After all, there had been dry summers when Kulakov was first secretary, but he had managed to find a way out of such crises, for instance by expanding the system of irrigation canals, a project later abandoned by Gorbachev because he lacked the requisite skill and enterprise. During the harvest season, Gorbachev never traveled to the distant and rugged parts of the territory as Kulakov (accompanied by him) had done and as Khrushchev and even Brezhnev, during the first phase of his rule, had done all over the USSR. It is not surprising that in 1975 there was yet another agricultural disaster in the Stavropol Territory.

In the days of Khrushchev Gorbachev would have been "kicked out" for poor economic indexes, bureaucratic complacency, and a failure to assume personal responsibilities. But by the mid-seventies, Brezhnev had given up on any reforms and written agriculture off, having decided that spending hundreds of millions of dollars on imported grain was more useful and less troublesome than investing the same, or perhaps even greater, sums in developing agriculture in Russia. Gor-

---

*A beverage famous for its curative powers since ancient times— named after the magical potion of the *narti*, a tribe of great warriors in the Caucasus.

bachev held his position of provincial Party boss during years of bureaucratic stability, when the Kremlin was placing much lower demands on satraps like him. Also, the Stavropol Territory ranked high in production of winter wheat, meat, vegetable oils, and fine wool for the State. There is so much fertile soil there that even the Soviet kolkhoz system could not do much damage; even in the years of the worst harvests, Stavropol Territory did fairly well in supplying the nation with agricultural products.

The local folklore about Gorbachev that we have gathered reveals traits of his character that vary from a rational approach to problems to arrogance, as a high official, toward rank-and-file Party members. (Nonmembers did not have access to him.)

Alcoholics who are connoisseurs remember him with gratitude and sentimental fondness and have even named a special kind of very tasty vodka after him, *gorbachevka*. It is distilled from a wild grass, is produced in limited quantities for the elite, and cannot be purchased even with foreign currency. The "magical" grass that gives *gorbachevka* its marvelous taste grows on a hill in the Stavropol Territory. When some zealous Stavropol officials wanted to demolish that hill because it impeded road construction, Gorbachev intervened and thereby immortalized his name among "professional" alcoholics. Now that he has become the Kremlin ruler and is imitating Andropov, he has declared another of the Kremlin's wars on alcoholism. If he wins it, which is hardly likely, his reputation among worshippers of "the green serpent" (Russian for "pink elephant") will be badly shaken.

Another example of his approach to problems dates from the early seventies, when he had just become first secretary of the Stavropol Territory. Harvests of cereal crops were falling off sharply; the cause was ascertained by local ecologists to be runoff of rainwater from the surface of the rich black topsoil. The land had been plowed deeply and there was plenty of rainfall, but the crops were nonetheless failing because not enough moisture was reaching their roots. The soil had been too densely compressed by the heavy-duty Kirovets tractors working the fields; under their weight, the porosity of the soil had been destroyed to the point that water could not penetrate it. Gorbachev, who had been given a few reprimands for the downturn in harvests, seized upon the recommendation of the ecologists that light tractors be manufactured. His proposal was supported by his sponsor in the Kremlin, Kulakov.

But both men ran into unexpected opposition from the military establishment because to manufacture light-weight tractors would mean, in practice, separating tractor production from tank production. Since World War II, all the biggest tractor plants in the USSR—the Chelyabinsk, the Kharkov, and the Kirov—have essentially been camouflaged tank plants, and only certain of their shops manufacture tractors. Many tank parts and even entire tank assemblies are used in tractors; this makes it possible to cut the production costs of tanks considerably and to use the agricultural budget as a cover for military outlays amounting to billions of rubles—a clever and impeccable kind of camouflage.

The dispute between the military men and the agronomers raged for two years; Gorbachev, supported by Kulakov, staunchly defended the interests of agriculture. Finally, the military made a mild concession: they would stick to the production of heavy-duty tractors, but they would "shoe" them with especially wide-tread tires or pneumatic caterpillar tracks. Unfortunately, the greater part of the rubber suitable for such caterpillar tracks went into military production; no more than a third of the quantity required was left for "civilian" caterpillar treads.

It is hard to say with any certainty whether that was a victory for Gorbachev or a defeat, but in any case he gained fame as a defender of the natural environment, and from 1970 through 1974 he even served on a committee charged with protecting the environment in one

of the houses (the Council of the Soviet) of the Soviet
parliament.

The following are two incidents of a very different
kind, showing Gorbachev as a consummate bureaucrat.

Judging by the reminiscences of Stavropolites, Gorbachev, despite his youth and university education,
"ruled" his province as a real old school Party vice-re-
gent, without the slightest trace of the "Party democratism" towards subordinates that would be attributed to
him when he became the country's general secretary.
Apparently Stalin remained his political ideal and the
model to emulate. Thus following Stalin's example,
Gorbachev, out of vanity and a desire to show up the
local Party stars, acquired a permanent bodyguard.
This was not at all customary for local secretaries in
those days. We have reliable information that Medunov, Party secretary of Krasnodar Territory, Gorbachev's neighbor and rival, had no permanent bodyguard
—at least, he did not appear in public with one. Moreover, Gorbachev's bodyguard was also his double.

Nikolai Shatalov, a former tractor mechanic in the
Stavropol Territory, remembers how in June 1972, after
he had been fired for criticizing his own boss at a Party
meeting, he was summoned to the headquarters of the
Stavropol Territory Committee of the Party on Lenin
Square, a five-minute walk from the old-style private
dwelling in which the Gorbachevs lived. When Shatalov's papers had been checked twice, he was taken by
the committee's instructor to a huge office on the second floor. The door was flung open and two men entered. They both had athletic builds and were the same
height. And they wore identical clothes—gray suits,
white shirts, identical ties, and identical shoes: black
and gleaming.

"I'm Gorbachev," said one of the "twins." "And
you're Shatalov?" He pronounced it "sha-ta-lov,"
semi-interrogatorily, dragging out the syllables one by
one. "The Party has always welcomed self-criticism
at all times and in all things, but you've gone too far.

You should be thrown out of the Party and sent to the devil. . . ."

Fortunately for Shatalov, this episode took place in the relatively liberal days of détente, so he was not sent to prison or a psychiatric hospital, and is today living in the United States.

The second story was told to us by a distant relative at whose home we stayed while on a summer vacation. Since he is still living in the USSR, we have called him by the initials V.K.

V.K., an old Party member and a war veteran, was living in Kislovodsk, a resort town in the Stavropol Territory well known for its mineral springs and mud baths. He had a kidney ailment but could not gain admission to a local sanitarium with facilities for hydrotherapy, although a doctor had prescribed precisely that kind of treatment for him. All the best sanitariums in Kislovodsk were accessible only to the Moscow elite. In response to requests and complaints by V.K., the Kislovodsk authorities said ironically, "Just look at what the man's asking for!" After that, he put on all his war medals and decorations and went to Stavropol to seek justice from the first secretary.

At first, Gorbachev flatly refused to see him, and he was told by the receptionist that he had no choice but to go back to Kislovodsk. But V.K. threatened that if Gorbachev persisted in his refusal, he, V.K., would go and lodge a complaint in Moscow, where in fact he had an influential acquaintance, a general under whom he had fought in the war. The threat produced the desired effect, and Gorbachev agreed to see him.

When V.K. entered Gorbachev's office, he saw before him a man who was relatively young but who, as V.K. put it, was already "a typical, thick-skinned bureaucrat." Gorbachev did not help him get a pass to the kind of sanitarium he needed, or to any other. All he did was explain to him, frankly and patiently, that there were some sanitariums for ordinary people and others for very high officials and other distinguished persons, and that it was correct to draw such a line between them. Stressing the point, he tossed in his favorite dictum: "There can be no two opinions about that!" Moreover, he acknowledged—just how sincerely is hard to judge— that he himself could not get a pass to any of the sanitariums where both the medical treatment and the service were of the very best quality, because, in his own words, he hadn't yet "grown to that stature." As the indignant V.K. was leaving, Gorbachev advised him to ease up on his quest for justice; "otherwise, something unpleasant may happen. We here in Stavropol will disregard those medals on your chest."

"An overfed hog" was what our relative repeatedly and angrily, perhaps too crudely, called Gorbachev. Just about that time Gorbachev had started putting on weight, whereas people recall that when he was Kulakov's right-hand man he had been lean and energetic.

The world-famous mineral springs of the Stavropol area, more than the fertile land and the rare kind of grass from which the remarkable vodka is distilled, were the chief source of political dividends for the local partocrats and above all for the Party boss of the territory.

The Krasnye Kamni sanitarium in Kislovodsk—for the cream of the elite—was hidden behind huge brown boulders of limestone spar. In one of them, a gigantic bas relief of Lenin had been carved. All along the outside walls were acacias and rose bushes; in the middle was a flight of concrete steps leading to the gray stone administration building, three floors of which were pleasingly asymmetrical. On each side of the flight of steps was a plaster statue, one of a boy and one of a girl; each held in its outstretched palm a lamp in the form of a frosted-glass sphere. Those statues linger in the memory of people who have visited the grounds, as we did on one occasion. One arresting detail: the girl is nude, but the younger man wears plaster swimming trunks—a gesture toward the moral purity of Soviet tastes.

We have noted earlier that the turning point in Mikhail Gorbachev's fortunes was associated with the visit of Andropov and his wife every autumn in the seventies to the Krasnye Kamni sanitarium. Both were diabetics, and the KGB chief had a kidney ailment that, as he used to say, the narzan mineral water "took away" for a whole year.

At Andropov's request, Gorbachev sometimes brought his wife with him to the Andropov cottage on the sanitarium grounds. She would accompany Andropov's ailing spouse on walks through the park, taking paths whose patterns were especially designed for therapeutic purposes—the so-called *turrenkur*.

By that time, the mid-seventies, Raisa Gorbacheva had completed a graduate correspondence course in Marxism-Leninism from Moscow University. As the rules for graduate study required, she had gone there several times a year, each time staying at the university dormitory in the Lenin Hills where she and her husband had spent their "honeymoon" year. While there, she no doubt compared, enviously and even bitterly, the sleepy, provincial way of life in Stavropol with the colorful, vibrant life of the capital, so full of opportunities to shop. According to one woman who knew her quite well in Stavropol, she would stand in line for hours on end in a store called The Children's World to buy scarce articles that were unavailable in Stavropol.

She liked most of all to travel to the capital with her husband for Party congresses, in order, in her own words, to "stock up on things." For token prices, delegates could get goods unavailable even to Muscovites: Persian lamb caps, mink coats, tins of caviar, and imported stereo sets. That same Stavropol acquaintance remembers that Madame Gorbacheva dressed and "ran the household" not in the Stavropol way but the Moscow way. She was very fond of expensive imported things, although Gorbachev himself adhered to the Party's democratic code of avoiding "conspicuous consumption," and in a rare exception to his usual indulgence of his wife's whims, flatly refused to wear the bright-colored sweaters and jackets that Raisa Maximovna wangled for him in Moscow.

For a Party boss to have as his wife a "Party lady" strong on Marxism-Leninism is not really all that satisfying an arrangement, since such a marriage could be lacking in warmth and intimacy. As one high Moscow official put it (he was not alluding to Gorbachev in particular), such a family atmosphere, necessarily permeated by ideological vigilance, "is like a life-long Party conference."

Raisa Gorbacheva, though, was not at all orthodox in matters of ideology. She had joined the Party when she was young and had later specialized in Marxism-Leninism, because, according to her calculations, those things would give her the best chance for a successful career. After getting her candidate's (roughly, Ph.D.) degree, she taught Party history at the Stavropol Teachers College, right up until Gorbachev's sudden elevation to Moscow in 1978. By that time, their daughter, Irina, had graduated from the Stavropol Medical College and had gotten married at a relatively early age to a classmate. As one Stavropolian remembers, the Gorbachev family life stayed on an even keel. The wife played the major role in the matter of Irina's rearing and exerted pressure on the husband, who by nature tended to be content to rest on his laurels and had no great designs for the future.

But Yuri Andropov's autumnal visits to Kislovodsk provided a rare, almost unique opportunity. Urged on by his wife, Gorbachev took advantage of that situation for career purposes. One might even say that the ambitious chief of the secret police awakened dormant ambition in Gorbachev, or, more precisely, ambition that had "gone to sleep" after the fiasco of his student days at Moscow University in the very first phase of his political career.

Being distrustful and suspicious (no doubt professionally suspicious, but naturally so as well), Andropov never entered into any relations with people beyond the on-the-job kind between a superior and his subordinates. He maintained a correct and polite but strictly businesslike and exigent attitude toward all his many associates in the KGB, never permitting familiarity or chats on private matters—family topics, for example. None of them dared show an interest in his wife's health or in how his children, Irina and Igor, were doing in their college work. Unlike Khrushchev and Brezhnev, each of whom brought to Moscow every single friend he had made in his childhood and youth, Andropov did not have enough friends to bring whom he could trust implicitly. Hence the great difficulties he encountered when, having become leader of the country, he had to choose reliable cadres: he simply didn't have enough of "his own people." When it came to showing his feelings and reactions, Andropov was an undemonstrative person, "with all his buttons fastened up," even rather prim and almost shy.

Gorbachev was perhaps the only person outside Andropov's family circle who quite often socialized with him. He was able to observe him not in official or on-the-job circumstances but when he was on vacation, in an atmosphere of leisure and relaxation, when the KGB chief was in pajamas and bedroom slippers instead of his usual dark suit and dark tie, chatting with his wife. When Gorbachev scheduled his own vacations in Kislovodsk to coincide with the Andropovs' visits there, whether by chance or deliberately, he established with the inscrutable top cop relations that were even more trusting and friendly, almost familial. For Andropov, his landsman and younger comrade Gorbachev was the only man of his kind with whom he felt completely at ease and could be frank—within certain limits, naturally. And Gorbachev knew how to please a superior, especially such a high-ranking one from the Kremlin: he never thrust himself upon Andropov but was polite and attentive, accompanying him on visits to the Teberda Forest Preserve and to places Andropov remembered from childhood.

In the late summer of 1977, when both the Andropovs

and the Gorbachevs were in Kislovodsk, the latter, in order to avoid too much familiarity, stayed not at Krasnye Kamni but nearby, in a less luxurious sanitarium. This must have pleased the chief of police especially, since right then he was launching his crusade against graft, waste, and the *embourgeoisement* of the Party elite. As the reader will recall, Andropov began that crusade with Brezhnev's protégé Sergei Medunov, who reigned in the neighboring Krasnodar Territory; using a compromising dossier that Gorbachev had helped him to put together. That joint endeavor brought the two natives of Stavropol, the older man and the younger, even closer together.

As for graft and malfeasance by officials, Gorbachev himself was not always "clean as a hound's tooth," owing in part to his wife's irrepressible appetite for the luxurious way of life *à la mode de Moscou*. We have learned from two reliable sources, one Stavropolian and the other Georgian, about a run-in that occurred between Gorbachev and another Andropov protégé. Namely, his neighbor to the south, police General Eduard Shevardnadze. With Andropov's help, under the guise of that same crusade against corruption, Shevardnadze had managed to topple a man who had been a good acquaintance of Brezhnev's since the days of the war from his post as first Party secretary of Georgia, and to replace him. Here it is important to note that neither Gorbachev nor Shevardnadze knew that they both had the same highly placed sponsor in Moscow. It was against the rules of the vigilant KGB chief to encourage the formation of alliances or factions, even among the people most devoted to him. He was the puppeteer and they were the puppets; all the strings ran directly to him, with no connections among themselves.

It must be said here that in Georgia, as in Azerbaijan, there *was* nepotism, bribery, graft in general, the "buying" of high positions (including ministerial portfolios), and a black-market industry successfully competing with State industry, all of which had reached a fantastic scope. As a matter of fact, both these Caucasian republics had de facto separated themselves from the economically centralized, socialized empire and become covertly capitalistic. General Shevardnadze, who like General Aliyev was a man of indomitable energy and remarkable inventiveness, had directed the campaign to restore his republic to the socialist camp under the overall command of the Kremlin with unvarying success.

His purges stirred up resistance in the most diverse segments of Georgian society, since the laxness of the State had been the very thing that fostered the growth of private initiative; and the underground capitalism had filled in the gaps left by the centralized economy. One might say, in summing up what Shevardnadze wrought in his native republic, that he had turned out to be a quack dentist: instead of a decayed tooth, he pulled a perfectly healthy one—because it had grown in the wrong place and illegally.

Frightened by the scope of Shevardnadze's campaign and by the harshness of the penalties being dealt out, a few small private Georgian firms making nickel and silver rings, chains, bracelets, and other costume jewelry, along with some shish-kebob restaurants and fruit-juice outfits, shifted their operations to the neighboring Stavropol Territory, where under the guise of State enterprise they successfully went on developing the "second economy." Shevardnadze, however, with the help of the KGB's central administration and its Stavropol branch, caught the Georgian fugitives at the scene of the crime. All that remained was to demand that the Stavropol Prosecutor's Office extradite the criminals to Georgia. Shevardnadze considered it as good as done and so was flabbergasted and outraged when he got a flat refusal from Gorbachev. No matter what legal arguments Shevardnadze used, confident that in the hierarchy he outranked the Party boss of a backwoods province, Gorbachev obstinately defended the newly arrived underground capitalists.

During that period (1975–77), we made several trips to Georgia on assignment from *Izvestia* and the magazines *Druzhba narodov (Friendship among Peoples), Iskusstvo kino (Film Art)*, and *Aurora*. The conflict between Shevardnadze and Gorbachev was then the talk of the town in Tbilisi, and local Party leaders whom we talked to chalked Gorbachev's unaccountable obstinacy up to the fact that he, like the majority of provincial bosses, was taking bribes; the private entrepreneurs of Georgia were famous for their largesse in that respect. Among the many jokes on the subject is one about a Georgian who, on a trip to Moscow, went to Lenin's Mausoleum. But instead of going inside to look at the mummified body of the *vozhd* in its glass coffin, he offered the sentinel a million rubles and told him, "Take him out!"

One of the people we talked to in Georgia related to us how Shevardnadze, in the presence of some of his aides (including the person we had talked to), made a phone call from Tbilisi to Gorbachev in Stavropol and threatened that if he kept on putting up a fight, he, Shevardnadze, would complain to Moscow. In an unusually indignant voice, he told Gorbachev straight from the shoulder: "Listen. I'm setting things straight in my own house, and you're interfering. Just think it over: Who are you, and who am I? Get out of my way right now! I'm warning you for the last time—I've got the backing of somebody who's big in Moscow. You'll make a couple thousand out of this, and you'll lose everything."

However, to Shevardnadze's great stupefaction and humiliation, Gorbachev prevailed in his defense of the Georgian capitalists he was sheltering. The first secretary of a mere territory, whom Shevardnadze considered as ranking lower than the Party leader (himself) of one of the fifteen national republics in the USSR, turned out to be more powerful and to have more influence than he, even when a direct violation of the law was involved. Gorbachev's "big man" in Moscow proved to be more potent than Shevardnadze's, although in both cases the "big man" was the same person: KGB Chairman Yuri Andropov. It was simply that, of the two protégés, Andropov gave a higher rating to Gorbachev, as a Russian, a landsman, and the only real confidant he had, who moreover, unlike the Georgian Shevardnadze, had an immediate prospect of making it into the Kremlin.

Such was the way in which the two Andropov protégés got to know each other well—in a collision. Yet this did not prevent Shevardnadze, after Gorbachev became general secretary, from making it into the Kremlin, where despite his total lack of diplomatic experience he replaced the aged Andrei Gromyko as foreign minister—the first police general ever to hold that post. Such "objectivity" on the part of Mikhail Gorbachev in the selection of his Kremlin cadres can only be ascribed to the fact that it is not by him personally, and not out of his people, that the top Kremlin elite has been put together but by strict adherence to Andropov's deathbed instructions, and out of *his* people. The only concession that was made to Gorbachev personally was to rid him of his chief rival; in the summer of 1985, Grigori Romanov was expelled from the Kremlin, and that was the end of his political life.

It would be a very great error—"a snare and a delusion"—to attribute, by way of hindsight, to Kremlin practices the principles of any code of ethics, even the code of Party morality. Ethics does not serve as a motive force in Soviet political careers. Sergei Medunov, the former Party satrap of the Krasnodar Territory, is now in prison; his former neighbor, Mikhail Gorbachev, is the Kremlin leader. But if the circumstances had developed in a slightly different way, the opposite could have happened. Medunov had no fewer points in his favor than Gorbachev, and Gorbachev was no less guilty of malfeasance than Medunov. The same applies to the Romanov-Gorbachev pair. In the Kremlin, political screening takes place by a process of random natural selection, to borrow the language of biology. And even if, nonetheless, one can detect certain patterns of regularity in it, they have nothing to do with Western political standards.

The Baby of the Politburo

The political rise of Mikhail Gorbachev was a by-product of the Great Kremlin Games, which in 1978 entered their decisive phase and brought into play some gambits that until shortly before had been banned since the Stalin era. Gorbachev made it to Moscow because fate had decreed a duel between his two chief Moscow patrons, Fyodor Kulakov and Yuri Andropov.

Kulakov was unquestionably the most capable and principled man in the Brezhnev Kremlin. Petr Egides, a former kolkhoz chairman, has the following to say about a conversation he had with Kulakov long before the latter was taken into the Kremlin. He asked Kulakov, "Do you think that if you were in the Politburo you could turn things around?"

Kulakov gave a wry laugh. "Oh, that's almost impossible."

"What is?"

"To get into the Politburo. The degree of probability is infinitely small."

"And as for turning things around?"

"Once you're there, the degree of probability that you might turn things around is somewhat higher, but the risk is infinitely greater. Still, in that case I would give it my best, although of course not right from the start. . . . Otherwise, life would lose all meaning. When a person is granted an infinitely rare destiny, he must show himself worthy of it. Not to try to make maximum use of it is a crime."

As we have seen, the impossible happened: Fyodor Kulakov was called to Moscow, where he became a CC secretary and a member of the Politburo. And every one of our Moscow acquaintances who, in the second half of the seventies, was in one way or another associated with the Kremlin establishment, talked about Kulakov as a man who was bold and stuck to his principles. One of them even called him "a second Khrushchev," but then added, "though without his recklessness." By that time, Brezhnev was already seriously ill; although his "predeath" agony was prolonged for another few years, in 1976–77 there were persistent rumors of intentions to send him into honorable retirement and replace him with Kulakov. Another, later version had it that Brezhnev was to be kept on in his nominal post as chairman of the USSR Supreme Soviet's Presidium and the position of general secretary given to Kulakov. Both pieces of scuttlebutt had a very real basis. Thus, an acquaintance of ours attended a lecture for Party members only, given at a research institute in Moscow by an instructor from the CC, who officially confirmed the second version and added that it was "only a matter of time."

However, on the night of July 16, 1978, Fyodor Kulakov died. The cause of his death, according to TASS, the official Soviet news agency, was "acute cardiac insufficiency and sudden cardiac arrest." At the same time, the KGB floated a rumor that after a failed attempt to seize power, Kulakov, the son of a peasant, had opened his veins in the manner of the Roman patricians. But people who knew Kulakov well rejected both these reports, declaring that he was healthy and as strong as an ox, had never had even a headache or a slight cold, and was an incurable optimist. The detailed but confused report on the cause of his death by a special medical commission, signed by seven medical luminaries headed up by the top Kremlin physician, academician Evgeny Chazov, boomeranged. Suspicions grew even stronger when Brezhnev, Kosygin, Suslov, and Chernenko failed to show up at the funeral of their colleague. Moscow was rife with sinister rumors that a murderer who coveted the post of the gravely ill Brezhnev for himself had got into the Kremlin.

Petr Egides, expressing not so much his own opinion as that prevalent at the time, says, "And suddenly Kulakov died, just like that. He died, vanished. And yet he was bursting with health, a sturdy man. And I, of course, have always been haunted by the feeling that he didn't sit well with the Kremlin mafia, and that he was 'vaporized' in the way Orwell described."

Did Kulakov actually attempt to carry out a palace coup while the top Kremlin leaders were vacationing on the concrete-covered beaches of the Black Sea, and did Andropov, as chief of the secret police, nip it in the bud? Or did Andropov simply eliminate a dangerous rival who could have come into power without a coup, and then use the story of a coup to explain to his Party supervisors the harsh measures he had taken to ward it off? Alas, we don't know, and it is hardly likely that anyone will know in the near future.

At Kulakov's funeral in Red Square on July 20, 1978, from which the top Kremlin leaders conspicuously absented themselves, the oration was delivered by Gorbachev. It was his first speech from the rostrum atop Lenin's Mausoleum, and it passed unnoticed. But his next speech, made seven years later at the funeral of another of his predecessors, Konstantin Chernenko, would be heeded by the entire world.

Kulakov's death was even more helpful to the Stavropol Party boss than his sponsorship had been. It left vacant the only post for which Gorbachev could qualify, by virtue of his agronomer's diploma (a fictive one, to be sure) and his agricultural experience (far from successful, be it noted): namely, the post of CC secretary for agriculture. Gorbachev, however, did not immediately succeed Kulakov. What stopped him? Why did he have to wait a whole six months before being shifted to Moscow?

First, because of his relatively tender years. That is of course the kind of shortcoming that disappears with the passage of time. But since the Politburo-Secretariat had gradually become an old folks' home, the average age of the members being sixty-seven at the time, there was no place there for the forty-seven-year-old Mikhail Gorbachev.

Second, Moscow was fairly crawling with specialists in agriculture who moreover had put down political roots in the capital and could count on the sponsorship of their Kremlin overlords, whereas Gorbachev had lost one of his patrons. Among the leading candidates for the vacant post were the minister of agriculture, who had the poetic last name of Mesyats (meaning "a moon on the wane"), and the head of the CC's agriculture department, Vladimir Karlov. Both were more suitable in terms of age for the post of CC secretary, and either would have been less conspicuous in the Kremlin's "Council of Elders": one was three years older than Gorbachev, and the other a whole seventeen years older.

Finally, there was one more obstacle in Gorbachev's path to Moscow—perhaps the main one. It would have been rather awkward to take yet another man from the Stavropol Territory into the Kremlin right on the heels of the first, considering that the USSR comprises thirty-five union and autonomous republics, eighteen national provinces and districts, and 128 territories and regions. In order to avoid criticism for geographic discrimination and administrative cronyism, the Kremlin tries to follow the rule of turnabout-is-fair-play. The one exception was made for the Ukrainian city of Dnepropetrovsk, where Brezhnev had spent "the best years of his life." When he became general secretary, he made it his main source for supplying the Kremlin with cadres. In Moscow, people joked that you're not born happy, you're born in Dnepropetrovsk.

Yet it ultimately proved to be a good thing for Gorbachev that he had been born in the Stavropol Territory and had spent a total of forty-two years there. His candidacy, proposed by Andropov, was supported by Mikhail Suslov, the guardian of Party morals and behind-the-scenes kingmaker, who in 1964 had directed the plot against Khrushchev and had divided up Khrushchev's power between Brezhnev (as general secretary) and Kosygin (as premier). Suslov may have remembered Gorbachev from Gorbachev's Moscow University days, when he had taken part in the ideological purge that Suslov covertly directed on orders from Stalin. And he had certainly known Gorbachev in the Stavropol Territory, which he himself had presided over in the days when it had been called the Voroshilov Territory in honor of Stalin's crony, and which he still visited now and then. Suslov liked Gorbachev's businesslike modesty, especially in contrast to the lordly ways of the "boys from Dnepropetrovsk." Suslov was annoyed by their dominance in their closeness to the ailing Brezhnev. He was especially irked that one of them, Andrei Kirilenko, was obviously gunning for his own place, trying to gradually nudge him out of the action and deprive him of his power as a kingmaker. Events were slipping out of the grasp of that lean ascetic, who was used to controlling them from the Kremlin cloakrooms. Personally, Suslov was not ambitious, even setting great store by his own modesty and unpretentious tastes. Although he was the tallest member of the Politburo, he made no fuss when photojournalists, acting on orders from above, shortened him slightly in official photos so that he would be on the same level as the rest of the Kremlin elite. When Svetlana Alliluyeva asked Suslov to let her and her dying Indian husband go to India, he was genuinely indignant. "What makes you feel such a strong attraction for a foreign country? My whole family and children," he declared, with great pride in their patriotism, "never go abroad and don't even want to. It's not interesting!" Stalin's daughter walked out of his office, "carrying away with me," she later wrote, "a frightful impression of that fossilized Communist living in the past who now runs the Party."

Even Brezhnev, at the height of his power, was rather afraid of his former mentor. If there was anyone in the Kremlin who could be called the last confirmed Bolshevik, it was Suslov, because his ideological orthodoxy,

Party purism, and austerity in daily life were totally genuine. It was precisely because of his dedication to Party principles that he never laid claim to high posts in the State but preferred to remain in the background, as befits a kingmaker. The role suited him perfectly, and he had hoped it would be a lifetime one. In short, Suslov had personal reasons for supporting Gorbachev's candidacy. If Gorbachev didn't get the post as CC secretary for agriculture, it would go to one of the Dnepropetrovsk mafiosi.

But the leading role in getting Gorbachev transferred to Moscow and in furthering his career there was played by Andropov. It was the KGB chief who, two months after Kulakov's death, introduced Gorbachev to Brezhnev. On the evening of September 19, 1978, a special train carrying General Secretary of the Party Leonid Brezhnev, accompanied by Konstantin Chernenko, to Baku, the capital of Azerbaijan, made an unscheduled stop at the resort town of Mineralnye Vodi on the bank of the Kuma River in Stavropol Territory. On the platform of the station they were met by KGB Chairman Yuri Andropov, who was at the time taking his regular course of treatments in nearby Kislovodsk, and Mikhail Gorbachev, Party boss of the Stavropol Territory. Here, during that brief stopover, Gorbachev's destiny was decided: by the end of the year he was in Moscow. And since that meeting was briefly mentioned in the Soviet press, it must be regarded as an historic event. On September 19, 1978, four men, each of them an official leader of the Soviet Union when his turn came, met on the platform of a little railroad station in the Caucasus: Brezhnev, Andropov, Chernenko, and Gorbachev.

There were three reasons why Gorbachev managed to get into the tightly closed circle of the Kremlin oligarchy, which rarely numbered as many as a dozen men. (By the time of his accession in 1985, the Moscow-based members of the Politburo had dwindled to eight.) He was brought in to replace Kulakov after the latter's tragic death; as a reward for his services in the Medunov affair; and to spite Grigori Romanov, whom Andropov saw (as he had Kulakov) as a rival in his struggle for power, but against whom he used a more "humane" means of elimination (the scandal at his daughter's wedding banquet).

Perhaps this is a good place to note one trait typical of Gorbachev's career up to this point: he has always been the youngest among his colleagues. At Moscow University he was one of the youngest students; most of his classmates had served in the armed forces during the war. He was the youngest Communist among the students, having joined the Party in his second year there, when he was only twenty-one. He was the youngest member of the university's Party committee, which was largely made up of gray-haired professors and administrators plus only a few students, and those, unlike Gorbachev, were upperclassmen. He was one of the youngest members of the Stavropol Territorial Committee, and when he became its first secretary in 1970 he was the youngest of the almost 200 provincial bosses in the USSR. (Incidentally, he was sixteen years younger than his neighbor and virulent enemy, Medunov.) A year later he skipped the "prerequisite course" as a candidate member of the CC and became a full member at the Twenty-fourth Congress of the Communist Party; at forty, he was the youngest person with full membership. In 1978, when he was called to Moscow and named one of the ten CC secretaries, he was again the youngest of his colleagues. Likewise, a year later, he became the youngest candidate member of the Politburo, a whole thirty years younger than its oldest "candidate," Vasily Kuznetsov, the Soviet vice-president.

Finally, in 1980 when he became a full Politburo member, he could have been taken as the son of any one of his colleagues but Romanov. He was twenty years below their average age and thirty-two years younger than the oldest member, Arvid Pelshe, a Latvian.

It is interesting to compare him with Chernenko, his predecessor as general secretary. Both were elected to the CC in the same year, 1971. From that time on, Cher-

nenko kept a lead over him of only two years: he became a CC secretary in 1976, a candidate member of the
Politburo in 1977, and a full member in 1978. But what
a difference between them, not only in age but in experience, or more precisely, in the experience of one and
the age of the other. What a great gap! Gorbachev was
born in the same year that Chernenko joined the Party.

Mikhail Gorbachev remained the youngest Politburo
and CC member right up until his inauguration as the
seventh Soviet leader and remains so today.

All that, however, is no reflection of his personal
merits. His youthfulness is relative; he has benefited
from the background against which his career has unfolded. And when the background was the depressingly
geriatric Kremlin, Gorbachev—who by 1985 already
had a five-year-old granddaughter—did in fact look like
the "baby" or "Benjamin" of the Politburo, as he was
wittily, if sentimentally, called by the English newspapers during his visit to Great Britain. (All that time
the world press, unfriendly toward Gorbachev's rival,
Romanov, was continuing to call him, pejoratively, an
"enfant terrible.") His constant presence among persons of an older age group cannot but have had an effect on his relations with them. For his part, it was a
matter of diligence, courtesy, and helpfulness—although without gross flattery and groveling—toward his
elders.

Sometimes these old men actually needed physical
help. Although they were surrounded by doctors and
aides, as American presidents are by bodyguards, Gorbachev came to their assistance at difficult moments.
Such a thing happened, for instance, on November 27,
1984, at a session of the nominal Soviet parliament.
Gorbachev propped up the falling Chernenko, and he
did it unobtrusively, with the tact that is typical of him,
in a way that was not humiliating either for himself or
for the badly ailing Soviet leader. The gesture came
across as a very human one, with even a touch of the
sentimental.

His older comrades in the Politburo repaid his agreeableness with unlimited trust, protection, and patronage. Some came from Brezhnev, much more from Andropov, and even some from Chernenko, who did not long remain in the post of top leader, which rightfully belonged to Gorbachev—if there is any such thing as a right behind the crenelated walls of the Kremlin. The whole system by which older men sponsored younger ones made Gorbachev the pet not only of his mentors but of fate itself, despite certain ups and downs in his political career. What others had taken by storm came to him gratis.

But there is another side to the coin. Persons like Gorbachev never belong to their own generation; they're already old when they're still young. Being not very independent and usually rather weak-willed, such a person does not make a political career himself: it is made for him by a series of patrons. They pass him on from hand to hand, like a baton in a relay race, and he ultimately becomes a puppet manipulated by others. But sooner or later the time comes when the mentors and sponsors have all died and their protégé is left to his own devices, personally responsible for everything. For persons who have always yielded to others, that is the most difficult time.

If one is to be precise instead of reaching for striking images, Gorbachev should not be called the "baby" of the Politburo but its pupil, a graduate of the Kremlin school in the phase of its decline and political degeneration. Moreover, he was that school's prize student, and he graduated with honors. But his political diploma was just as fictitious as his two earlier ones: from the Law School of Moscow University and the Agriculture Department of the Stavropol Institute. The Kremlin school teaches you not how to govern a country but how to pretend that you're governing it. It teaches not initiative but obedience, not originality but stereotypes, not sincerity but hypocrisy. It was just those Kremlin lessons that Gorbachev learned so diligently. Nor could it have been otherwise: "social existence determines consciousness," and this is all the more true of a stagnant social existence such as that in the Kremlin, one so refractory to new ideas. Incidentally, that is one of the reasons why, after Chernenko's death, the Kremlin's septuagenarians, with their pathological fear of the "young ones," agreed to name Mikhail Gorbachev as their presiding officer, as one who would be "first among equals." In six years they had had time to get used to him; he suited them, and it seemed to them that, by his very nature, he belonged to their generation.

After all, he had been called to Moscow not really as a replacement for, but rather as an opposite of, his former sponsor, that tragic figure Kulakov, who was obstructing Andropov's path to power and at the same time disturbing the peace and quiet of the complacent and cynical gerontocrats of the Politburo. Gorbachev gave no one cause for alarm. He is a typical product of the Party-bureaucratic system, an even-tempered careerist, a moderate and accommodating colleague. He easily adapted to each period he lived through, taking on its coloration like a chameleon. He has been a man for all seasons: a Stalinist in the age of Stalin, a Khrushchevite in the age of Khrushchev, a Brezhnevite in the age of Brezhnev, an Andropovite in the age of Andropov.

He has kept on his mask as an Andropovite for the Gorbachev era, and at the very outset of that period he made good use of it, because of his last patron's growing posthumous popularity among the people.

At the Kremlin school, with its monotonous classes and boring teachers, the brief fifteen-month course taught by Andropov made the strongest impression on Gorbachev, although it might seem that it was the least suitable to his rather complacent temperament. But here again, what mattered was not the student but the teacher, and this one was trying to awaken an entire empire from a lethargic sleep. His classes were not wasted on Gorbachev, especially since they no doubt reminded him of the Stalinist lessons he had learned while still a student at Moscow University.

9. Stalin's Shadow Over the Kremlin

> Have you ever heard of our former commandant? No? Well, it isn't saying too much if I tell you that the organization of the whole penal colony is his work. We who were his friends knew even before he died that the organization of the colony was so perfect that his successor, even with a thousand new schemes in his head, would find it impossible to alter anything, at least for many years to come.
>
> —FRANZ KAFKA,
> In the Penal Colony

LET US RETURN to the long-drawn-out battle between Romanov and Gorbachev that preceded the latter's victory. In order to win, it was necessary that each of them change his tactics and behavior, psychological and political. Romanov had to become more polite, tolerant, and patient, if only toward his comrades on the Central

Committee, whom he frightened with his too-manifest rudeness. Gorbachev, on the contrary, had to become sterner and harsher, taking into account the aesthetic conception of a ruler that was entertained by both the populace and the Kremlin elite. Still more important, however, was a change in political tactics. For Romanov, it was essential to moderate his Stalinist zeal so as not to frighten the Kremlin oldsters, all of whom had vivid memories of the colossal Party purges of their youth. (Although it was those purges that had brought them power, they had been frightened, because the Stalinist broom swept indiscriminately, and survival in those days had been simply a matter of having a lucky lottery ticket.) Gorbachev, by contrast, had to appear to be more of a Stalinist than he had seemed up to then.

It was easier for Gorbachev to accomplish his task than for Romanov to accomplish his. First, Gorbachev was eight years younger than his rival, which meant he was more adaptable. Second, he was more amenable by nature and used to obeying and yielding his will to others, to his wife or to one of his successive mentors, it didn't make any difference. Third (and this is perhaps the most important), in order to harden his position in the direction of Stalinism, it sufficed to become again what he was in his years as a student in Moscow when he was a devout Stalinist. (Nor could it have been otherwise: at the time that was the only way to make a career.) His present ideological flabbiness was the result of the great political shocks he had lived through: Stalin's death and his exposure by Khrushchev, the overthrow of Khrushchev, and Andropov's secret-police coup. He was not born a man for all seasons: he was made that way by changing circumstances.

Romanov was his opposite. Both his character and his political ideas had long ago crystallized into a single, immovable block of ice. He was unable to modify either his habits or his Stalinist outlook in the slightest—not even for the sake of gaining supporters in the Kremlin. All he could do was look on as his enterprising rival quickly mastered his own weapon, Stalinist terminology.

In that respect, Gorbachev, like a clever and assiduous epigone, even surpassed all the other Kremlinites, including Romanov. Several anachronisms from the lexicon of the Stalin era that he retrieved and put back into political circulation especially surprised his compatriots, although for Westerners, an explanation may be necessary in order to understand them and judge the importance of their revival.

As early as the spring of 1984, Gorbachev issued a restricted directive that served as the basis for his official announcement several months later, at an all-union Party conference in Moscow, of a return to the so-called Stakhanovite movement:

> Next year we will observe the fiftieth anniversary of the Stakhanovite movement, which played an outstanding role in the history of socialist construction. To carry on the tradition of the Stakhanovites means to channel the energy and initiative of the masses into the solution of key problems of stepping up the efficiency of the economy.

Actually, if the Stakhanovite movement played any outstanding role at all, it was only in Stalinist propaganda, or in the personal fate of Alexei Stakhanov himself. Put into service as a battering ram in the Soviet economy, the Stakhanovite movement was one of the hugest of those programs of deception with which the Stalinist system regularly conned both itself and naïve foreigners like George Bernard Shaw, who regarded himself as "a knowing old bird" and an old skeptic.

The Stakhanovite movement was launched on the night of August 31, 1935, when Alexei Stakhanov, a miner in the Donets coalfield in the Ukraine, hewed out 102 tons of coal in one shift, more than fourteen times the norm. Three weeks later, he set a new record: 227 tons of coal, or thirty-two times the norm. Stakhanov's "feat of labor" was taken up by other miners, and soon the Stakhanovite movement spread through all branches of industry and agriculture. Stalin approved of the workers' "spontaneous initiative," and norms were sharply raised throughout the country.

Just at that time, GBS came to Russia, and a meeting with one of the famous Stakhanovites was set up for him. The Irish playwright and wit was somewhat taken aback not only by the Stakhanovite movement but by the Stakhanovites' popularity among the blue-collar workers. In Great Britain, workers broke the record-breakers' heads with brickbats for such things as over-fulfilling norms. But Shaw's doubts were short-lived. He ended up convincing himself—and, upon his return to London, his readers—that in Russia everything was topsy-turvy. For example, in prisons, Shaw fondly supposed, the main job of the administrators was "to persuade prisoners who had served out their term to leave the prison."

The story of Stakhanov himself—his rise to eminence in the Stalin era, and his fall in the Khrushchev period —is curious. After he had set his "records," he was sent to Moscow to study, was "elected" a deputy to the First Congress of the USSR Supreme Soviet, and was given a position in the Ministry of the Coal Industry. But in 1957, during de-Stalinization, Khrushchev sent Stakhanov back to the Donets mines for his part in one of Stalin's biggest swindles. For it had been discovered that a whole shift of gnomes, Stakhanov's fellow miners, had worked alongside him. It was the only thing, short of divine intervention, that could have explained his fantastic records.

And now, half a century later, Gorbachev is resurrecting from well-deserved oblivion that sleight-of-hand man Stakhanov, along with the movement named in his honor, and is proposing to carry on the tradition of the Stakhanovites. The tradition of self-deceit?

Another anachronism Gorbachev has retrieved from that same era is the one about the flea. He persistently shows off with it among close associates, and he has even used it to mystify the British minister of trade, Paul Channon. During his tour of England, he told Channon, "If you send us a flea, we'll put horseshoes on it."

But symbols employed on both sides of the Iron Curtain do not always coincide in meaning. For instance, in the time of our childhood, in the fifties, none of us, no matter how curious we were, had ever heard the names of the Wright brothers, George Stevenson, or Guglielmo Marconi. But we knew very well that the first airplane was built by Zhukovsky, the first steam locomotive by the Cherepanov brothers, that the radio was invented by Alexander Popov, and that in general all great discoveries in science and technology had been made by Russians. In the Stalin era, the main character in a story by Russian writer Nikolai Leskov, a master gunsmith nicknamed Lefty, was added to the long list of Russian "natural" geniuses as a real person.

The story tells of how, during Alexander I's travels in England (more than a century and a half before Mikhail Gorbachev's visit there), the tsar was presented with a mechanical steel flea. But it was so tiny that one had to use a microscope to see it dance the quadrille. The next tsar, Nicholas I, was not a Westernizer like his older brother but a Russophile. And when he discovered the English flea among the things he had inherited, he gave orders that something should be thought up "so that the English not outdo the Russians." So the steel flea was sent to the old city of Tula, a center of the gunsmiths' trade. There Russian master craftsmen, headed by Lefty, outdid the English and shoed the flea—although then the flea could no longer dance. But that part of the story was usually omitted, leaving the impression that the Russians had outdone the English. In the Stalin era, a crude, chauvinistic image was fashioned from Leskov's charming and tragic story (at its end, the talented Lefty dies, a victim of alcoholism, bureaucratic indifference, and police brutality). And it was that image that

Gorbachev remembered during his tour of Great Britain. Gorbachev's remark to the British minister of trade was intended to mean, However amazing the achievements you have shown us, if necessary we can outshine you. In other words, send us a flea and we'll put tiny horseshoes on it. But since Channon was ignorant of Russian folklore, he might have assumed that the future Soviet leader was talking about a real flea and was proposing that the English send it alive to the Kremlin, where he and the other Politburo members would shoe it and send it back to London.

But it is hard to tell exactly what prompted Gorbachev to take up again these anachronisms from the Stalin era. Was it only a tactical dodge in the power struggle, intended to show the old-fashioned members of the Politburo that he was not too modern a man? Or is Gorbachev's real approach to the country's economic and political problems reflected in those two images? Or again, was that a nostalgic reminiscence of his youth and at the same time, in a certain sense, an indication of what the future will bring, since the empire's cautious policy of re-Stalinization was making its tomorrows look more and more like its yesterdays? Most likely, it was all of these together which produced the reappearance of such archaisms as the "Stakhanovite movement" and the shoeing of an English steel flea by a Russian *muzhik*.

When he became head of the empire, Gorbachev began to speak out plainly, revealing his earlier concealed political ideals. It had taken more than three decades for the man who had been a Moscow University student in Stalin's sunset years to set about putting into practice the lessons he had studied then.

Two months after his inauguration, at a grand meeting celebrating the fortieth anniversary of the victory over Nazi Germany, Gorbachev, early in his speech, named the man to whom, in his opinion, the country was most indebted for the victory. In fact, that man bore direct responsibility for the military catastrophe and for millions of the lives lost in the first months of the war—not to mention his other crimes—yet Gorbachev evoked his memory solemnly, listing the posts he had held and giving his name in full: Joseph Vissarionovich Stalin. It was a political manifesto, one the audience had been expecting and one that they welcomed with applause so thunderous that for a time Gorbachev could not go on speaking; he tried, but the applause drowned him out.

Gorbachev was the first Soviet leader since the tyrant's death to utter Stalin's name in such tones of reverence.* Khrushchev had never mentioned him except in negative terms. (On a few occasions, to be sure, he had backtracked and mumbled a compliment to the tyrant, but only out of tactical considerations, as everyone understood at the time.) Brezhnev named him only once, among other military commanders; yet even then he was interrupted by unexpected applause. Neither Andropov nor Chernenko uttered his name in public a single time. That Gorbachev named him so positively astounded many people. He was politically rehabilitating Stalin and at the same time enlisting his posthumous support. Yet not even he had been able to gauge accurately the response he would get. "It is not given to us to predict what response our words will provoke," wrote the great Russian poet Tyutchev. Gorbachev had predicted it, but had slightly underestimated it. His favorable evocation of Stalin's name stirred rapture and gratitude in the hearts of many of his compatriots.

Paradoxically, although Stalin belongs to the past, many people in Russia feel that the Russian future should also belong to him. The Kremlin is taking very practical steps in that direction with resolve that grows with each passing year. The steady progress of the coun-

---

*In that same speech, Gorbachev scored another first. He was the first post-Stalinist leader to revive Stalin's chauvinist terminology and ethnically single out "the great Russian people" as "an inspiring example" for all the other pooples of the USSR. Fortthis, too, he was loudly applauded.

try's re-Stalinization in all aspects of its domestic and foreign policy is at once the most ominous and the most intriguing thing happening right now in the Soviet empire.

The beginning of that process can be dated at October 1964, when Khrushchev was overthrown by a palace coup and the putschists, his former comrades in arms, categorically disowned the so-called "thaw," Khrushchev's liberal policy of de-Stalinization. The coup itself, viewed historically, may be seen as the empire's way of reacting to Khrushchev's anti-Stalinist policy. And the surprising thing is not that the plotters managed to overthrow Khrushchev so easily but that he wasn't overthrown even sooner. (In 1957, an earlier faction of Stalinists, headed by Molotov, did manage to vote him out of office at a Politburo session, but Marshal Zhukov restored him to the Party throne.) What really staggers one, however, is that Molotov, the most steadfast, unbending, and devout of Stalinists, was at the age of ninety-four restored to Party membership, twenty-two years after he had been expelled, and that it happened in the summer of 1984, while the power struggle in the Kremlin was raging. About Molotov's restoration, there was no disagreement.

After the anti-Khrushchev plot, the process of re-Stalinization required one more palace coup to pick up speed and become the Kremlin's official policy: the secret-police revolution begun by Andropov, continued quietly by his followers behind the back of Chernenko, and revived with new vigor under Mikhail Gorbachev.

Consider by way of contrast to these events the words of Roy Medvedev, an interview given by him to *Newsweek*:

It is a critical step in the transfer of power in the nation and the party to a new generation of leaders, whose careers began after the death of Stalin and whose political pasts are free of ties to the black times of Stalinism.

Every single word in the above is a falsehood. As we have seen in the example of Gorbachev, his political career began while Stalin was still alive, and he is not free of ties to the Stalin era. The only difference between the new generation of Kremlin leaders and the earlier one is that the former did not go through the tragic experience of that era and has neither any personal fear of Stalinism nor the instinct of self-preservation that restrained Brezhnev, Chernenko, and even Andropov. That is why Gorbachev has proven more outspoken than his predecessors and has opened his era with a kind of oath of loyalty to Stalin.

Why and how does that dead autocrat still hold sway over Russian hearts, Russian hopes, and the Russian imagination? Who was Stalin for the Russians, and what has he become for them?

The census (the only appropriate word) of the population he annihilated in the USSR numbers at least twenty million. Just as many people were killed in World War II, and the failure to prepare for that war was entirely Stalin's fault. That epidemic of murders spread to all segments of the population, but some of the people, the country's natural elite, were slaughtered almost to a man: the prerevolutionary officials, the merchants, the clergy, the technical and cultural intelligentsia, the peasants who owned their own farms (kulaks), and that same Leninist Party to which Stalin formally belonged and that he annihilated with special, personal savagery.

That holocaust of the people of his own country has no parallel in history, and can therefore in no way be explained as due to communist ideology. There was no such holocaust under Lenin; and there would not have been one if any of his other compeers—Trotsky, Bukharin, Rykov, Zinoviev, Kamenev, or Pyatakov—any but Stalin—had come to power. That Stalin was a dangerous man was recognized by Lenin; in his "testament" he wrote that he would prefer to see anyone but Stalin in the post of general secretary. Trotsky was not equal to the situation because of his intellectual vacilla-

tion; he abandoned Lenin at a time that was fateful for
the country and yielded the power to Stalin without a
struggle. In a postscriptum he provided some brilliant
definitions of his enemies: "counterrevolutionaries,"
"gravediggers of the Revolution," "epigones of Bolshevism," "apparatchik-usurpers," "unlawful heirs of
October," "Thermidoreans," "a faction of national
socialist clerks," and others no less sarcastic and accurate. George Bernard Shaw, who called Trotsky "the
king of pamphleteers," was right, as was Lenin, who regarded him as a great revolutionary and organizer. The
trouble was that, unlike Lenin, the number-two man in
the Party was a negligible quantity as a politician.
Lenin's premature death and Trotsky's political worth-
lessness cleared the way to power for Stalin.

So much for the subjective causes of the Stalinist
Thermidor; but there are objective, historical ones as
well.

In all of Russian history there was no man so beloved
as Stalin. His funeral was attended by millions, and the
people's grief was sincere—as is today's nostalgia for
the days of Stalin.

Stalin, a Georgian, met native Russian needs better
than either of his chief political rivals, Lenin and Trotsky, one of whom he vanquished after he was dead, the
other while he was still alive. It took millions of human
lives to transform the internationalist ideas of Marxism
into the great-power ideas of national socialism à la
Stalin. "In Russia, Bolshevism has disappeared, and its
place has been taken by a Slavic type of Fascism,"
Mussolini wrote in 1939. The titanic phenomenon of
Stalin was begotten by Russian history, as Russia's
response to the Western ideas that Marxism certainly
represented (regardless of our attitude toward it), in
order to counteract them in a monstrous way and utterly
destroy them on Russian soil. In the person of Stalin,
the Revolution (to use de Tocqueville's expression) completed the evolution of the old regime, adapting it to
modern times and destroying the original revolutionary
idea. As a result, the Russian empire was not only re-

stored after its temporary decline during the Revolution but expanded at the expense of remnants of empires that had collapsed (Austro-Hungary, the Third Reich, Japan). General de Gaulle wrote of Stalin, "Face to face with Russia, Stalin sees it as more mysterious, more powerful, and more stable than all theories and regimes."

It is not surprising that Stalin's favorite hero was not Lenin or Marx, the official Soviet saints, but another Russian despot, Ivan the Terrible (more accurately, the Dread), whose headsmen didn't have time to sharpen their axes but lopped off heads with dull axe-blades. On orders from Stalin, Sergei Eisenstein made a film about the monster-tsar. But the film struck Stalin as not laudatory enough, and it was banned; the great director fell out of favor.

The way Ivan the Terrible figured in the historical memory of later generations provides a special key to understanding the present rehabilitation of Stalin by the Russian people, who are the bearers of the imperial idea. A century and a half ago, writer and historian Nikolai Karamzin wrote of him:

> The fame of Ivan outlived his notoriety in *the memory of the commoners*. The moans had ceased to be heard, the victims' bodies had rotted away, and the old legends were eclipsed by new ones; but Ivan's name glittered in his Code of Law and was a reminder that three Mongolian realms had been acquired. The proofs that hideous deeds had been done lay in the archives, but for centuries the populace saw Kazan, Astrakhan, and Siberia as living monuments to the conquering tsar. It revered in him the famous hero through whose labors the might of our State had been built up, and our civil society formed. The name of the *Tormentor,* given him by his contemporaries, was rejected or forgotten; and Ivan has since been called, because of those dark rumors about his cruelty, merely the Dread . . . —rather in praise than in reproach.

A like metamorphosis is now taking place with Stalin: he is being transformed from an historical fact into an historical myth. People remember not the victims of the gigantic purges of the thirties but the industrial victories of those times; not the bitter defeats during the first months of the war but the triumphant fanfare at its end. They have fond memories of the iron discipline and exemplary order that the dictator established in the country and that it now lacks. With overweening national pride, they recall the empire's greatness in Stalin's day as compared with its present decline.

The more symptoms of decline are displayed by the world's last empire—from ferment along its borders (as in Poland) to the lag behind the West in military technology, from the Russians' demographic degeneration (especially because of the epidemic of alcoholism) to their economic crisis, which has already become permanent—the more the imperial people fix their nostalgic gaze on the time of its growth and flourishing, and the higher the stakes put on Stalinism by those at the helm. In Russia, Stalinism is seen by both rulers and ruled as a medicine (strong, to be sure, but indispensable, very effective, and quick-acting) for the economic depression, the sloth of the populace and the bureaucrats' graft, for rising infant mortality, for the threat from the Poles, the Chinese, the Jews, the Americans, and from themselves.

That is why the process of re-Stalinization cannot be regarded as voluntarism, as an arbitrary act, on the part of the new pleiad of Kremlin leaders headed by Mikhail Gorbachev. Quite to the contrary, that process is the result of pressure from below, where Stalin's underground fame—after he had been officially ostracized by Khrushchev—sprang up like mushrooms after a rain and almost reached the level of his cult during his lifetime. People had got their idea of what a leader should be from the "ideal" image of Stalin, with his majestic remoteness, his monumental autocracy, and his strictly rationed contacts with the populace, through edicts, orders, and biannual appearances (on the two great national holidays) atop Lenin's Mausoleum. Stalin's snow-white generalissimo's dress uniform with gold embroidery and his snow-white service cap with gold laurels around the band were deeply imprinted in the grateful memory of the common people and were preserved there as a model of imperial impressiveness, which recently has made for such flare-ups of nostalgia. It became a fad among taxi drivers to hang his photograph on their sun-shields; on trains making long runs you could buy homemade calendars, modeled after those depicting a saint's life, with pictures from Stalin's life on each page. Nationalist writers made him the hero of their works; retired marshals depicted him fondly in their memoirs; and one poet even published verses calling for the erection, in downtown Moscow, of a Pantheon to which the remains of the disgraced *vozhd* would be transferred:

> Let whoever enters this place know
> How he depends on Russia in all things.
> Among us is the Generalissimo
> With his great marshals, statelier than kings.

Even Solzhenitsyn, who had anathematized Stalin in his weighty tomes *Gulag Archipelago,* several years later wrote an appeal to the Kremlin leaders calling upon them to follow the patriotic example of Stalin.

Stalinism is viewed as a panacea for all those imperial ailments that the imperial people notice every day, both around them and in themselves. If by a miracle the tyrant were to come back to life and, like Napoleon at Fréjus, to land on the shore of the Black Sea, the Baltic, or even the Bering Strait, he would be assured of a triumphal progress through the length and breadth of the land. The dwellers of the Kremlin would carry him on their shoulders, and his stay there would not be limited to one hundred days.

The spontaneous popular rehabilitation of Stalin has

run far ahead of the official one. For example, *The War,* a novel by Ivan Stadnyuk that vindicates Stalin, was discredited by *Pravda* when it first appeared ten years ago, but it has now won the State Prize. Among ordinary readers it became a best-seller immediately upon publication. This spontaneous rehabilitation is not to be seen as only a political phenomenon; it must also be seen from a Freudian and Kafkan point of view, as a consequence of mourning for a dead father who filled his children with fright but at the same time with love, since he relieved them of personal responsibility and left them politically infantile, with a kind of Peter Pan complex. For the Russians, with their atheistic mentality, Stalin was a man-god,* a superman; after his death the people everywhere manifested the orphan's syndrome. Stalin appeared as the Great Leader, the Father of Peoples, and the Savior of His Country in novels, on TV, in movies, and in verse:

> For all Russia, in May and October,†
> He was what we checked our feelings by,
> As he stood there, holding one hand upward,
> Equal to the Thunderer on high.

Stalin's posthumous glory is quite different from what waits beyond the grave for the tyrants of most other nations—either curses and mockery or, in the best case, oblivion. Stalin, though, is like Sleeping Beauty, and Russian princes of all political bloodlines, from the top Kremlin leader (Gorbachev) to the Kremlin's chief oppositionist (Solzhenitsyn), are hastening toward him from all directions to awaken him to political life again.

There is of course a difference between odes to the despot in verse and prose, and an official dithyramb to him by the present Soviet leader. Is this not an instance

---

*As opposed to the god-man, Christ (Dostoyevsky's antithesis).
†This refers to Stalin's appearance, twice a year, on Lenin's Mausoleum during the national holidays of May Day and the anniversary of the Bolshevik Revolution.

of how grass-roots democracy functions in a totalitarian state, when it is not the people who follow the leaders but the leaders who follow the people?

Let us give due credit to Brezhnev. Although he came to power through a plot by Stalinists against an anti-Stalinist, all during the first half of his rule he resisted the extremism coming from below. Combating right-wing opposition in the Kremlin, he expelled the most dedicated Stalinists—Polyansky, Shelepin, Shelest, Tolstikov, Pavlov, and others—from the Politburo and its closest affiliates. Brezhnev succeeded in this series of countercoups only because, while vanquishing his opponents personally, he yielded to them ideologically, making compromises with the trend they represented. (The trappings of power were dearer to him than political ideas were.) Thus the country's re-Stalinization proceeded slowly, but steadily and irreversibly. It picked up in tempo during Brezhnev's last years, when he was only the nominal leader and by reason of old age and poor health could no longer oppose the rehabilitation either of Stalin personally or of Stalinism as the political ideal of a broad range of the Russian people, from pensioners and dissidents to the top officers of the KGB and the armed forces, to many Politburo members.

In a relatively short period of time, beginning in the late seventies, the neo-Stalinists have managed to restore the "tried and true" methods of governing the empire. Dissent has been rooted out; the secret-police system has been strengthened and tightened up; and the emigration leak has been plugged, since it is impossible to maintain constant pressure in two communicating vessels when one of them is leaking. Propagandists have stepped up anti-Semitism, spy mania, and xenophobia, and all contacts between Soviet citizens and foreigners have been cut off—declared illegal and criminally punishable.

Most important, however, for the first time since Stalin's death but strictly in conformity with his recipe, the empire has annexed a country that had been on the other side of the Iron Curtain: Afghanistan. Hence that military-political action should not be put in the same category with the Soviet incursion into Hungary in 1956 or into Czechoslovakia twelve years later: those were strictly police actions to restore order in nations already subject to the empire.

Afghanistan had never been such a subject nation, although in the late twenties Stalin made the first attempt to annex it to Russia. The following account of that first Afghan adventure comes from one of the chief implementers of Stalin's schemes for Asia, Georgi Agabekov, former chief of the eastern sector of Soviet intelligence and its resident in the Near East. (He later fled to the West, where he was murdered by Soviet agents.)

On orders from Stalin, eight hundred crack Red Army troops, wearing Afghan uniforms and armed with many machine guns and some field pieces, were concentrated on the bank of the Amu-Darya near the town of Termez, ready to cross the river to the Afghan side. Barges, other flat-bottomed boats, and motorboats from all up and down the river were brought there for the crossing. Early in the morning, an escadrille of six planes carrying bombs and armed with machine guns took off from the Termez Airport. Gaining altitude, they headed for the other bank of the river where the Afghan border post of Patta-Gissar was located. It was guarded by some fifty Afghan soldiers. Hearing the drone of the motors and figuring the planes were on their way to Kabul, many of the soldiers dashed out of their quarters to look at them. But after circling the border post twice, the planes swooped down and strafed the doomed men. Bombs that were dropped on the post building killed the remaining soldiers, burying them under the debris. The whole operation took only a few minutes.

Meanwhile, the Red Army troops calmly embarked in the barges and other boats and crossed to the Afghan bank. At another border post, Sia-Gert, a garrison of one hundred, armed only with sabres, was entirely wiped out by machine-gun fire. The next morning, the Soviet troops stormed the town of Mazar-i-Sharif. But, forgetting that they were supposed to be posing as Afghans, they went into the attack shouting the traditional Russian "Hurrah!" After the town was captured, its streets resounded with obscene Russian curses. On every hand lay the disfigured corpses of the town's defenders, numbering about three thousand. The next day, still in Afghan uniform, the Red Army troops continued their advance, shooting and killing everyone in their path so no one would know of the Soviet invasion. Stalin had hoped to put together a pro-Soviet Afghan government, using local extremists, but when this failed, he ordered the Soviet troops to withdraw. On their way back through Mazar-i-Sharif, they seized all the astrakhan, or lambs' wool, from the town's warehouses, as a kind of reimbursement for expenses incurred by the Kremlin in organizing that expedition.

We have told about this little-known Afghan venture of Stalin's in order to stress the continuity of the Kremlin's expansionist policies. Making adjustments for modern technology, it was a smaller-scale version of the well-known account of the invasion by eighty-five thousand Red Army troops of Afghanistan just before Christmas 1979. A half-century after Stalin's failure in Afghanistan in the late twenties, his heirs took revenge for it.

The big questions are these: Who in the Kremlin is carrying on that imperial Russian tradition? Who made the decision to send Red Army troops into Afghanistan? Who is now waging the war there, which is growing fiercer with each passing year? And, finally, why do the Russians need Afghanistan? After all, not even Stalin had initiated that Central Asian policy; he merely continued it. For example, in the late nineteenth century, Russia seized the independent states of Khiva, Bukhara, and Khokand, which were neighbors of Afghanistan. Marxism, which many Western commentators hold responsible for the invasion of Afghanistan, was then known in Russia to only a few dozen people at the most. But traditional Russian geographic imperialism was already several centuries old by that time. Here, strange as it may seem, the instinct of self-preservation comes into play: an empire must either expand or collapse. A static, steady state is impossible for an empire: it expands in order not to collapse. And an empire that is old, weakening, or in a state of permanent crisis is even more aggressive, just as a weak enemy is sometimes more dangerous than a strong one.

However, in addition to the traditional imperial appetite, undiminished with age, when the Russians seized Afghanistan in late December 1979 they were also prompted this time by strategic motives, although the strategy in question was obsolete in our century of ICBMs. But the Russians are not the Japanese: it is not just their technology that is lagging behind but their mentality—politically by entire centuries and militarily by several decades at a minimum.

We here mention some far-fetched explanations for the rape of Afghanistan merely in order to promptly discard them as implausible or too remote to be taken into account in a current analysis. Among them are the Soviet Union's desire to gain access to the Indian Ocean and the warm-water ports of the southern seas, or to seize the oil fields of the Arabian Peninsula, which are so vitally important to the West.

Some fringe benefits accrued from the occupation of Afghanistan. The military have acquired a splendid proving ground they can use under combat conditions, and not in war games during military exercises. The Red Army, which had grown stale during four decades of peace, has now been given a huge shakeup and brought into a higher state of combat readiness than before. Also, it was not only the armed forces that needed a boost to their fighting spirit, but the people as well. The war in Afghanistan has provided a patriotic fix for a country whose Communist ideology has long since become nothing but empty words that stir no one. The

Soviet press is making broad use of examples from Afghanistan for propaganda purposes.

Even in their totality, however, these fringe benefits do not constitute sufficient reason for a military venture that is costly in all respects: it has brought losses of human lives and matériel, the indignation of world public opinion, American political and economic sanctions, and so on. There is yet another reason, the main one.

While waging war in Afghanistan, the Soviet Union is beefing up its military presence on the Chinese border, where more than a million troops (one-quarter of the Soviet armed forces), armed with missiles and nuclear weapons, are stationed. It is systematically squeezing China out of Indochina and skillfully provoking Vietnamese imperialism to that end (the Vietnamese seizure of Laos and Cambodia, and skirmishes on the Chinese-Vietnamese border). In addition, it is waging a peaceful offensive in India, getting it entangled in a spiderweb of treaties and obligations and at the same time heating up India's hostility toward China and its ally, Pakistan, India's rival.

In the context of all these military and "diplomatic" moves, the occupation of Afghanistan can be perceived as part of an overall, ramified plan for encircling China: Afghanistan is of no other strategic value. From the viewpoint of Kremlin leaders from Khrushchev to Gorbachev, China has been and is Russia's principal enemy in a military and demographic sense, especially in view of China's ever-closer economic, military, and political relationship with the United States, Japan, and Western Europe. Paradoxically, Afghanistan has fallen victim to Russia's constant fear of China. The one hundred thousand Soviet troops in Afghanistan are simply reinforcements for the millions on the Chinese border.

That is why the Kremlin has attributed special importance to the Vakhan Pass, the great ancient East-West route that crosses the roof of the world, the Pamirs, at a height of seven thousand meters. In the thirteenth century, the hordes of Genghis Khan's grandsons broke through that pass into Persia and southern Europe; in that same century, the Venetian traveler Marco Polo went peaceably through it in the opposite direction, discovering China for Europe. Centuries later, that strip of no-man's-land with an overall area of only twenty thousand square kilometers has become the object of rivalry between the Russians and the Chinese. From the viewpoint of both countries, the barren valley with its nomadic Khirgiz tribes would bring to the one that owned it great strategic advantage as a launching pad for an attack on the enemy. In 1979, the Kremlin had received reports that Afghan Maoists from the Eternal Flame group, together with Chinese agents, were driving the Khirgiz from their grazing lands and gradually occupying the Vakhan. Documents supposedly seized from Chinese guerrillas and circulating among the Soviet leaders indicated that with the agreement of the Afghan president, Hafizullah Amin, who was a CIA agent, joint detachments of Chinese and American troops were to enter Afghanistan through the Vakhan. According to a credible story, those documents provided the *ultima ratio** for the Kremlin leaders, or rather for those leaders physically able at the time, to take part in discussions of the plan to seize Afghanistan.

There were not many of the latter. By late 1979, both of the USSR's nominal leaders, General Secretary Brezhnev and Premier Kosygin, were *hors de combat*. The health of each was so bad that their doctors had little hope for their recovery. In Kosygin's case, their prognosis proved to be right: he never recovered from his stroke, and he died in the hospital. In Moscow, there was yet another rumor that Brezhnev had died, and this time it was closer to reality than ever before. A few months later, Brezhnev did return to activity, but it was

---

*The rationale had already been worked out and had been applied when first Hungary, then Czechoslovakia, were occupied: It was said then that the Red Army had beat the Bundeswehr to the punch by a mere few hours.

limited and involved only ceremonies; he was already incapable of handling any business. Both Arvid Pelshe
and Andrei Kirilenko were also sick at the time, and
Mikhail Suslov was undergoing an operation. The decision to send "a limited contingent of Soviet troops"
into Afghanistan "to render international assistance to
the Afghan communists" was made privately by Andropov, Gromyko, Gorbachev, and a military triumvirate
consisting of Marshal Nikolai Ogarkov, Marshal Victor
Kulikov, and General Alexei Epishev, chief of the
armed forces' political department—and Minister of
Defense Ustinov, who was blindly obedient to that
troika. (Although the overall direction of the campaign
in Afghanistan was handled by the KGB under Andropov, the technical planning was done by the military, in
particular by General Epishev, who had visited Afghanistan twice in 1979 at the head of large military delegations to check the details of the impending action on the
spot.) Chernenko, Grishin, and Tikhonov were notified
of the decision *post factum,* when there was nothing
they could do but agree. The majority of Politburo
members—the five patients in the Kremlevka, the elite
hospital, and the three who lived outside of Moscow
(Romanov in Leningrad, Shcherbitsky in the Ukraine,
and Kunayev in Kazakhstan)—learned of the Soviet occupation of Afghanistan only from the newspapers.

We know, then, where to assign responsibility for
that occupation. Although it took place in the last phase
of the Brezhnev era, the authorship of that deed must be
ascribed to the empire's regent, Andropov (by that time
all-powerful), his supporters, and others he could count
on. As for Brezhnev, even if he had wanted to take part
in making that decision, he wouldn't have been able to
because of his physical state.

Coincident with that military action, a propaganda
campaign was launched in the Soviet Union. Conceived
as a musical accompaniment, it provides a glimpse into
the Kremlin's designs. One week after the invasion got
under way, one of the major Soviet newspapers pub-

lished an article by well-known Russophile writer Valentin Rasputin that was full of historical allusions and contained warnings in a militaristic vein like the following: "Is Fate not bringing closer to us the time when we shall again go forth onto the Field of Kulikovo to defend Russian soil and Russian Blood?"

The battle against the Tatars at Kulikovo is ranked by Russian historians with two other great battles: Borodino in the war against Napoleon and Stalingrad in the war against Hitler. It took place six hundred years ago. But the Russians, who in their historical aberration often identify the future with the past, figure that sooner or later it will have to be fought again, perhaps in the near future. Kulikovo was a battle not between countries but between races and continents; and it is on just such a global scale that Russia sees its future conflict with China and the countries aiding China. In the Russians' apocalyptic vision, it will be a tragic battle fought by one against all. This is being said not at all by way of justification but rather by way of explanation: Russia is the aggressor, but an aggressor with the mentality of a victim.

Incidentally, in the battle of Kulikovo, which is regarded as a Russian victory by that country's historians, nine out of every ten Russian soldiers were killed. We mention this apropos of a question that at first caused quite a stir among American journalists: How soon will Afghanistan become a Soviet Vietnam?

Apparently, Vietnam is lodged so deeply and painfully in the American consciousness—we are judging this as mere onlookers, since at the time of that war we were still in the USSR—that comparison with it has become a commonplace in the American political lexicon. The Vietnam analogy is brought up apropos of almost any military conflict. If Afghanistan is a Russian Vietnam, then Lebanon was an Israeli Vietnam, and the Falkland Islands almost became a British Vietnam while the British fleet was on its way toward Argentina. This is not to mention any threatened American involvement in a conflict outside its borders, be it in Lebanon, El Salvador, or in Nicaragua. (One gathers that the only reasons the journalists didn't compare Grenada to Vietnam were the rapidity of the military operation and the tininess of the island.) Precisely the Vietnam syndrome kept Americans from viewing the military situation in Afghanistan clearly and without bias; and it was hard to resist the temptation to wish their own misfortunes on the enemy!

Even though the blitzkrieg of Afghanistan did not come off as planned, unlike those of Czechoslovakia in 1968 and Hungary in 1956, and even though the war in Afghanistan has become the longest the Russians have waged in the past two centuries, Afghanistan has not turned into a Soviet Vietnam, and it looks as if that won't happen.

First of all, Russia has always been less sensitive to losses of human life than the developed democracies of the West, whose sensitivity is an admirable trait in all respects but the military, where it is an Achilles heel. But Russia has no such Achilles heel, and never has had. That fact is borne out by many historical examples, from the battle of Kulikovo—which victory, as we have seen, cost Russia nine out of every ten of its soldiers—to World War II, another victory, in which the Russians lost twenty million lives (and an additional twenty million during Stalin's Great Terror). Of the many examples, one is closest to us as former Leningraders: What other country would have continued to hang on to its second-largest city when that city's almost entire population had perished as the result of a nine-hundred-day siege? One vindication of the sacrificial offerings that were made to the Moloch of the State is found in the aforementioned neo-Stalinist novel by Ivan Stadnyuk, *The War*; that book's epigraph is a quotation from Athenian commander Themistocles: "We would perish, if we hadn't perished."

The Soviet Union has no free press to report its losses in Afghanistan. Nor does it have any public opinion

—no oppositionists, or liberals, or pacifists, or deserters, and not even its own Daniel Ellsberg. It has only the fear that has welded the Soviet empire together. So that even if, in a ten-year occupation of Afghanistan, the Soviet Union were to lose 58,000 troops, as America did in Vietnam, that: 1. would not be made known to the Soviet people; 2. would not provoke mass protests; 3. would not compel the Russians to leave Afghanistan, or even to make concessions to the guerrillas, or hold talks with them. But the Soviet Union will never lose as many soldiers in Afghanistan as the United States did in Vietnam. First, the sorties made by the *mujaheddin* (holy warriors) against the occupying troops are only sporadic and are much exaggerated by the American press. Second, the military aid they are getting cannot be compared to the massive supply of weapons that were furnished to North Vietnam and the Viet Cong by two great powers, China and the USSR. Finally, North Vietnam was waging war in South Vietnam, whereas on Afghan territory there are not two Afghanistans but one, occupied by the Russians, within which there are dozens of little mutually hostile guerrilla groups, poorly armed and poorly trained.

Undoubtedly, the guerrillas' sorties against the Soviet occupying forces will continue, provoking repressive actions against the non-combatant population (one-quarter of which, about four million, has already left the country) and further brutalization by the Red Army. The following remark made by a tsarist minister—although, to be sure, he made it on a different occasion—can be applied to Afghanistan: "Russia needs Armenia, but she has no need of Armenians." That is why neither the attacks of the kamikaze guerrillas, nor American and Pakistani aid to them, or condemnation of the genocide in Afghanistan by world public opinion can snatch the prey back from the predator and restore freedom and independence to Afghanistan. World War III will not begin because of Afghanistan, and the Kremlin knows that full well. It is in this context that one should interpret the direct threats made by Mikhail Gorbachev to the president of Pakistan during their talk at Chernenko's funeral, threats reinforced by many Soviet air raids on Afghan refugee camps and Afghan guerrilla bases on the territory of Pakistan. And the impression carried away by the Pakistani president after his talk with Gorbachev, namely, that the Kremlin would stop at nothing to put down the Afghan resistance, must be regarded as completely accurate. It's a sad thing to say, but Afghanistan is doomed.

Afghanistan is the most striking example of the empire's return to Stalinism, although the fate of Soviet political prisoners—the young poet Irina Ratushinskaya, the blue-collar worker Anatoly Marchenko, Iosif Begun, the teacher of Hebrew, and thousands of others —is a no less vivid example. The Kremlin's brutal treatment of its subjugated peoples and of its own subjects already amounts to Stalinism, although as yet without its Stalin, not the Stalin who is buried beside the Kremlin Wall but a new, living, vigorous one who, although he may bear a different name, will have the same political ideals. The conditions for his appearance are now optimal, and he is the most sought-after man in Russia. It would be premature to take comfort from the fact that none of the present Kremlin Stalinists has such a markedly paranoid individuality as Stalin himself. For he now has so many followers in the Kremlin, and they are multiplying so steadily that they can win by sheer force of numbers. And sooner or later one of them will take into his own hands their collective might, or rather, the might of the ideological and political heritage of Stalinism that they as a group represent and on which their power depends.

Meanwhile, as if to prove that it can again flourish on Russian soil, Stalinism has sprouted there without Stalin, three decades after his death. The whole question is: Will it reach the scale of such political paroxysms as Stalin's annihilation of the peasantry during the period of collectivization, or the Great Terror of 1937, or another "program" dreamed up by Stalin that only his timely death prevented from becoming equally colossal, namely, the Doctors' Plot, which was to serve as a prelude to the "final solution" of the Jewish problem in the German manner?

When, on a dark October night in 1962, under reinforced guard, the dead Stalin was removed in disgrace from Lenin's Mausoleum, where he had contrived to lie for almost a decade until his crimes were exposed by Khrushchev, and buried in an "ordinary" Party-elite grave in Red Square, the then-dissident poet Yevgeny Yevtushenko published in *Pravda* an impassioned poetic appeal to triple the guard at that grave, "so that Staliin will not arise and, with Stalin, the past." As the passage of time has shown, the poet's alarm was well-founded, but the guard, alas, has proved not to be strong enough.

10. The Kremlin, the Empire, and the People: The Paradox of Russian-Style Populism

> Everybody says, "the Kremlin, the Kremlin." I've heard about it from all of them, but I myself have never seen it. Many, many times by now (a thousand), drunk or hung over, I've walked through Moscow from north to south, from west to east, from one end to the other, all the way through, and whichever way—and I've never seen the Kremlin one single time.
>
> —BENEDIKT EROFEYEV,
> The Moscow Petushki Shuttle

> I just don't know whether the character of the Russian people created such rulers, or whether such rulers formed the character of the people.
>
> —ASTOLPHE, MARQUIS DE CUSTINE,
> Russia in 1839

HARDLY HAD THE train for Moscow left the station in the city of Gorky when in one compartment a disturbance broke out. A passenger shouted at a rather old, gray-haired woman, "I recognize you! You're the wife of academician Sakharov. I don't want to ride on the same train with you and breathe the same air!"

He was soon joined by several other indignant passengers. "Admit it!" one of them sharply demanded. "You really are Sakharov's wife, aren't you?"

When the woman nodded in the affirmative, he yelled, "Then get off this train!"

By this time, the train had picked up speed and was rushing toward the capital of the Soviet Union.

The woman was Elena Bonner, the wife of academician Andrei Sakharov, the famous Soviet civil rights leader, the father of the Soviet hydrogen bomb, and a Nobel Peace laureate. Frightened, she ran out of the compartment and to the restroom. There, she locked herself in so that she could collect her thoughts and decide what to do next.

When she came back, a crowd of passengers had already gathered near her compartment. One of them shouted, "Stop the train immediately! She threw something into the toilet. She's a CIA agent. We have to search the roadbed and find what she threw out!"

At that point, the conductor finally showed up. Although he expressed his full agreement with the passengers' indignation as citizens, he stood guard over the law. With a jerk of his head toward Elena Bonner, he reminded them, "After all, *she* is a passenger, too. She has a ticket, and we don't have the right to put her off the train."

But the furious passengers wouldn't accept that legal argument, so the conductor took her along to the crew's compartment. However, that was not the end of it. The word that Elena Bonner was aboard spread through the entire train. And until late at night, instead of sleeping, passengers from other cars peered into the crew's compartment and shouted curses and insults through slots in the door.

That episode on the train, almost like something out of Hitchcock's *The Lady Vanishes* or Agatha Christie's *Murder on the Orient Express,* might be chalked up as a provocation by the KGB except for one fact: Periodically, it was repeated by many other such indignant citizens. On the street, in waiting lines, and in movie houses, they raised a hue and cry over the Sakharovs, insulting them and threatening to kill them. Finally, the Sakharovs stopped going outside their home altogether. They are even afraid to go to the next-door bakery shop, where some people once shouted at Andrei Sakharov, "Your kike wife has to be killed!"

In Gorky, Elena Bonner, putting her medical knowledge to use (she was a nurse at the front during World War II), once helped to cure a neighbor's small child of an acute allergic reaction. But instead of showing gratitude, the child's father later showed up at the Sakharovs' and shouted at her, "I'd rather let him die from his sores than to let you touch him even one more time with your filthy hands!"

So it is that two of the Russians most celebrated abroad lead, in their own country, the existence of renegades and pariahs. And in the matter of their ostracism, the Kremlin and the hoi polloi are in perfect agreement. Indeed, the hoi polloi are probably more irresponsible and less tolerant than the Kremlin: if they had their way, Andrei Sakharov would now be, not in exile, but in prison. And that's in the best case.

The above incidents happened quite recently, after the dissident movement led by Sakharov had ceased to be a political entity. His own misfortune can hardly be compared with that of his confederates, the majority of whom were sent to Siberia, are in prison psychiatric hospitals, or were expelled from the country. Some were even murdered: Gely Snegirev, Oles Tikhy, Konstantin Bogatyrev, Vladimir Ivasyuk, Alla Gorskaya, and others. But there was a time in the seventies when the dissidents seemed to themselves and to many Western journalists and politicians (for example, President Carter) to constitute a real opposition to the Kremlin.

Actually, that was a myth engendered by wishful thinking—one that a few Russian romantics and ambitious individuals tried to endow with traits of reality. In so doing, they had to redirect their efforts: they counted primarily on response in America and Western Europe, not in Russia, where there couldn't be any except for the kind we have just described.

Hence, within the totalitarian state, there arose an artificial climate for a few dozen persons (there could be no more than that) that was maintained by the sensational interest it held for the free press, by the sympathy of Western public opinion, by the atmosphere of détente, and by political intrigues. Fired from their jobs, cut off from their professions, hounded by the authorities, and isolated from Russian society, which avoided them like lepers, the dissidents lived entirely on Western moral, ideological, monetary, and material subsidies. The fame accorded the dissidents in the West was sort of compensation for their lack of political prestige and influence in their own country.

Even before it was crushed by the KGB, Soviet dissent had been rejected by Russian society itself, just as the human body rejects a foreign or artificial organ that disturbs its normal functioning. Any movement, to succeed, must be an organic part of the country in which it springs up. Even if it is the tiniest capillary, it must be a part of the nation's circulatory system.

It is appropriate here to mention once more the first Soviet dissident, Nikita Khrushchev, and his opposition to Stalinism. He was a rebel sitting in the prime minister's seat. But even at such a high level, dissent was rejected, first by the intolerance of the general populace and then by the palace coup of Leonid Brezhnev and his colleagues, who easily got the ship of state back on course and into the main channel of Russian history. It is really astonishing that at the time Khrushchev was removed from office—the only Soviet leader to which that happened—he did not have a single supporter in the entire CC except for his son-in-law, journalist Alexei

Adzhubei, who alone fell into disgrace along with him. Khrushchev was closer than the other Kremlin leaders to the common people and often socialized with them, treated them as equals, and had a concern for their well-being; yet he was the object of their equally common contempt, and finally became persona non grata in the very country to which he had diligently given "loving care." By contrast, Stalin, whose "appearance to the people" (as in a vision of Christ) was a rare, biannual event, has been restored to high political status, first by the populace and now by the government, despite the fact that he exterminated or imprisoned millions of people, whereas Khrushchev rehabilitated them and set the survivors free. Truly, no man is a prophet in his own country.

Soviet dissent arose at the juncture between the two regimes, Khrushchev's and Brezhnev's. It was a carry-over from the Khrushchev era, which after his over-throw went underground. It was not squashed once and for all until the early eighties, when the KGB apparatus squeezed out and replaced the Party-bureaucratic clique and began to officially restore the cult of Stalin and his political methods. The trials of the Soviet dissidents were a posthumous defeat for Khrushchev, this time not by his former colleagues but by Russian history.

As a rule, attempts at radical change in Russia do not weaken tradition but make it stronger and harsher. The liberal age of Boris Godunov ended in the Time of Troubles of the seventeenth century and the accession of the House of Romanov. When, three hundred years later, the Romanov dynasty was overthrown by a bour-geois, democratic revolution, the latter's gains did not have long to live: within only a few months they were all destroyed by the succeeding Bolshevik Revolution. That year, 1917, with its two revolutions, was for Russia a time for a free choice between democracy and totalitar-ianism. That choice was made, and the Great Terror of the thirties continued and intensified the civic baccha-nalia triggered by that year's events.

In another Russian paradox, the slaughterhouse built by Stalin at one and the same time gave Russian anarchy tremendous scope and organized it as a function of the State. Dark, sadistic, unacknowledged instincts were provided with a lofty rationale, ideology. The Russian anarchic spirit, reawakened by democratic reforms after the fall of the monarchy's totalitarianism, was channeled by a bureaucratic totalitarianism. It was still called socialism as a result of momentum, but that was by now a mere token name.

Every time a totalitarian system in Russia is weakened or destroyed, it arises again, in response to a special kind of need, to "popular demand," to historical necessity, but inevitably. We see here the action of a law of subliminal populism in a totalitarian regime. Because totalitarianism in Russia is not a usurpation of power and not political voluntarism but a unique form of populism—the result of a choice by the commonalty. Even the neo-Stalinist mood that is now so widespread in Russia arose from, among other things, an instinctual desire for discipline, order, and *vozhdism* (Russian-style absolutism), that is, from the people's distrust and fear of freedom. In Russia, freedom promptly and irreversibly degenerates into anarchy, and those experiences of carnage are subconsciously retained in the people's memory and make for a very powerful instinct of self-preservation.

We hope that what we have just said—together with, for that matter, everything before it and after it—does not sound supercilious. We ourselves are Russians; but since we believe in democracy, we had to leave Russia. And now we are looking at freedom not in a moral context but in an historical one, where it is not better or worse than lack of freedom but is either applicable or inapplicable to a specific situation—in this case, that of Russia.

Undoubtedly, moral law and ethics are absolute and categorical: it's hard to dispute that affirmation by Immanuel Kant. But as history has repeatedly shown, attempts to transfer Western political, juridical, and moral norms to Russia forcibly and without modification have usually produced results the opposite of those desired. Justice, truth, and the rule of law must spring from Russian soil. To transplant them artificially is senseless: they won't take root.

And they haven't taken root.

One thinks of such native-born geniuses as Peter the Great, Leo Tolstoy, and Vladimir Lenin, who suffered defeat when they tried to re-educate their own people. One thinks, too, of Napoleon, who was sure that his campaign in Russia would succeed because he had promised freedom to the Russian serfs and was counting on their support. But he had to pay dearly for that mistake: the slaves took up arms to defend Russian tyranny, because they themselves had created it. (They were the opposite of the Poles, who went over to the side of the conqueror and liberator.)

A slave can be freed only by himself, when he wants to and *if* he wants to. To free a slave by coercion is impossible.

Other peoples can and must be defended against Russia. But not the Russian people, who don't want to be so defended, and don't need it. You can't defend anything against itself, be it an individual person or an entire country.

In 1968, when Soviet troops went into Czechoslovakia to quash the incipient revolt there, the standard arguments among the Russian people were, "We spilled blood for them when we liberated them from the Germans, and now they've betrayed us," and "They're eating our bread, yet they've decided to go over to the Americans." Needless to say, popular support for the occupation was unqualified and unanimous, as it had been in the case of Hungary twelve years before and would be in that of Afghanistan eleven years later.

A few months after the blitzkrieg of Czechoslovakia by the Red Army, the Soviet and Czechoslovak ice hockey teams played an international match. That ath-

letic joust turned into a purely political one. The Soviet
team, which technically was certainly the stronger one
that year, quailed and retreated before the whirlwind of
Russophobia that the Czechoslovak players were caught
up in. On the ice, the victimized country took revenge
on the aggressor country. When that political hockey
match was over, all the inhabitants of that Central
European country spilled out into the streets, shouting
nationalist and anti-Soviet slogans as they feted their
victory over Russia. And the occupying force of six hundred thousand troops could do nothing about that spontaneous explosion of pride and hatred. The Soviet
soldiers in Czechoslovakia were as helpless as the Soviet
players in the hockey match.

We were living in Russia at the time, and we remember how the Russian fans split up into two factions. (On
that occasion, everybody was a fan, including people
who beforehand hadn't known the difference between
hockey and soccer.) "The people" were fans of "their"
team, while Russians of the intelligentsia were fans of
the Czechoslovak team. The intelligentsia had taken it
hard when the Prague Spring was crushed under the caterpillar tracks of Soviet tanks, and they needed some
kind of revenge for the crushing of their own hopes of a
softening of the Kremlin's regime. It is curious, however, that they had based their "great expectations" of
another thaw in connection with the Prague Spring and
their "small expectations" of revenge in the hockey
match on forces outside their own country: in the first
instance, on the Czechoslovak reformers, and in the second, on the Czechoslovak athletes.

"The intelligentsia has been put in a frightful,
unheard-of position: the common people, *for* whom
they are fighting, hate them; and the authorities, *against*
whom they are fighting, are proving to be their protec-
tors, whether they like it or not." That was written in
1909 by Russian philosopher Mikhail Gershenzon. And
indeed, one can easily imagine what would have happened on that train from Gorky to Moscow if the man

representing the authorities, the conductor, had not protected the wife of Sakharov, a desperate fighter for the rights of "the people" in the USSR, but instead had let the people themselves, the passengers, take the law into their own hands.

When Stalin himself, in early 1953, hatched the Doctors' Plot, drunkards on the streets, in waiting lines, and in streetcars shouted, "The Jews tried to kill Stalin!" Perfectly sober people refused treatment at hospitals by Jewish doctors for fear of their lives. This attitude became commonplace among ordinary people, although Soviet propaganda, for all the anti-Semitic bacchanalia it had set in motion, had not yet decided to draw such blatant conclusions. Mustafa Dzhemilev, whose people, the Crimean Tatars, were all deported by Stalin for "collaboration with the fascists [Nazis]" and who is now serving his sixth prison term because he has fought for their return to their homeland, recalls that while escort guards were shoving that entire people into cattle cars, they shouted at them, "Instead of shipping you out, we should be shooting you!" And many other instances of "the people's" extremism could be given.

No one knows his own people as well as their boss, the Kremlin. As W. H. Auden wrote in "Epitaph on a Tyrant," "He knew human folly like the back of his hand." The kind of conclusions one may draw from such knowledge are something else again. Thus, Stalin stirred up and made use of all the dark, slavish, cruel, xenophobic instincts of the Russian people. But Lenin diagnosed these instincts very accurately and tried to combat them. The following remarks of his about "the people" cannot be quoted in the Soviet press (and we know this from personal experience, because the censors deleted them from articles of ours, even though they had been made by the most-revered of all Soviet saints):

We are still so much slaves that we are being used to turn other races into slaves. We are still putting up with a government at home which is not only using all the ferocity of a butcher to squash any striving toward freedom in Russia but is using Russian troops to forcibly encroach on the freedom of others.

No one can be blamed for having been born a slave. But a slave who not only holds back from striving for his own freedom but tries to justify and put a better face on his own servitude (for example, by calling the strangling of Poland and the Ukraine "defending the fatherland")—such a slave provokes legitimate feelings of indignation, scorn, and loathing toward himself as a lackey and scum.

When the Korean airliner was shot down on orders from the Kremlin, we were already far across the ocean from our native land. But unlike foreign correspondents in Moscow, we were not in the least surprised by the reactions of the Soviet "man in the street" to that event —one so extraordinary in the international scene. We quote from *The New York Times, The Washington Post, The Baltimore Sun,* and *The Christian Science Monitor,* although much the same kind of responses from Soviet citizens were recorded by correspondents of *Daily Telegraph, Le Monde,* and *Il Corriere della Sera.*

> "That was done correctly."
> "The plane went too far."
> "What happens, happens."
> "If an aircraft was shot down, it could only be because it posed some real threat—perhaps it was spying."
> "If I may be frank, we were absolutely right to shoot down the Korean plane."

Even when one American journalist brought up the fact that the lives of 269 passengers were lost along with the plane, it did not shake the conviction of the people he questioned on the streets of Moscow that their government had been in the right.

"Look. Tell your readers that they should be absolutely clear on one thing. On issues like this we are very tough. You enter our airspace like this, and you get shot down."

"Well, the air defenses were simply doing their duty."

"Besides, would the Americans really react differently in our place?"

It is understandable that Western journalists should have been puzzled by this unfeigned concurrence on the part of these people with their military and civilian leaders. Let's just suppose that Franz Kafka had given his novel *The Castle* a Soviet setting. In that case, he would have had to discover what links there were between the medieval "castle" on Red Square and the ordinary citizens of the empire dwelling beyond its impregnable walls—especially in those extraordinary cases when the Kremlin diverges so sharply from Western moral and political standards and provokes indignation throughout the world. After due investigation, Kafka would have had to recognize that in spite of certain frictions and differences in their view of things, there is an historical bond, umbilical and unbreakable, between the Kremlin and the Russia outside that citadel's walls.

The present Kremlin regime, which is perceived by a Czech, a Pole, an Estonian, a Hungarian, or an Afghan as the worst form of imperial totalitarianism, is a creation of the Russians, one that meets their historical tradition and idea of law. If not, we would have to resort to a mystical explanation for a system, which, under various names that have not altered its essence—autocracy, dictatorship of the proletariat—has for centuries survived intact on the territory of Russia. The empire has put its people, backward in many respects, on a level with advanced nations; it has given the Russian nation a feeling of equality or even of superiority and has made it a force to be reckoned with. Hence, for the Russians, relinquishing the empire would mean relinquishing their own historical significance as a great nation, and from their point of view would be tantamount to suicide.

"If we did not sprawl from the Bering Strait to the Oder, we wouldn't be noticed," wrote Petr Chaadayev, a Russian philosopher of the nineteenth century, about the "historical nullity" of his own country. Indeed, the features that lend distinction to Russia are not historical but geographic: it has developed in breadth, not in depth. That development began as far back as the fourteenth century, when Prince Ivan Kalita "gathered in the lands" around Moscow. According to the estimate made by Norwegian polar explorer Fridtjof Nansen, every seven years from 1500 until his day, Russia had gained an amount of territory equal to that of his own country, the Kingdom of Norway. Imperialism is a traditional, basic, integral trait of Russia—its chief one, that country's national stimulus and international style. It is not the specter of communism that is haunting Europe, as Marx and Engels mistakenly predicted, but Russian history. And it is haunting more than Europe: for Russia, expansion has always been a substitute for internal development. Those countries that the empire has attached to itself—from Czechoslovakia and Hungary to Lithuania and Afghanistan—have found themselves forcibly involved in the expansionist process of Russian history, which is completely alien to them.

We remember how, when we were schoolchildren, the teacher would proudly move his pointer across a political map of the world; and we learned by heart that the Soviet Union took up one-sixth of the earth's land surface, and that there was plenty of room on its territory for 2.3 United States, or forty Frances, or ninety-two Great Britains. We freely acknowledge that at the time that gave us a feeling of patriotic pride. It was not just official propaganda: it was a nationalistic sentiment. In the USSR, geography takes the place of history, politics, and ideology. Geographic patriotism leads to geographic imperialism and vice versa.

Thus, with rare exceptions, all great Russian writers were sincere imperialists in their political (or more precisely, their geographic) views. Gogol wrote rapturously that his country sprawled over half the world. Pushkin, in an ultrapatriotic, militaristic poem, glorified the Russian troops' suppression of a Polish uprising and their capture of Warsaw. Griboyedov, the author of the brilliant comedy *Woe from Wit*, drafted several colonialist treaties for the government; and while implementing one of them, as Russian ambassador to Teheran, he was killed by a raging mob of Moslem fanatics. Dostoyevsky had passionate visions of the capture of Constantinople. On his deathbed, the great poet and philosopher Fyodor Tyutchev eagerly asked for details of the conquest of Khiva, a Central Asian khanate adjacent to Afghanistan. And these were the best minds of Russia. What, then, was to be expected of government officials or the people?

Russians have a wanderlust in their blood. Some of Russia's conquests cannot be explained from an economic, political, strategic, or any other reasonable point of view. What we have here is an obsession with space—an obsession arising from constant restlessness and historical nomadism. Russia prides itself on its vast expanses, but there are only kilometers in it, and the Russians can only take fright at those barren expanses devoid of both people and things. Actually, Russia is just Moscow, which with its iron hand keeps countless provinces and colonies on a leash. Russia regards what is a defect in its physical constitution as its chief virtue, striving to preserve and strengthen it at any cost.

Aristotle was of the opinion that there are objects either so tiny or so huge that they cannot be perceived or taken in by the eye, so in a sense they do not exist. Russia is too huge to be a reality. It is a geographical and political fiction; as such, in the eyes of the Russians, it must expand its borders to become more lifelike. It has been doing this very successfully for quite a few centuries, regardless of who is ruling.

What is most astounding, however, is how the Russians themselves view its wolfish imperialist appetite.

Among the factors in the history of Russia, one of the most tragic and painful is the recurrent invasion of its territory by enemies. Russia was under the Tatar-Mongol yoke for almost one-third of its one-thousand-year existence; we don't even know if that can be grasped by the imagination of a Westerner. Mongols, Swedes, Poles, Lithuanians, French, and Germans, century after century, right up until World War II, have made devastating raids into Russia and even captured the capital. The memory of those national catastrophes has been preserved in two forms. First, in an acute xenophobia, so that even anti-Semitism must be regarded not only as a result of official propaganda but also as an expression of the Russians' aversion to aliens. Second, in what might be called a stronger-than-usual instinctual need for the State as a protective institution. To the Russians, their own imperialism seems to be a defensive mechanism, not an offensive one. Psychologically, their aggressive drive is a sublimated fear.

Russia's fear of the nations around it—China, Japan, Western Europe, and the United States—is compounded by an equally great fear of its subject peoples: the hangman's fear of his victims, the master's of his slaves, the persecutor's persecution complex. The Russian empire is a boomerang, which comes back to wound the one who threw it. As Marx acutely observed, "A nation that enslaves other nations forges its own chains." The chains forged by the Russian people are the strongest and best in the world, regardless of what name they have borne: the *oprichnina,* or elite security troops, in the age of Ivan the Terrible, the Third Department under Emperor Nicholas I, or the KGB today. Setting moral categories aside, the empire itself must be listed among the great creations of the Russian people, along with *War and Peace, The Brothers Karamazov,* Mendeleyev's Periodic Table, the ballet, and the sputniks.

The empire's demographic paradox is that it was created as a *Russian* empire but has come to be a *multinational* one in which the Russians have been pushed into the background quantitatively and are now in fact a national minority, although politically they have remained in the foreground with the help of the "organs" of coercion. Given the demographic decline of the Russians and the population explosions in some of the ethnic groups subjugated by them (especially the Moslems of Central Asia and the Caucasus), that incongruity will stand out ever more clearly as the years pass, so that we shall be able to compare the Russia of a few decades from now with present-day South Africa, where an ethnic minority rules a great majority. The very existence of such a colossal apparatus of coercion as the KGB is occasioned first and foremost by the need to keep its satellite peoples pent up within the empire, or more accurately, the peoples along its boundaries in the double border zone: the union republics within the USSR and the socialist countries outside it.

Not only have there been strongly nationalist uprisings against the empire in countries close to its borders (repeated revolts by the Poles, Ukrainians, Hungarians, Czechoslovaks, and now the Afghans); there have been other uprisings in regions close to the empire's center that have had a multinational complexion. For example, the savage peasant wars waged under the leadership of Stenka Razin during the reign of Tsar Alexei Mikhailovich in the seventeenth century, and those fought under the command of Emelyan Pugachev during the reign of Catherine the Great in the next century, were primarily uprisings of non-Russian ethnic groups—the Mari, the Chuvash, the Mordvinians, the Tatars, the Cossacks—against Russian domination.

The Russians themselves are immune to infection with rebellion; and any revolt by subject nations is perceived by both the Kremlin and the populace as first and foremost anti-Russian—which, by the way, is absolutely true.

The widely entertained notion of the Kremlin rulers as usurpers is thus only partly correct. If today a miracle were to happen and free parliamentary elections were held in Russia, the power would either be kept by the same leaders or it would go to even more pronounced hardliners and extremists because, as we have seen, in some respects the imperial people favor stronger and more aggressive actions than are considered permissible by the government, whose political awareness and responsibility (or more accurately, fear of international consequences) are often greater than those of the people. With certain qualifications, one can apply to the present situation in Russia the well-known dictum of Joseph de Maistre, who served as the Kingdom of Sardinia's envoy to the court of Emperor Alexander I: "Every people gets the government it deserves." In some cases, to be sure—in the time of Khrushchev, and even of Brezhnev—the people had a better government than they deserved, which is why they were unable to appreciate the merits of either man, especially of Khrushchev, whom they treated with disdain, called "a clown" and "Nikita," and consigned to oblivion.

Although Brezhnev ruled for eighteen years, he left the people indifferent. By contrast, when Yuri Andropov came to power, it was "love at first sight"—which hardly does credit to the political tastes of the imperial people if one judges them by Western standards. By way of feedback, that is, under the influence and pressure of popular tastes, the Soviet Government, too, over the past decades, has been changing in the direction of the people's ideal: Stalin. Such is the mechanism of subliminal populism in the totalitarian empire: the *vox populi* is heard by the Kremlin Olympians, and the key political decisions taken there are often in line with the tastes, notions, and desires of the general public.

The bond between the Kremlin and the populace, although invisible and by no means easily and quickly discernible, is really quite strong, perhaps even stronger than in the developed democracies, because it is primal and natural. That bond is manifested both in concurrences—concern for the condition of the empire, national pride, paranoid suspicions that the world outside is a hostile one, and the like—and in disagreements. Among the latter is the general public's disdainful attitude toward the countries and peoples of the Third World, with whom the Kremlin must play along for strategic or propagandistic reasons. Sometimes that bond takes the form of a tacit agreement between the Kremlin and the people, like the one embodied in the well-known formula, "They pretend they're paying us, and we pretend we're working."

However, in matters of production and economics in general, there are disagreements, mutual grievances, and friction between the Kremlin and the Russians living "outside the walls of the citadel." The people regard their leaders as parasites and exploiters, and the leaders regard the people as loafers and drunkards.

There are in fact great gulfs between the Kremlin rulers and the hoi polloi they rule: social, economic, and "life style." Only the Kremlin has access to the kind of information readily available to the general public in any democratic country. Only Kremlin-dwellers can get the drugs and medications that can be bought in any Western pharmacy. The gourmet foods and staples for which ordinary Muscovites, like primitive hunters and gatherers, spend whole days of searching, and which are completely unavailable to Soviet provincials, may be found on the tables, in the refrigerators, or in the cupboards of Kremlin-dwellers in the same abundance as in the home of the average U.S. citizen. (No wonder a Politburo member lives fifteen years longer than the average Soviet male.) Politburo members are driven to the Kremlin and to their dachas in the countryside near Moscow in official, armor-plated ZIL limousines with green-tinted bulletproof windows and radio-telephones. Each ZIL is preceded by a KGB Chaika and followed by another security car. Those black stretch limousines, handmade for an elite of twenty men, race at high speed along the middle lane, which is also reserved for that elite, of the highway or street, and passersby stare in wonder at the truly "royal procession." These men are so isolated from the general public that Gromyko, in the words of his own daughter, "for twenty-five years has not set foot in the streets of Moscow" and sees Russia "only from his car window." On one occasion when he went into a café, Brezhnev had completely forgotten that there was such a thing as a monetary system. And Gorbachev is seriously hoping to inspire the Soviet people, who have lost faith in everything, to the labor idealism and production feats of the thirties.

All these things necessarily stir up an undercurrent of hatred among the people toward the "Red bourgeoisie," which is why Andropov's anticorruption campaign, begun at the top, enjoyed such solid support. Of course, that campaign was actually a struggle for power. Yet looked at from a slightly different angle, it was also a campaign for the redistribution of scarce goods, which in the USSR are available only to the Party-government elite and its staffs (writers, journalists, scientists). As a replacement for what Milovan Djilas called "the new class" of partocrats, who had been in place long enough to age not only physically but politically, Andropov began to create a *new* "new class"—people who had come late to the table and were now hurrying to make up for lost time. One might call the process a rejuvenation of the cadres, a blood transfusion, a redistribution of class privileges from the old "new class" to the new one, an exchange of places between outsiders and the favorites of the ruling elite—whatever, depending upon one's angle of vision and criteria.

The most graphic example of the contradiction in all this was between the family of Andropov and the man himself. In the last phase of his campaign against corruption he had finally got to Brezhnev's daughter and, taking advantage of her fondness for *la dolce vita,* had had her charged with appropriating jewels belonging to someone else. But it suffices to compare the scene at

Brezhnev's funeral with that at Andropov's to see how far Andropov's own children had strayed from the proletarian austerity preached by their father. At the former, Brezhnev's family—including his daughter Galina, who was being harassed by Andropov—wore mourning; the clothes were badly tailored and hardly distinguishable from those of other Soviet citizens. But at Andropov's funeral, where the Soviet people got their first look at his family, his son, his daughter, daughter-in-law, and other unidentified relatives were dressed as if for a fashion show. They astounded TV audiences —even Western ones, not to mention Soviet viewers— with the luxurious elegance of their imported fur coats: Russian mink, polar fox, ermine, and other trademarks of that same "Red bourgeoisie" in combating whom Andropov had won popularity among the common folk. One could apply here the ironic formula of the Polish poet, Janush Shpotansky, "In his knightly combat against corruption he was so carried away by noble ardor that he came to only when he caught himself with his hand in the till."

The ordinary Soviet citizen is much less informed than his Western counterpart about the kind of life led by the VIPs in the Kremlin. For instance, the Soviet public had no inkling that Khrushchev, on an official visit to Scandinavia, took along his entire family, including children and grandchildren and totaling twelve persons—a visit that the Western press called "a family picnic."

Again, the Soviet populace had no idea that Brezhnev had a passion for fast, expensive foreign cars. For an ordinary citizen of the USSR, even a Soviet-made car is such a luxury as to be almost impossible to come by: first, because of the price; second, because of the short supply. So for him it would have been all the more intriguing to learn that in whatever country Brezhnev went to on a State visit, he expected to be presented with a late-model car manufactured there. His hopes were almost always realized, and he gradually accumulated

an entire fleet of foreign-made limousines, including a
Rolls-Royce. That particular limousine gave the exiled
poet Joseph Brodsky a subject and rhyme for his epitaph on Brezhnev:

> *He could have killed more than he could have fed*
> *but chose to do neither. By falling dead*
> *he leaves a vacuum and the black Rolls-Royce*
> *to one of the boys who will make the choice.*

For that matter, it is very unlikely that Brezhnev's
Rolls-Royce was passed on to his successors, one after
the other, particularly since there were three of them in
the short period of twenty-eight months. Besides, there
were enough foreign cars in his collection for all the
Politburo members, so it wasn't necessary for anyone to
drive the Rolls, with all the miles it had on it. In 1972,
when Nixon went to Moscow, he brought Brezhnev a
black Cadillac sedan: Anatoly Dobrynin, the Soviet ambassador to the United States, had told Kissinger that a
Cadillac would be the right gift for Brezhnev. The next
year, on his return visit to America, Brezhnev was given
a dark-blue Lincoln Continental with luxurious black
velour upholstery. His gift from Willy Brandt, the chancellor of West Germany—again in accordance with a
gentle hint from the Soviet ambassador—was a Mercedes 450 that cost the Bonn government twelve thousand dollars. Brezhnev tested the Mercedes right then
and there. He got into it, slammed the door shut and, ig-
noring the German road signs, drove off down a wind-
ing road at a furious speed, hit a deep pothole, and
stopped the car. Then he declared that its silver-gray
color wasn't to his taste, so it was promptly replaced by
a steel-blue one. It was a tearful, bitter disappointment
for Brezhnev, already in his second childhood, when toward the end of his life the new chancellor of West Germany, Helmut Schmidt, failed to follow suit. Whether
because of his own parsimony (he had been minister of
finance under Brandt) or, more probably, because of

pressure after the transition from détente to another cold war, instead of the late-model car that had been officially ordered through diplomatic channels, he presented the Soviet ruler with an antique hunting gun. Brezhnev didn't know what to do with it: although he was an avid hunter, he had no knowledge or appreciation of such antiques.

Brezhnev was in every sense of the word a "dear guest" for his Western hosts. His visits not only laid a heavy burden on the treasuries of the countries that were supporting détente but personally cost his foreign hosts a pretty penny. It would seem that only Kissinger, by some kind of miracle, managed to avoid personal outlays for the guest from the Kremlin who had such a penchant for foreign things. But some of his aides found themselves out of pocket.

Brezhnev once scrounged from one of them a watch that had taken his fancy, in spite of all the aide's protestations that the watch was a gift from his wife and therefore precious to him. Because of that dispute about the watch, the Soviet-American talks almost came—indeed, momentarily did come—to a halt; and were only started again when Brezhnev got the watch. In 1976, at the first meeting between Brezhnev and Gerald Ford at the Vladivostok Airport—this one, too, set up by the indefatigable Kissinger—after Brezhnev tried on the U.S. president's wolfskin coat, he pestered him for it until he got it.

In his own gift-giving, Brezhnev did not make any concessions to the principle of a "fair exchange." In one instance, after having been given an expensive automobile, he reciprocated with a scarf handwoven by artisans in his home town; in another, with a Russian samovar and tea service.

It is the official practice in the Soviet Union to take a disdainful attitude toward consumerism, especially toward products made in the hostile capitalist world. Young people are sternly criticized in the Soviet press for coveting foreign-made jeans, shorts, T-shirts, tape recorders, and other things from the "degenerate" West. The following patriotic lines by Vladimir Mayakovsky, the "classic" Soviet poet, are quoted for their edification: "We Soviet people have our own pride—we look down on foreign things." So it is very difficult for the wives of Kremlin leaders, with their all-consuming passion for foreign-made things, to shop at Western department stores and buy articles of Western make for the whole family and at the same time not to lose any of their "Soviet pride," especially since journalists and photographers waylay them everywhere.

Although they have many privileges in their own country, Kremlin wives are bound by very rigid restrictions. The wife of former Soviet UN official Arkady Shevchenko was well acquainted with Gromyko's wife. Here is what she told her husband about the lengths Mrs. Gromyko had to go to in order to gratify her consumer appetites and that she had to conceal from her own husband.

"What do you think Lidiya Dmitriyevna and I do when Gromyko brings her to New York? Go to museums? No, we shop. I shop for her. I give her money, our money. And you have Gromyko's protection, just as I have hers."

Khrushchev, before he set out on his trip to the United States, by his own admission spent a good many days pondering whether "to take or not to take" his wife, Nina Petrovna, along. He regarded traveling accompanied by women as "unbusinesslike, and a pettybourgeois luxury."

Nonetheless, he did decide to take her. Before their departure, Khrushchev gave her many instructions on how to behave in general and at official receptions in particular; what to say (the strictest prohibition was "Not a single word about politics!"); and that at receptions she was not to take even a drop of an alcoholic beverage, including champagne, because "there is no more disgusting spectacle on earth than that of a drunken woman." (To the male population of the

USSR, the spectacle of a drunken *man* is much more attractive.) Madame Khrushcheva coped very well with the difficult role of First Lady of the USSR. And on subsequent trips, Khrushchev slackened the reins of his personal rule over her and granted her greater freedom of action, counting on her innate tact and dignity.

Although Brezhnev took his wife on trips abroad (the populace called her "a free supplement to the Brezhnev edition"), she was strictly forbidden to talk about politics, economics, her own husband, details of his background, or anything related to life within the USSR. The only things Victoria Brezhneva was permitted to discuss were the weather and her family; and even when it came to the latter, she was obliged to keep the talk perfunctory, avoiding intimate details. She had to dress in the "dignified" manner prescribed for Kremlin wives, which included wearing high-heeled pumps, even though at home she preferred low-heeled shoes that offered more stability. The Brezhnevs' sociable and garrulous daughter told what an agony it was for her corpulent mother to wear the narrow pumps that protocol demanded. Since her feet were usually swollen from walking and from the heat, putting them into those pumps was like putting herself into an instrument of torture. Madame Khrushcheva had herself undergone similar torments earlier. But whereas she, during unofficial receptions, would at least inconspicuously take off her pumps and ease her aching feet, Victoria Brezhneva dared not do it. In short, for the Kremlin's first ladies, trips abroad were hardly enjoyable or something to be looked forward to.

But the old-fashioned, strict code of conduct for the behavior of Kremlin wives abroad was quickly modernized and brought closer to the more permissive etiquette of Europe by Raisa Gorbacheva, who is two whole generations younger than her "colleagues." When she went with her husband to England just before Christmas 1984, she, alone of all Kremlin wives, had her own schedule of receptions and tours, independent of the official one. Thus, instead of visiting the grave (or at least the museum) of Karl Marx as she should properly have done not only as the future First Lady but also as a specialist in Marxism-Leninism, Raisa Gorbacheva went to look at the crown jewels and took her husband along with her. A vain and fashion-conscious woman, she has done away with the time-honored tradition of conservative, dignified dress for Kremlin wives at official receptions. (One remembers Madame Brezhneva's dark uniform and the jabot she never failed to wear.) Raisa Gorbacheva prefers modish silk blouses and stylishly tailored suits and alternates a white mink stole with a musquash coat. She created a sensation when she appeared at a reception at the Soviet embassy wearing a cream-colored satin dress and gold-embroidered slippers. A reporter for one of the English newspapers wrote, "What a contrast with the other wives of Soviet leaders, who looked as if they had just come from the construction site of a dam in Siberia!"

Even by Western standards for the behavior of a first lady, Raisa Gorbacheva slightly overdid things when, on some days, she changed her outfit several times. Her visit to London was her big début; she reveled in the attention she received from the Western press.

Unlike his predecessors, Mikhail Gorbachev has given his wife the freedom to do whatever she wants abroad. For one thing, the Gorbachevs are more emancipated and up-to-date than the old-fashioned couples of the Brezhnev generation, when the wife was always the homemaker and the husband the breadwinner. But also Raisa Gorbacheva has always been the dominant one in their small family, and when she entered the esoteric circle of Kremlin wives, she retained that leading role.

In England, carried away by her passion for jewels, which in itself is blameworthy in an honored representative of the "workers' and peasants' State," Raisa Gorbacheva purchased a pair of diamond earrings costing $2,500 at Cartier's and coolly paid for them with an American Express card. It was a wildly unprecedented event. Never before had even the leader of the Soviet

Union had an American Express card. That Madame Gorbacheva had one meant either that she had an account in a Western bank or, much more likely, that the Soviet government, which does have such accounts, was paying for her purchases. All members of the Politburo and the Secretariat are entitled to have an open account in the State Bank, from which they can withdraw whatever amount they want whenever they want it—a right that, needless to say, is kept secret from the public. But it must be in rubles, not hard currency that can be invested, especially abroad!

With her gesture, Raisa Gorbacheva laid bare before Western correspondents and papparazzi the privileged and parasitic existence of the Kremlin oligarchy as a caste—a fact that its members have long striven to conceal by a whole system of internal taboos and a strict protocol, elaborated over the years, governing their contacts with the Russian citizenry and their behavior abroad. Only a person of the young and present-day generation of Kremlin wives could have violated that very strict prohibition so thoughtlessly.

Mikhail Gorbachev represents an entirely new breed of politicians not yet very noticeable in the political arena of Russia who, unlike the members of the old Brezhnev-Chernenko Politburo, did not experience either Stalin's Great Terror or the devastating war years or the country's exhaustion by Stalin's directives in the first postwar years. So they perceive their very special privileges as something to which they are naturally entitled, almost by right of inheritance. The Gorbachevs have for so long a time, and so securely, dwelled in that paradisiacal world of wall-to-wall privilege (one carefully screened off from the general Soviet public), that they haven't even developed the habit of concealing them from anyone. Their life-style in that elite milieu is a modernized Soviet version of the lordly life and high-handed manners of the nobility in old Russia. One only has to see how Mikhail Gorbachev, before making his entrance at receptions in the Kremlin or in foreign countries, shrugs out of his overcoat without even looking to see who is behind him to take it—or, likewise without looking, flings his cap to one side, into the hands of the invisible (to him) person waiting on him—to realize how deeply the arrogance and haughtiness of the high official, the lack of democratic behavior toward others, has struck root in him. Such lordly manners, which with him have become reflexes, were not displayed by a single Soviet leader before him.

However, in a bid for popularity and support among the general citizenry, Gorbachev has exhibited the window-dressing of democratic behavior: rehearsed, "exemplary" meetings with "simple folk" on streets, in factories and plants, and even in their apartments; and appearances with his wife at the Moscow Art Theater or the Kirov Theater not in the "royal box" but in orchestra seats, amid ordinary theatergoers. As we know, at such meetings "the people" consist of bodyguards assigned to the *vozhd* by the KGB's Ninth Administration. (Exceptions were Lenin and Khrushchev, who in fact met with ordinary Soviet people.) Naturally, this "going to the people" by Gorbachev is described in detail by the Soviet mass media, as it is in rumors floated from above and circulated widely. Such are the ways of fostering the cult of modesty, ironical by its very nature, of the new Soviet leader.

However, all the details of Raisa Gorbacheva's shopping sprees in England and France, which were so avidly described in the free press, remain unknown to ordinary Soviet citizens. They realize of course that their Kremlin masters lead lives rather different from their own; but the Kremlin reality so painstakingly concealed from them is far beyond what they imagine it to be. In any case, if the Soviet press had reported that Raisa Gorbacheva purchased a pair of diamond earrings costing $2,500 or that the "ambassadeur de charme" attended two Paris fashion shows at the Saint Laurent and Pierre Cardin houses, and that she like her husband is a regular customer of Gucci,* it would have caused a furor in

*Naturally, that world-famous firm has no franchise in the Soviet Union.

Moscow and throughout the USSR. It is no coincidence that throughout the entire summit in Geneva in November 1985 of all the journalists dogging Raisa Gorbacheva's footsteps there was not a single Soviet. One Soviet reporter, asked about arrangements to cover Mrs. Gorbacheva, brusquely told an American correspondent: "That's your problem. We don't write about her."

In general, the Kremlin at present is like a two-faced Janus: it turns two totally different masks to the West and to its home audience, and neither one reflects its real features. Take Gorbachev, for instance. If during his well-orchestrated, PR tours of the British Isles, France, and Switzerland, he appeared as a "Gucci Communist," then in his domestic appearances he emulated Lenin, who had a true simplicity and democratism.

Yet even without knowing all the details of the life in the Kremlin, the common people regard their leaders as so many "lucky guys" who have "latched onto" good things that are hard to come by and who, except for Stalin, are not especially different from ordinary folk. But among a people grown accustomed to servitude over a thousand-year period, even dislike for the faceless leaders in the fortress on Red Square is passive, inert, and somehow contemplative, as it finds expression in folklore. Here is a bit of dialogue from one of the many jokes about the Kremlin.

"I dreamed that the whole Kremlin was on fire, and the Politburo members had been hanged from the towers."

"Well? What happened next?"

"I don't remember."

"Too bad. The beginning was good."

Political apathy has grown in recent years because of the frequent changes of Kremlin leaders, who came into power even before the masses had learned how to tell one from another during the holiday parades in Red Square. Today, hardly anyone can tell you the names of more than two or three Politburo members or would be able to recognize many of them when they are on exhibit on holidays. According to a recent communication from Moscow, out of 123 persons asked, only four could give Gorbachev's full name.

But how many people now remember what Chernenko looked like or what his first name was? The portraits of all Kremlin predecessors are taken out of circulation immediately after their solemn funerals in Red Square; they disappear, at one and the same time, from the people's memory and from official Soviet history. Only one thing is done for them: The Kremlin, by way of rendering posthumous honors to itself, names cities, streets, steamships, and schools after them. But as time passes, people get used to the names and forget their origins. For posterity, those names become as much of an etymological puzzle as the name of the Russian capital, Moscow.

The Kremlin repays the people for their apathy in kind, with alienation, isolation, and indifference to their needs; by exploitation for economic and military ends; and with irritation when that exploitation does not yield the wanted results, owing to the people's irresponsibility, laziness, and drunkenness.

In recent years, drunkenness has taken on the proportions of a national disaster. Each new Kremlin leader is faced with the ever-more acute problem of combating alcoholism.

No one is planning to wage war against us. All the talk about the "Pershings" and strained [international] relations is a bluff. Why wage war on us if within 12 to 15 years we shall simply have collapsed as a sovereign State? A State in which more than half of the adult population consists of alcoholics and drunkards essentially unable to function and unable to put up a defense.

Those words were not written by Andrei Sakharov or Alexander Solzhenitsyn. They are quoted from a letter drafted by a group of Soviet scientists from the Novosibirsk Akademgorodok, a branch of the USSR Academy of Sciences. The letter was addressed not to the UN, or to the world at large, or to the U.S. president, or to *The New York Times* (the usual addresses of letters written by Soviet dissidents) but to the Central Committee of the Party. Although it was couched in the sharpest and most pessimistic terms, its authors were not subjected to harassment. To the contrary, that letter was taken up for discussion at a Politburo session in the middle of May 1985. In the absence of Grigori Romanov, who had already been expelled, the session was presided over by Mikhail Gorbachev and attended by three newly elected members, all protégés of Andropov: Victor Chebrikov, Egor Ligachev, and Nikolai Ryzhkov. The Politburo took the following steps to combat alcoholism: curtailment of vodka production and of the hours during which it could be sold, with a simultaneous raising of the age limit for purchasers; fines for drunkenness in public places; beefed-up antialcoholic propaganda; increased medical care for alcoholics; and the serving of mineral water instead of alcohol at formal receptions in the Kremlin. Those measures were by no means the draconian ones the people had been expecting with mixed feelings of fear and hope and that had been strongly recommended by the Novosibirsk scientists. Rather, they were halfway measures, palliative and perfunctory.

Why didn't the Kremlin decide to wage open warfare on this national calamity? Out of fear of their own people? Because the situation was hopeless?

Russian drunkenness is nothing new, but in recent years it has grown to epidemic proportions and has tragic and ominous consequences. There has been a sharp drop in male longevity, to sixty-two years. Infant mortality has risen just as sharply, to forty per thousand. Of the babies born in 1982, one out of six (16.5 percent) was abnormal. A full 85 percent of all felonies such as murder, rape, and armed robbery were committed by people under the influence of alcohol; and "hooliganism" is always the result of too much drinking. In the villages of Siberia, where everyone drinks —from the collective farm chairman to the stable boy— there are virtually no male pensioners because almost no one lives to be sixty, the age of retirement. The number of women who drink is also very high: according to the estimates of the Novosibirsk scientists, 97.6 percent* as against 99.4 percent of men. In 1980, the level of alcoholic consumption in Russia was 2.5 times that in other countries where it is consumed: 10.5 liters of pure alcohol per capita annually. And according to a graph drawn up by the scientists, by the year 2000 the level will reach 20 liters per capita.

> The most frightening result of this twenty-year period of drunken madness is the progressive degeneration of the nation. . . . That degeneration of our people is the worst tragedy in the entirety of its thousand-year history. Tragedies have occurred in the past, but a healthy posterity was born which was capable of moving ahead. But what kind of people are we leaving behind us? . . . In 1983 so many abnormal babies were born in our country, that by 1993 no less than 15 percent of our children will be attending such schools [for abnormal children]. . . . We must clearly realize that alcoholism is a program for squeezing us, as a nation, off the face of the earth.

We have quoted again from the letter by the Novosibirsk scientists (a copy of which we obtained from the USSR through secret channels) in order to emphasize the Kremlin's passivity toward this most tragic problem faced by the country. (Or rather, by its Russian population: in Central Asia, the inhabitants don't drink at all, and people in the other ethnic groups drink far less than their "older brother," as the imperial people were officially called in the Stalin era). We were recently asked

---

*Academician Fyodor Uglov tells of a female alcoholic who bore five children fathered by five different men: all five were abnormal.

by a fellow American journalist, "If Stalin could take the peasants' land away from them, along with their hogs and cows, obviously he or his successors could take the bottle away too, couldn't they?"

Here is Stalin's answer, given in 1927, in an interview with some foreign workers' delegations:

> Of course in general we would be better off without vodka, since vodka is an evil. But then we would have to go into bondage to the capitalists temporarily, which would be an even greater evil. Therefore, we have preferred the lesser evil. Today, vodka yields us five hundred million rubles in revenue. To give up vodka now would mean giving up that revenue. Besides, there are no grounds for claiming that alcoholism would decrease, since the peasants would begin to make their own vodka, poisoning themselves with moonshine.

The question comes down to whether, in the eyes of the Kremlin, the damage from alcohol is outweighed by the advantage gained from it. It is a complex question, since neither the damage nor the advantage is fully susceptible to statistical analysis. No doubt, alcohol is an important source of revenue. The yield from each bottle of vodka is several hundred percent, making it more profitable than gold mining. "Total prohibition" would deal a heavy blow to the Soviet economy. The profits from vodka are a kind of voluntary tax that the government can constantly raise in either of two ways. It can lower the quality—and hence the cost—of the product by replacing relatively expensive spirits distilled from grain with a cheaper kind distilled from sugar beets, potatoes, or syrup. Or, under the pretext of combating drunkenness, it can raise the price of alcoholic beverages, as it has done in Gorbachev's current anti-alcohol campaign. Finally, in addition to these two devices, there is an even more jesuitical way of combating drunkenness: through charges and fines. If a person is arrested for drunkenness, he pays a penalty of twenty-five rubles for the detox stations, is charged a standard fine of 30 rubles, and is deprived of quarterly and annual bonuses. At one packing plant in Stavropol, when Mikhail Gorbachev was Party boss there, it was calculated that a bottle of vodka could cost (and sometimes did cost) as much as 260 rubles, or $371.80.

According to some estimates, revenues from that "tax" exceed the officially acknowledged outlay for national defense. Alcohol, however, is a double-edged weapon: it accounts for a 7 percent loss in the Soviet GNP, compared with 2.5 percent loss in the United States. If we add to that the aforementioned rise in infant mortality, the drop in longevity, demographic shifts among ethnic groups, the dropoff in the combat-readiness of the armed forces,* the deterioration of morals, the rise in crime, and the degeneration of the Russian genotype, we realize that the economic advantage alone would not offset the moral and physical damage from alcohol.

One could go deeply into Russian history to try to explain the historical, societal, and geographic causes of Russian alcoholism. One might even mention climate as a cause, since in Russia people often do drink to keep warm. Its contemporary universality could be ascribed to the systematic destruction of nondrinking and moderate-drinking segments of the population in this century: the nobles, landowners, officials from the old regime, priests, kulaks, intellectuals, Old Bolsheviks, and others. For example, in rural areas, most of the drinking was done by the poor peasant, Chekhov's *muzhik*. He might have drunk to drown his sorrows and because he was poor. Or maybe he was poor because he drank instead of working. We do not claim to replace the classic approach to the Russian Revolution with one based on alcoholism—the destruction of the non-

---

*Up to the point where three tank crewmen with the Soviet occupying forces in Czechoslovakia in the spring of 1985 traded their tank for a case of vodka.

drinkers by the drinkers—but we must nonetheless note that as a result of the October Revolution and the reigns of terror that followed it, radical changes took place in the makeup of the Russian nation. Today's Russians are for the most part the descendants of those who always drank, the workers and peasants. So that the present-day rate of alcoholism in Russia is due, among other things, to a vicious inherited trait.

But this organic approach has never satisfied those who favor the theory of intervention in Russian affairs by evil forces from the outside: a worldwide plot against Russia. (In Solzhenitsyn's metaphorical version, this is the theory of the horse and rider, where the horse is the Russian people, which has been mounted by a tyrannical rider, communism.) Advocates of the mystery-story approach to Russian history have always sought, and easily found, an answer to the question of who has been plying the Russian people with drink. (Each new answer, however, has been different from the last.)

It is reliably known that Peter the Great plied his guests with drink. Guardsmen with tubs of *sivukha* (raw brandy) circulated among the guests at his riotous evening entertainments, and specially posted sentries made sure that everyone drank. Dostoyevsky believed that the *muzhiks* were made drunkards by the Jews, who had a monopoly on the trade in alcoholic beverages, opened taverns in the villages, and sold their customers *peisi-khovaya* vodka, distilled from raisins. To this day, Soviet propagandists blame alcoholism on the tsarist government. They even regard its present epidemic proportions as a vestige of the accursed past. And some people in the Soviet Union believe that the root of the evil lies in those "hundred grams" that were issued to each Soviet soldier before going into battle during World War II.

Eugene Muslin, a journalist with Radio Liberty, believes that the Soviet rulers apply the "law of social dissipation," using alcohol, among other things, to divert, dissipate, or drain off the social aggressiveness of

the population. When we objected to Muslin that the
dissipation theory was too rational for the Kremlin
leaders to apply, his answer was that indeed they do not
apply it rationally but out of an instinct of self-
preservation. That Party bureaucrats are among the categories of the Russian population who drink the least
supports that notion.

The theory of dissipation, however, is too rigid. It
presupposes the existence, in the Kremlin partocracy, of
beings from another planet. Yet if the theory of dissipation is true to any extent, it applies to both sides. In
other words, there is a tacit agreement—or, to use Rous-
seau's famous phrase, a "social contract"—no less ad-
vantageous to the people than to the State. As one
popular verse has it, "He doesn't need to be deceived/
He's happy to deceive himself."

Let us suppose that the Kremlin does, consciously or
unconsciously, deceive its own people in various ways,
including plying them with drink. But the people deceive
the State in turn, by means of the black market, thefts
of government property, "off-the-record" work, and
production losses due to alcoholism, thus getting back
—fully, partially, or with interest—what the State has
taken from them. What is achieved in this way is, if not
social harmony, at least a kind of economic balance,
with each side feeling it has won while the other has
been deceived.

If we come at the theory of dissipation from the other
end, we can see how the population itself applies it. The
consumer of vodka can, with its help, disperse (at least
for a time) his own fears, feelings of humiliation and
social injustice. He diverts his rebellion from a prohibited area to a legal one. Thus Nekrasov, a nineteenth-
century Russian poet who was very knowledgeable
about the peasantry, wrote that the Russian *muzhik*
drinks instead of rebelling. Today, as then, the drunk
on the street elicits the warmest sympathy from passersby. And in conflicts between a drunk and a sober
man—especially a policeman—the onlookers *always*

side with the drunk, whatever the nature of the conflict. In 1839, the Marquis de Custine wrote:

> In Russia, depravity interblends with liberalism. Here every rebellion seems legitimate—even a rebellion against reason. In a country where the social order is based on oppression, every disorder has its martyrs and its heroes.

And he adds, as if in the name of Russian drunks, "Here disorder would be progress, because it is the offspring of freedom."

We must acknowledge our own inability to provide an adequate explanation for this matter. Just as the problem as to whether the chicken came before the egg or vice versa has remained unresolved, so has the now-classic question about Russia: Did the Kremlin breed such a people, or did the people engender such rulers? It is a vicious circle from which we have simply found no way out.

So let us go once more to the letter sent by the Novosibirsk scientists to the Kremlin leaders for our concluding words on what is now Russia's biggest problem.

> In *Mein Kampf,* on the subject of the right policy to be applied in the eastern Slavic territories, Hitler wrote: "For them [the Slavs] there should be no hygiene and no inoculations—only vodka and tobacco."

We are now carrying out that order of Hitler's.

Vladimir Solovyov and *Elena Klepikova* are a husband-wife writing team now living in New York. Until the late Seventies, when they left Russia under threat of arrest, both belonged to the Soviet literary establishment and were members of the prestigious Writers' and Journalists' unions. After being expelled from these organizations for speaking out against censorship and anti-Semitism, they founded the first independent news agency in the USSR, whose bulletins were published in the United States and Western Europe. Their previous book was *Yuri Andropov: A Secret Passage Into the Kremlin*.

Selected Bibliography

References are given in parentheses: a Roman numeral indicates a chapter, and if there is a direct quotation, the page of the book in question is indicated by an Arabic numeral. (For the most part, there are no references to these books or periodicals in the notes.)

In English

Alexandrov, Victor. *The Kremlin, Nerve-Centre of Russian History*. New York: St. Martin's Press, 1963.

Ascherson, Neal. *The Polish August*. New York: The Viking Press, 1982. (V)

Ash, Timothy Garton. *The Polish Revolution: Solidarity*. New York: Charles Scribner's Sons, 1984. (V)

Barron, John. *KGB Today*. New York: Reader's Digest Press, 1983. (IV)

Beichman, Arnold, and Michael Bernstam. *Andropov, New Challenge to the West*. New York: Stein & Day, 1983.

Bialer, Seweryn. *Stalin's Successors: Leadership, Stability and Change in the Soviet Union*. Cambridge University Press, 1980.

279

Binyon, Michael. *Life in Russia*. New York: Pantheon Books, 1983.

Brumberg, Abraham, ed. *Poland, Genesis of a Revolution*. New York: Vintage Books/Random House, 1983. (V)

Butson, Thomas G. *Gorbachev: a Biography*. New York: Stein & Day, 1985.

Clubb, Oliver. *KAL Flight 007 and the Superpowers*. Berkeley: University of California Press, 1985. (I)

Cohen, Stephen F. *Rethinking the Soviet Experience*. New York: Oxford University Press, 1985.

Conquest, Robert. *The National Killers: the Soviet Deportation of Nationalities*. New York: Macmillan, 1970. (VIII)

Corson, William R., and Robert T. Crowley. *The New KGB: Engine of Soviet Power*. New York: Morrow, 1985. (IV)

Crankshaw, Edward. *Khrushchev, a Career*. New York: The Viking Press, 1966.

Custine, Adolphe, Marquis de. *Journey of our Time*. New York: Pellegrini & Cudahy, 1951.

Dallin, Alexander. *Black Box. KAL 007 and the Superpowers*. Berkeley: University of California Press, 1985. (I)

Dornberg, John. *Brezhnev: The Masks of Power*. New York: Basic Books, 1974.

Finder, Joseph. *Red Carpet*. New York: A New Republic Book/Holt, Rinehart and Winston, 1983. (VI; 318)

Fischer, Louis. *The Life of Lenin*. New York: Harper & Row, 1964.

Frankland, Mark. *Khrushchev*. New York: Stein & Day, 1967.

Gorbachev, Mikhail S. *A Time for Peace*. New York: Richardson and Steirman, 1985. (VIII)

Henze, Paul B. *The Plot to Kill the Pope*. New York: Charles Scribner's Sons, 1984. (V)

Hough, Jerry F. *Soviet Leadership in Transition*. Washington, D.C.: The Brookings Institution, 1980. (I; VI)

Hyland, William, and Richard W. Shryock. *The Fall of Khrushchev*. New York: Funk & Wagnalls, 1968.

Kaiser, Robert. *Russia: the People and the Power*. New York: Atheneum, 1976.

Khrushchev Remembers. Little, Brown, Boston, 1970 (IV;417)

Khrushchev Remembers. The Last Testament, Little, Brown, Boston, 1974. (I)

Kissinger, Henry. *White House Years*. Boston: Little, Brown, 1979.

Kissinger, Henry. *Years of Upheaval*. Boston: Little, Brown, 1982. (VI)

Klose, Kevin. *Russia and the Russians: Inside the Closed Society*. New York/London: W. W. Norton, 1984.

Konrad, Syrop. *Spring in October. The Polish Revolution*. New York: Praeger, 1957. (V)

Markov, Georgi. *The Truth That Killed*. New York: Ticknor & Fields, 1984. (IV)

Medvedev, Roy. *Khrushchev*. New York: Anchor Books/ Doubleday, 1984.

Medvedev, Zhores. *Andropov*. New York/London: W. W. Norton, 1983. (IV; 40)

Murphy, Paul J. *Brezhnev, Soviet Politician*. Jefferson, N.C.: McFarland, 1981.

Nagorski, Andrew. *Reluctant Farewell*. New Republic/Holt, 1985.

Nixon, Richard M. *The Memoirs of Richard Nixon*. New York: Grosset & Dunlap, 1978. (Introduction; 610)

Pipes, Richard. *Russia under the Old Regime*. New York: Charles Scribner's Sons, 1974.

Reddaway, Peter, and Sidney Bloch. *Psychiatric Terror*. New York: Basic Books, 1977.

Rositzke, Harry. *The KGB: The Eyes of Russia*. Garden City, N.Y.: Doubleday, 1981. (IV)

Shevchenko, Arkady N. *Breaking with Moscow*. New York: Alfred A. Knopf, 1985. (II, VII, X)

Shipler, David K. *Russia: Broken Idols, Solemn Dreams*. New York: Times Books, 1983.

Smith, Hedrik. *The Russians*. New York: Quadrangle, 1976.

Solovyov, Vladimir, and Elena Klepikova. *Yuri Andropov: A Secret Passage into the Kremlin*. New York: Macmillan, 1983.

Steel, Jonathan. *Soviet Power: the Kremlin Foreign Policy from Brezhnev to Andropov*. New York: Simon & Schuster, 1983.

Steel, Jonathan, and Eric Abraham. *Andropov in Power: From Komsomol to Kremlin*. Garden City, N.Y.: Anchor Press/Doubleday, 1984.

Sterling, Claire. *The Time of the Assassins*. New York: A

William Abrahams Book/Holt, Rinehart & Winston, 1984. (V)

Suvorov, Victor (pseud.). *Inside the Soviet Army.* New York: Macmillan, 1982. (VI)

Tatu, Michel. *Power in the Kremlin: From Khrushchev to Kosygin.* New York: The Viking Press, 1970. (VI; 89)

Ulam, Adam B. *Stalin: the Man and his Era.* New York: The Viking Press, 1973.

Weschler, Lawrence. *The Passion of Poland. From Solidarity through the State of War.* New York: Pantheon Books, 1984. (V)

Willis, David K. *Klass: How Russians Really Live.* New York: St. Martin's, 1985.

In Russian

In this book, when a book or periodical originally published in Russian has been quoted from or referred to, the Russian-language edition has been used, even if an English translation of it has been published. This has been done in order to avoid the inaccuracies that are inevitable in translation. For this bibliography, all titles of Russian-language books have been translated into English. The names of periodicals are given in transliteration.

Agabekov, G. S. *The Cheka at Work.* Berlin: Strela, 1931. (IX; 258–61, 276–83). Agabekov was the former chief of the Eastern Sector of the OGPU's Foreign Department, and its resident in the Middle East.

Alekseyeva, Ludmilla. *A History of Dissent in the USSR: The Latest Period.* New York: Khronika Press, 1984.

Alliluyeva, Svetlana. *Twenty Letters to a Friend.* New York: Harper and Row, 1968. (VI; 64, 146, 150–51, 170, 174–76)

———. *Only One Year.* New York: Harper and Row, 1970. (VIII; 41–43)

Amalrik, Andrei. *The USSR and the West in the Same Boat.* London: Overseas Publications Interchange, 1978.

Andropov, Yuri. *Selected Speeches and Articles.* Moscow: 1983. (I; 224–25, 230)

Anti-Semitism in the Soviet Union: Its Roots and Conse-

quences. Jerusalem, 1979. (VI)

Avtorkhanov, A. *The Enigma of Stalin's Death: Beria's Plot.* Frankfurt am Main: Posev, 1971.

Avtorkhanov, A. *The Origins of the Partocracy.* 2 vols. Frankfurt am Main: Posev, 1973.

———. *The Strength and Feebleness of Brezhnev.* Frankfurt am Main: Posev, 1979. (Introduction, 27)

Bakinskiy rabochii, 1970–85.

Bazhanov, Boris. *Reminiscences of a Former Secretary to Stalin.* France: Editions de la Troisième Vague, 1980.

Belyayev, A. *The Whole Army of Scribblers.* Moscow, 1983. (Introduction)

Bocharov, Gennnadiy. *The Passionate Seconds of Life. Afghanistan: the Young Heroes of the Revolution.* Moscow, 1980. (IX)

Brodsky, R. M., and O. Y. Krasivsky. *The True Face of Zionism.* Lvov, 1983.

Burlatsky, Fyodor. *War Games.* Moscow, 1984.

Chalidze, Valery, ed. *Internal Contradictions in USSR.* nos. 1–10. New York, 1981–84. (IV; X)

Chuyev, Feliks. *The Song of the Falcon's Wings.* Moscow, 1970. (IX;20–21)

Dneprovets, A. *Yeshov's Reign of Terror: We Cannot Forget.* West Germany: TsOPE (Central Association of Political Emigres from the USSR), 1958. (III;38–43)

Doyev, A. B. *Today's Judaism and Zionism.* Frunze, 1983. (VI; IX)

Epishev, A. A. *A Sacred Duty, An Obligation of Honor.* Moscow: DOSAAF Publishing House, 1983. (IV; IX)

Erofeyev, Benedikt. *The Moscow-Petushki Shuttle.* Paris: YMCA Press, 1981. (X; 7)

Fedotov, G. P. *The New City. A Collection of Articles.* New York: Chekhov Publishing House, 1952. (VI; 204)

Gaidar, Timur. *Thunderstorms in the South.* Moscow: Military Publishing House of the USSR Ministry of Defense, 1984. (IX)

———. *Under the Afghan Skies.* Moscow, 1981. (IX)

Gershberg, Semyon. *Stakhanov and Stakhanovites.* Moscow: Political Literature Publishing House, 1985. (IX)

Gladkov, Alexander. *Meetings with Pasternak.* Paris: YMCA Press, 1973. (VIII; 49)

Heller, Mikhail, and Alexander Nekrich. *Utopia in Power: A History of the Soviet Union from 1917 to Our Day*. 2 vols. London: Overseas Publications Interchange, 1982. (IX)

Izvestia, 1977–85.

Kashuba, G. P. *Encounters in Afghanistan*. Moscow: DOSAAF Publishing House, 1981. (IX)

Khrushchev, Nikita. *Memoirs*. 2 vols. New York: Chalidze Publications, 1979, 1981. (I; IV; VI)

Komarov, Boris (pseud.). *The Destruction of Nature: The Aggravation of the Ecological Crisis in the USSR*. Frankfurt am Main: Posev, 1978.

Kommunist, 1977–85.

Kontinent, nos. 1–45.

Korneyev, L. A. *The Classic Essence of Zionism*. Kiev, 1982. (VI, IX)

Kostin, N. D., ed. *A Shot Fired at the Heart of the Revolution*. Moscow: Political Literature Publishing House, 1983. (I)

Krasin, Victor. *The Trial*. New York: Chalidze Publications, 1983.

Krasnaya Zvezda, 1979–85.

Krupskaya, Nadezhda. *Recollections of Lenin*. Moscow, 1957.

Kushnik, Gubert. *Afghanistan as Seen by an Eyewitness*. Moscow, 1982. (IX)

Landmarks. Moscow, 1909. (X; 89)

Lenin, V. I. *Complete Collected Works*. Moscow. (X; vol. 5, 357 and vol. 26, 108)

Leningradskaya pravda, 1975–85.

Marx, Karl, and Friedrich Engels. *Works*. Russian ed., vol I. (III; 418)

Mikunis, Samuil. *Insight: Memoirs of a Former Secretary of the Communist Party of Israel about His Life in the Kremlin*. Israel: Tel Aviv, *Vremya i my*, 1984.

Mlynar, Zdenek. *A Cold Wind Blows from the Kremlin*. New York, 1983. (VIII; 11–26)

Morozov, M. *Leonid Brezhnev*. In German. Stuttgart, 1973.

Nekrich, Alexander. *Punished Peoples*. New York: Khronika Press, 1978. (VIII; 44–46)

Ogarkov, N. V. *History Teaches Us Vigilance*. Moscow: Military Publishing House of the USSR Ministry of Defense, 1985. (VI)

Olgin, P. *The Undeclared War Against Poland.* Moscow: Political Literature Publishing House, 1984. (V)

Ostrogorskiy, V. *Beware: the Deutsche Welle!* Moscow: Political Literature Publishing House, 1985. (Introduction)

Pasternak, Boris. *Correspondence with Olga Freidenberg.* New York: Harcourt Brace Jovanovich, 1981. (VIII; 280–83)

Pravda, 1968–85.

Problemy Vostochnoi Evropy, nos. 1–12. (V)

Prokhanov, Alexander. *A Tree in Downtown Kabul.* Moscow, 1982. (IX)

Prudnik, I. V. *Zionist Lobbies in the U.S.* Minsk, 1984. (VI; IX)

Romanov, G. V. *Selected Speeches and Articles.* Moscow: Political Literature Publishing House, 1983. (II)

Selikhov, Kim. *The Undeclared War.* Moscow, 1983. (IX)

Shatunovskaya, Lidiya. *Life in the Kremlin.* New York: Chalidze Publications, 1982. (VI)

Shevchik, A. N. *Anti-Communism on the Air Waves.* Minsk, 1984. (Introduction)

Shlepanov, A. N., and L. A. Smirnova. *"Stealing Minds" in the Past and in the Present.* Moscow, 1983. (VI)

Snegirev, Vladimir. *A Dawn Scorched by Gunpowder.* Moscow, 1984. (IX)

Solzhenitsyn, Alexander. *Letter to the Leaders of the Soviet Union.* Paris: YMCA Press, 1974. (IX)

———. *The Calf Butted the Oak Tree.* Paris: YMCA Press, 1975.

Stadnyuk, Ivan. *The War.* Moscow: Military Publishing House of the USSR Ministry of Defense, 1981. (Introduction; 462–63; IX)

Stavropolskaya pravda, 1970–85.

Syrokomsky, V., ed. *The Barrier of Incompatibility.* Moscow, 1983.

Takakhasi, Akio. *The President's Crime: the Provocation Involving the South Korean Plane Was Carried Out on Reagan's Orders.* Moscow: Novosti Press Agency, 1984. (I)

Trotsky, L. *My Life: An Essay in Autobiography.* Berlin: Granit, 1930. (III, vol. 2, 247)

———. *Stalin.* Novy Zhurnal, nos. 155–58, 1984-85. (VI; IX)

———. *Portraits.* New York: Chalidze Publications, 1984.

Tsvigun, Semyon. *The Secret Front.* Moscow, 1973. (IV)

Vachnadze, Georgiy. *Behind the Scenes of one Dirty Trick. Who Ordered the Terrorists to Kill the Pope?* Moscow: Political Literature Publishing House, 1985. (V)

Voslensky, Mikhail. *The Nomenklatura: The Soviet Ruling Class.* London, 1984. (III; 362)

Vremya i my, nos. 1–85.

Zarya Vostoka, 1970–85.

Zemtzov, Ilya. *Political Dilemmas in the Struggle for Power.* Jerusalem, 1983.

———. *Corruption in the Soviet Union.* In French. Paris: Hachette, 1976.

———. *Party or Mafia? A Stolen Republic.* Jerusalem, 1976. (IV)

Zhaba, S. P. *Russian Thinkers on Russia and Humankind.* Paris, YMCA Press, 1954.

Zhukov, G. K. *Reminiscences and Reflections.* Moscow, 1969. (VI)

Zimin, A. (pseud.) *Socialism and Neo-Stalinism.* New York: Chalidze Publications, 1981. (IX)

Zivs, S. L. *The Anatomy of the Lie.* Moscow, 1982. (Introduction; VI)

Zolotarevsky, L. A. *Reporting from Afghanistan.* Moscow, 1983. (IX)

Notes

It is to be expected that readers of this book should question the authors' sources, considering that the Kremlin is one of the most mysterious power centers on our planet. Nonetheless, there are leaks of information from there. Thus, even when we were writing our earlier Kremlin book—the one about Andropov, the most secretive of the Soviet leaders, if only by virtue of fifteen years of service with the KGB—we found at least two dozen people in the West, mostly émigrés and defectors from the USSR and Eastern Europe, who had met with him personally. Then too there were those who had gone to school with Andropov's son, who had had a friendship with his daughter, or who had been acquainted with a friend or relative of his. Finally, some of that material was taken (as well as some in this book) from the "political diary" that, beginning in the late sixties, we kept regularly while in the USSR, and that we managed to smuggle out of that country. By the way, in our book on Andropov, we predicted almost the entire makeup of the present top echelon in the Kremlin, beginning with Gorbachev and including Eduard Shevardnadze, Geidar Aliyev, Victor Chebrikov, Vitaly Vorotnikov, and others who are still regarded in the West as shadowy figures, despite the heightened interest in them.

Naturally, much more is known about Gorbachev, Shevardnadze, Aliyev, and other members of the Kremlin establishment who are less "classified" than Andropov, than is known about him. For example, there are now people in the West who attended Moscow University at the same time as did Mikhail Gorbachev. There are even more who knew him and remember him from the days when they were living in the Stavropol Territory, where he spent the greater part of his fifty-four years. (He lived there from birth until the age of nineteen, and from his twenty-fourth to his forty-seventh year, making a total of forty-two years, compared with twelve years in Moscow, five as a student at Moscow University and seven so far in the Kremlin.)

For instance, Vladimir Maksimov, now editor-in-chief of the émigré journal *Kontinent* (Paris), was for a period of three years (1956–59) on the staff of the Komsomol newspaper in Stavropol, which at the time was under the supervision of Mikhail Gorbachev as a member of the City Committee. Maksimov remembers his then boss as a "hard-working executive," a "discreet young man," and "by no means an ascetic." Says Maksimov: "He was fun-loving, and liked a good time in every sense of the word, including women and vodka. He never missed an opportunity to enjoy such things." (*Milan Europeo*, July 13, 1985.)

We note in passing that we have been faced rather often with the problem of verifying accounts of one matter or another by analyzing them and checking them against others. In a number of cases, we have had to forgo as doubtful some amusing stories about life in the Kremlin.

In this book we have refuted old wives' tales about Kremlin figures that have become staples in the Western press. For example, the many rumors about Grigori Romanov's amorous adventures and bouts with the bottle we regard as smears circulated by his political opponents, first by Andropov, then by Gorbachev. In that same category of disinformation we put the rumors about the involvement of Brezhnev's daughter in the affair of the stolen jewelry, about the suicide of General Semyon Tsvigun, deputy chairman of the KGB, as well as that of CC Party Secretary Fyodor Kulakov. There have also been "reverse rumors" lending gloss to the images of individual Politburo members: Andropov, Aliyev, Gorbachev. Whenever possible, we show that they have the same source as the smears. In general, it would be a mistake to underestimate the propaganda resources of the Kremlin and the KGB.

For instance, with Gorbachev's accession to power, his

idealization (not to say idolization) in the West increased and, at the same time, became more organized. Before his trip to France in the summer of 1985, the Soviet propagandists provided a special film on him for the French. A few months later, by the time of the Geneva summit, his articles and speeches had been translated into English; and a collection of them was promptly published as a book in the United States. No doubt, if his planned trip to America takes place in 1986, at least one, and probably more than one, propagandistic book about him will be published to coincide with his visit.

In all cases we have used only accounts that were known to us either from several sources or from a single source in which we place complete trust and which has been subjected to political analysis. Incidentally, in some instances Kremlin events have been reconstructed by means of analysis; when that has been done, we have shown, at the same time as the results of the investigation, the very process of it. The process is no less intriguing than the results themselves; for example, the investigation detailed in Chapter 3, of the blank spaces in the biographical material on Chernenko. Our critical attitude toward various kinds of "stories" scattered through émigré publications and elsewhere in the Western press has probably deprived the book of some amusing and colorful episodes, but we simply could not use them because we did not regard them as sufficiently authentic.

Those gaps, however, are more than filled by information we have obtained via secret channels from several reliable sources in the Soviet Union with whom we have managed to maintain contact since the days when we founded The Solovyov-Klepikova Press in Moscow, the first and only independent press agency in all of Soviet history. Its bulletins and news items were widely published in the international press. *The New York Times* alone printed three long articles about our agency and how it functioned (April 28, May 4, and May 30, 1977), with a front-page photo of its founders. When news about it came back to the USSR via the Russian-language broadcasts of the Voice of America, the BBC, and *Deutsche Welle*, we found ourselves on the receiving end of a flow of unique information unavailable to any Western journalists in Moscow, including reports on what was happening in the Kremlin's upper reaches.

After we were obliged to leave the Soviet Union under threat of arrest, we continued the work of our "agency," regularly publishing political commentary on the country we had left behind us in leading American and European newspapers. Also, thanks to the same radio stations mentioned above, our articles, with abridgments, were retranslated into Russian and broadcast to the USSR, from where we continued to get very valuable information. In spite of the strict measures recently taken there against leaks of Kremlin information, we are still getting news from the Soviet Union, though with less regularity than a few years ago, part of which we use in our newspaper and magazine articles. In several cases, that information has been confirmed a few months later by Western correspondents in Moscow; so far, none of it has been refuted, unlike the many Kremlin rumors that are born on the morning news broadcasts and die on the evening ones. For example, we predicted Andropov's accession to power and later that of his entire team (Gorbachev, Chebrikov, Aliyev, Shevardnadze, and others). And we followed, stage by stage and in detail, the struggle between Gorbachev and Romanov behind the back of the nominal Soviet *vozhd,* Konstantin Chernenko. The fact that there had been such a struggle was fully confirmed when the victorious Gorbachev ruthlessly expelled Romanov from the Kremlin and sent him to a hospital for alcoholics.

As we see it, the reliability and freshness of the information in our articles—and not just the originality of the political analysis—explains the readiness of American syndicates and newspapers to buy those articles. We would not have presumed to mention that readiness if we had felt it was due only to our personal merit. Unfortunately, however, we cannot list the names of those who have helped us and are still helping us make sense of the tangled web of Kremlin realities, so shrouded in secrecy. Indeed, in our articles and books, including this one, instead of disclosing our sources we have been compelled to camouflage them in every way possible.

The quality of our postal connection with Moscow leaves much to be desired. Whereas a letter from Rome takes a few days to get to New York, and one from just about anywhere in the Soviet Union to just about anywhere abroad takes several weeks to arrive, with our roundabout postal connection it sometimes takes several months for mail from Moscow to reach its destination in the free world. Much depends on opportunities which may or may not turn up. In any case, during the period when this book was being written, in order to get as much information as possible about the latest developments in Moscow after Mikhail Gorbachev came to power—and, along with him, the "Andropov team" that he captains—we made two flights across the ocean and several side trips to points close enough to the epicenter of the empire's life to make them dangerous. In short, if someday the time comes when it will be safe for our Soviet "coauthors" to tell how our articles and books on the Kremlin were put together, theirs will be real tales of adventure.

Although we are not in a position to acknowledge here our gratitude toward our chief collaborators, we would like to thank the following "citizens of the free world" who in different degrees and in different ways helped us in our work: Nina Bouis, Nodar Eristazi, Sid Goldberg, Bela Kirali, Dr. Andrei Loeber, Eugene Muslin, Ivan Stepanovich Raskolnikov, Aishe Seitmuratova, Shlomo Sikorsky, Larisa and Frantisek Silnitsky, Maria Zakharovna Solovyova, and Bert Todd.

Our special thanks go to Guy Daniels, our translator and friend; Heide Lange, our literary agent; and Cynthia Vartan, our editor.

Since this book is intended for Western readers, we have deliberately Westernized some terms and modernized or archaized others in order to make Kremlin realities more understandable. Thus, in a number of cases we have replaced Soviet appellations with conventional Western ones. For example, we call The USSR Supreme Soviet "the parliament," the chairman of its Presidium "the president," the chairman of the Council of Ministers "the premier," *oblasts* "provinces," the first secretary of the Party Committee of an *oblast* "the Party boss" (usually), the armed forces "the Red Army" (on occasion), the chairman of the KGB "the chief of the secret police" or "the KGB chief" (when not leaving his title as is), the chairman of the City Soviet (Council) of Workers' Deputies "the mayor," and so on. Over the past few decades, some organizations and positions have acquired new appellations (e.g., the KGB and the general secretary, who in the Khrushchev era was called the first secretary). In order not to confuse the reader, we have usually kept to the present-day appellations; for example, we almost always call the Party's supreme ruling body the Politburo, even when speaking of the period when it was called the Presidium.

And there are other isolated instances of simplifications. For example, we have included, in the "troika" of KGB generals in the Politburo, General Eduard Shevardnadze, who was in fact minister of internal affairs (chief of the regular police) in Georgia. But his functions differed little from those of his neighbor and friend Geidar Aliyev, KGB chairman in Azerbaijan. The difference between those two positions was (and is) strictly formalistic.

We even use the word *Kremlin* in a sense different from that given it in Soviet dictionaries. There it denotes the architectural complex in the center of the imperial capital, while what we mean by it is the empire's political center, that baker's dozen of its leaders, the members of the Politburo, rather like the Inner Party in George Orwell's novel *1984*. For that matter, anyone who has read this book will hardly need additional explanation of the word *Kremlin*.

Introduction: the Limits of Understanding

On Svetlana Alliluyeva's return to the USSR, see the more detailed discussion of it in our article "Svetlana Stalin's Return is No Mystery" (*The Los Angeles Times,* November 29, 1984). In the matter of Stalin's listening to foreign radio broadcasts, we have used a quotation from Ivan Stadnyuk's *The War*. Although it is cast in the form of a novel, the author had access to secret Kremlin archives of the Stalin era. Moreover, the factual nature of the incident he describes has been confirmed by several other authors, including some memoirists.

1. A Throne on a Deathbed

The tape-recorded conversation between the pilot, Vasily Kazmin, and ground control is quoted from publications of the U.S. government; the commentary on it by Victor Belenko, a former Soviet pilot, is taken from his article in *The Reader's Digest,* January 1984. The Soviet explanations of the KAL tragedy—statements issued by TASS, interviews with (and statements by) Marshal Ogarkov, Gromyko, Andropov, *et al.*—can be found in *Pravda, Izvestia,* and *Krasnaya zvezda (Red Star),* September 3–8, 10, 12, 20, and later. The incident involving the American U-2 spy plane is recreated on the basis of Khrushchev's memoirs (MS at the Harriman Institute of Columbia University, collated against the Russian-language and English-language editions). The transcript of the remarks made at Andropov's meeting with workers at the Sergo Ordzhonikidze Plant in Moscow is quoted from *Izvestia* of February 1, 1983, and a collection of articles and speeches by Andropov. A detailed account of Andropov's career, which also covers other actions taken by him that are mentioned in later chapters of this book, may be found by the reader in our book on Andropov.

2. The Duel at the Tyrant's Coffin

The story of the power struggle between Mikhail Gorbachev and Grigori Romanov described in this chapter (also in Chapters 6 and 7) was detailed by us at various stages of its development in newspaper articles, beginning with "Chernenko's Fictitious Rule" (*The Chicago Tribune,* May 16, 1984) and thenceforth in other articles; for instance, in *The Boston Globe,* October 8, 1984; *The Baltimore Evening Sun,* November 26, 1984; *Svenska Dagbladet,* September 24, 1984; and so on. Thanks to news regularly received from the USSR, we were able to describe, in J. B. Priestly's phrase, "the bullet in flight," with its very uneven trajectory. Our commentaries stood out starkly against the background provided by the American press in general, where at the time correspondents were writing about the struggle between generations in the Kremlin. The Romanov speech from which we quote was published in *Leningradskaya pravda,* February 26, 1984.

3. An Intermezzo With Konstantin Chernenko

The comments by Andropov's advisors on Chernenko are quoted from an article by Joseph Kraft, "Letter from Moscow" (*The New Yorker,* January 31, 1983). Other recollections of him are taken from *The New York Times,* June 20, 1979, and February 13 and 14, 1984; the Sunday London *Times,* February 19, 1984; and *Time* magazine, February 27, 1984. Chernenko's comments on Brezhnev are quoted from *Pravda,* November 13, 1982; the quotations from Brezhnev's memoirs are taken from the version of them published in the magazine *Novy Mir* (no. 5, 1978, and no. 11, 1982). The interview with Andropov was printed in *Der Spiegel,* April 25, 1983. The biographical sketches of Chernenko appeared in *Pravda,* February 14, 1984, *Literaturnaya gazeta,* February 15, 1984, and the Sunday London *Times,* February 12, 1984. The article by Elena Chernenko appeared in *Pravda,* February 19, 1984, and the historical sketch by Lieutenant General Vasily Donskoi in *Krasnaya zvezda,* April 10, 1984. On Chernenko's term of service with the border troops, see another sketch in *Ogonyok (Guiding Light),* May 24, 1984.

Information on the "blood weddings" of the Dnepropetrovsk secret police may be found in the book *Yezhovshchina (Yezhov's Reign of Terror)* listed in the Russian bibliography and in articles written and interviews conducted by the Israeli Sovietologist Mikhail Agursky published in *Posev (The Sowing),* no. 7, 1979, and no. 7, 1982; *Le Monde,* March 2, 1984; *The Daily Telegraph,* November 26, 1979; and *The Washington Post,* June 15, 1984.

The obituary of Zadionchenko appeared in *Pravda,* November 21, 1972, and an article on it by British Sovietologist Leonard Shapiro appeared in *Survey,* vol. 21, no. 3, Summer 1975.

4. The Empire's Secret Government: The KGB

For further details on Aliyev, see, in our book on Andropov, the chapter titled "Andropov's Caucasian 'Rehearsals': The Police Blitzkrieg in Azerbaijan and in Stalin's Homeland." (This chapter also discusses Eduard Shevardnadze's role in those affairs.) See also the book *Partiya ili mafiya. Razvorovannaya respublika (The Party or the Mafia? A Stolen Republic),* by Ilya Grigoryevich Zemtsov, who worked in a section of the Azerbaijani CC and was well acquainted with Aliyev. Syrian President Assad's message of condolence is quoted from *Pravda,* February 12, 1984.

5. The Kremlin's Hamlet Complex: What to Do Or Not to Do About Poland?

With respect to the number of Polish officers killed in the mass murder in the Katyn Forest, our figure of 4,321 is based on data from the exhumation carried out under the direction

of a Polish physician on the staff of the Red Cross. In official
statements issued by the Third Reich, however, the body count
is twelve thousand, and in most of the materials dealing with
the subject published in the West, it is more than ten thousand. All in all, about fifteen thousand Polish military personnel were killed by the Soviet state security "organs," but the
majority of such killings did not take place in the Katyn Forest.

On General Jaruzelski, see, in addition to the Walter
Cronkite interview of him that we quote from, interviews with
Jaruzelski by Barbara Walters (*Nightline,* July 21, 1983) and
Tad Szulc (*Parade,* July 18, 1982) and articles by Michael T.
Kaufman (*The New York Times Magazine,* December 9, 1984)
and by Kay Withers (*Newsday,* November 23, 1983). Articles
on Jaruzelski by us appeared in *The Chicago Tribune* (July 11,
1981; July 28, 1982; December 13, 1982; August 24, 1984);
The Baltimore Evening Sun (December 31, 1981; December
13, 1982; August 17, 1983); *The Wall Street Journal* (June 11
and July 13, 1981); *The Los Angeles Times* (September 11,
1981); *The Boston Globe* (July 14, 1981); *Newsday* (November
10, 1984); and the New York *Daily News* (July 12, 1981;
November 8, 1981); and others. Their tenor may be judged
from their titles: "Will Poland Find a 'National Savior' in
Time?"; "The General: Dictator and Savior"; "Moscow
Fears a War with Poland"; "In Defense of General Jaruzelski"; "The General is Poland's Hero"; and so on.

The characterization of Jaruzelski by Helmut Schmidt, the
former chancellor of West Germany, is taken from "A Talk
with Helmut Schmidt" by Craig R. Whitney (*The New York
Times Magazine,* September 16, 1984). Most of the other
quotations are taken from the Polish periodicals *Tribuna
Ludu* and *Politika.* For details on the political murders in the
Ukraine that we mention, see the article "That Democrat, Andropov . . . ," written by Petr Grigorenko, a former Soviet
general, published in the newspaper *Novoe Russkoe Slovo,*
July 29 and 30, 1982.

6. The Origin of the Kremlin Mafias

The references to Stalin as commander in chief appeared in
Pravda, January 1 and 25, 1985; and the Chernenko speech
from which we quote was published in that same newspaper

on September 28, 1984. In addition to the articles by Marshal Ogarkov that we mention, see his book *Istoriya uchit bditel'nosti (History Teaches Us Vigilance)*, which was published in 1985, after Ogarkov's rehabilitation from the disgrace into which he had fallen because he had supported Romanov.

7. The King Is Dead, Long Live the King!

Andrei Gromyko's nominating speech when Mikhail Gorbachev was "elected" general secretary was issued as a special brochure by the Political Literature Publishing House.

8. Meet Mikhail Gorbachev

The interview with Lev Yudovich from which we quote was published in *The Wall Street Journal*, March 12, 1985; and the description of the meetings at Moscow University is taken from Alexander Nekrich's article "The Campaign against the Cosmopolites," which appeared in *Kontinent*, no. 28, 1981. The item about the brief get-together of Brezhnev, Chernenko, Andropov, and Gorbachev at the railroad station in Mineralnye Vody was printed in *Pravda*, September 21, 1978. The biographical information about Gorbachev that was never published in the central Soviet press appeared in *Stavropolskaya pravda*, February 6, 1979. Information about the conflict between Gorbachev and the military establishment was taken from articles by Boris Komarov (the pseudonym of Zeyev Volfson), "Ecology in the USSR Today" (*Posev*, no. 2, 1985) and "Lake Baikal in the Era of Socialism" (*Novoe Russkoe Slovo*, June 14 and 15, 1985) and one by Alexander Rar, "The Darling of the Party" (*Russkaya mysl' [Russian Thought]*, April 18, 1985). The brief memoir by Petr Abovin-Egides appeared in *Kontinent*, no. 42, 1984.

9. Stalin's Shadow Over the Kremlin

On the Stakhanovite movement (and on Gorbachev's declaration), see *Pravda*, August 23, 1984, May 4 and 19, 1985, among others. See also the book *Vzglyad skvoz' gody. Zapiski stakhanovtsev (A Glance over the Years: Notes of the Stakhanovites)* (Moscow, 1984). Gorbachev's remark about the flea is quoted from an article by Serge Schmemann in *The New York Times Magazine*, March 3, 1984. The quotation from the story "Lefty" is taken from *Sobraniye sochinenii N. S. Leskova (The Collected Works of N. S. Leskov)*, vol. 7 (Moscow, 1958) p. 34. The speech in which Gorbachev praises Stalin and "the great Russian people" was published in *Pravda,* May 9, 1985, and *Kommunist,* no. 8, 1985; the reaction of the audience was included in a broadcast on Moscow television on May 8, 1985. The quotation from Roy Medvedev is taken from the aforementioned interview of him published in *Newsweek.* Karamzin's characterization of Ivan the Terrible is quoted from his *Izbrannye sochineniya (Selected Works),* vol. 2 (Moscow, 1964) pp. 410–11. S. Smirnov's verses were printed in the magazine *Moskva,* no. 10, 1967, and Valentin Rasputin's "warning" is taken from his article in *Sovetskaya kultura,* January 4, 1980. On Gorbachev's threats to the president of Pakistan, see *The Sunday Telegraph,* March 31, 1985. Yevgeny Yevtushenko's poem on Stalin was published only once in the USSR (in *Pravda,* October 2, 1962, on personal instructions from Khrushchev) and has never been reprinted in any of Yevtushenko's books, including the recently published three-volume edition of his work. On the Red Army's invasion of Afghanistan: at the very outset of the Soviet aggression, we began publishing articles in the American press about the motives for it and the reasons why Afghanistan would not become a Russian Vietnam. See the following articles by us: "Geographic Imperialism" (*The Washington Post,* March 3, 1980); "The Man Who Came to Dinner in Red Square" (*The Christian Science Monitor,* December 4, 1980); "Moscow Will Have No Vietnam" (*The Chicago Tribune,* December 8, 1980); "Oil? Ports? No, Fear of the Dragon Stirs the Bear to Act" (*The Los Angeles Times,* December 29, 1980).

10. The Kremlin, the Empire, and the People

The episodes involving Andrei Sakharov and Elena Bonner are taken from an account by their very close friend Natalia Gesse (her article in the *Novoe Russkoe Slove,* March 3, 1984, and an interview with her on Radio Liberty, published in the *New York Post,* May 21, 1984). The quotations from the letter written by a group of Soviet scientists are taken from a copy of that letter that we received from the USSR via secret channels. For more details on the subject of Soviet dissent, see our essays: an Op-Ed article in *The New York Times,* October 4, 1977, and "The Russian Dissidents: A Political Obituary," (*The Michigan Quarterly Review,* Winter 1980). On alcoholism in the USSR, see our articles, "The Lush's Paradise" (*The American Spectator,* October 1981) and "The Paradox of Russian Vodka" (*Michigan Quarterly Review,* Summer 1982). The episode of the evacuation of the Crimean Tatars is taken from an article by Zinaida Grigorenko, "The Sixth Prison Term of Musfata Dzhemilev" (*Novoe Russkoe Slovo,* May 18, 1984).

Index